The Quest for Charles Rennie Mackintosh

A Moment White

The Man Who Played Robert Burns

East End to West End

Worlds Apart

A Year Out in New Zealand

Solo Performers

On the Trail of Robert Burns

The Luath Burns Companion

Immortal Memories

The Quest for Robert Louis Stevenson

The Quest for Charles Rennie Mackintosh

JOHN CAIRNEY

Luath Press Limited
EDINBURGH
www.luath.co.uk

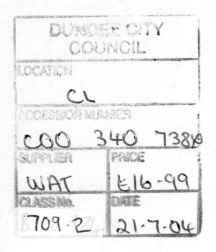
First published 2004

The paper used in this book is recyclable. It is made
from low-chlorine pulps produced in a low-energy,
low-emission manner from renewable forests.

Printed and bound by
Creative Print and Design, Ebbw Vale

Typset in 10.5 Sabon by S. Crozier, Nantes

To Bob Adams, OBE, playwright, wit and good friend who made a start possible in 1974.

A prophet is not without honour save in his own country and in his own house. And because of their unbelief he did not work many miracles there.

Matthew, Chapter 13 Verses 5 to 7

Doubtless there is a danger to the untrained designer in direct resort to Nature.
For the tendency in his or her case is to copy outright,
to give us pure, crude fact and not to design at all.
Still, there is hope in honest error:
none in the icy perfections of the mere stylist.

John Dando Sedding

Contents

Acknowledgements

Make a detailed record of the buildings of that genius, Mackintosh, before it's too late.

Percy Thomas, President RIBA, 1935

The author wishes to state his obligation to the following in the writing of this book and sourcing of illustrative material:

Douglas Annan, The Annan Gallery
Brian Armstrong, Glasgow City Council
the late Sir Harry Barnes
Colin Baxter
Roger Billcliffe
Clare Brotherwood
William M Buchanan
Jude Burkehauser
Lynda Clark, Hunterian Museum and Art Gallery
John Coleman
Alan Crawford
Robin Crichton
Sarah and Justin Crozier
Dr David Daiches
The Earl of Elgin
Murray Grigor
Dr Janice Helland
the late Dr Thomas Howarth
Lesley Johnson
Anthony Jones
Wendy Kaplan
David Kernohan
Jean Lim
Dr Lorn Macintyre
the late Robert Macleod
David McKail
Graham Metcalfe
May Mitchell, Strathclyde Police Museum
Alistair Moffat
the late Margaret Morris
Timothy Neat
Alannah O'Sullivan
Iain Paterson
Dr Sylvia Pinches
George Rawson
Professor Pamela Robertson, Hunterian Museum and Art Gallery
Tom Robertson
Graham Roxburgh
the late Benno Schotz
Ailsa Tanner
Peter Trowles, The Glasgow School of Art
the late Allan Ure
the late Professor Andrew McLaren Young
Janet Copsey and staff, The University of Auckland Library
Stuart Robertson and Patricia Ingram and all at The Charles Rennie Mackintosh Society

Preface

What exactly is the Modern Movement? Was it not the movement started only a generation ago by that remarkable
Scotsman, the late Charles Rennie Mackintosh? Ask Continentals about this. You will find that they regard Mackintosh
as the arch-apostle of the Modern School just as Karl Marx is
regarded as the arch-apostle of Communism.

John Begg, 'Quarterly', 1936

AS THE DEDICATION of this volume implies, I was begun on the
pursuit of Mackintosh by RW (Bob) Adams in his capacity as
Managing Director of the AH McIntosh Furniture Company in
the Kingdom of Fife. In the early Seventies, Tom Robertson and
Drew Bennet of their design team approached him with the idea of
producing domestic furniture 'after the style' of Charles Rennie
Mackintosh and not, as Cassina in Milan under Filipo Alison had
done, as exact replicas. The Fife firm chose to go for a slight vari-
ation in the chairs to make them more ergonomically acceptable
while at the same time retaining their distinctive and pleasing
'Mackintosh' shape. To my mind this was completely defensible
and in line with contemporary needs. The question remained: was
a facsimile, made by modern methods from original Mackintosh
drawings, as the Italian company elected to do, a genuine Mackintosh chair or not? The Scottish company added their own touch.
Significantly, when the Museum of Modern Art in New York
mounted their *Furniture by Charles Rennie Mackintosh* Exhibition in 1974, all the furniture shown was by Cassina.

When I first came to do the research on Mackintosh as a vehi-
cle for performance I had nothing to go on but a book by Thomas
Howarth, the letters from Port Vendres kept by Glasgow University, and miscellaneous articles in old architectural magazines and

periodicals. It was a slim field of resource by any standards. I got the Howarth book from the library and was given access to the letters and the lectures because the late Professor Andrew McLaren Young of the Fine Arts Department of the University thought that a script to be performed by an actor, even if he were a graduate of that same university, was an ephemeral affair and did not constitute commercial publication in the strictest sense. However, he insisted that his young assistant, Roger Billcliffe, look over my shoulder – just in case.

Nowadays, all researchers of Mackintosh stand on Roger's shoulders, or at least seek the hand of Pamela Robertson, who was then a very young Miss Reekie. I was fortunate to have both at hand to help me in adapting a script, which became *Mackintosh the Man,* a 90-minute Dramatised Lecture Reading for three actors, with triple-screen audio-visual illustrations created by Graham Metcalfe and Roland Kennedy, and directed by Murray Grigor. This was first presented by Shanter Productions at an Architectural Seminar sponsored by the McIntosh Company at the Adam Smith Centre, Kirkcaldy on December 6, 1975 by permission of its manager Chris Potter and the Kirkcaldy District Council. As this was the first seminar ever held in Scotland on behalf of Mackintosh, it might be in order to list the complete programme for the day and those taking part.

11am	Beveridge Suite
	Coffee with display of Mackintosh and McIntosh furniture.
11.05	Welcome on behalf of Kirkcaldy District Council by Councillor R King.
11.30	Cinema
	Opening remarks by RW Adams.
	Screening of *Mackintosh* – short documentary film by Murray Grigor.
NOON	Theatre
	A Critical Forum on Mackintosh and his Work.
	Chairman – Dr Maurice Lindsay of the Scottish

Civic Trust.
Speakers:
Robin Haddow – Mackintosh, the Architect.
Henry Hellier – Mackintosh, the Designer.
Emilio Coia – Mackintosh, the Artist.
1pm   Lunch
2.30pm   *A Study in Form – by Murray Grigor*
A visual exploration of Mackintosh design on
triple screens with synchronised soundtrack.
3pm   Comment by Murray Grigor.
3.30   Roger Billcliffe introduces John Cairney in
Mackintosh the Man with Rose McBain as
Margaret Macdonald and John Shedden as
Narrator and others.
4.30   Comment by Anthony Wheeler, Past President
RIA (Scotland).
4.45   Closing Remarks and Vote of Thanks by
RW Adams.

The reception from a packed audience of Scottish architects was encouraging and further performances of the reading took place in the following year in Glasgow, at the Martyrs' School, the Art School, the Glasgow Art Club, Queen's Cross Church, and at Hill House, Helensburgh. A television version, fleshed out by a full cast, was later shown by STV in 1979, but all it did was to convince me that the real drama was in the story of the man himself. There is everything in it – a great love story, personal complications, professional conflicts, triumphs and disasters and an engulfing tragic ending.

However, 30 years ago, Mackintosh the man was obscured by Mackintosh the Architect, and even more so by Mackintosh the Designer and Decorator. The Saatchi and Saatchi Mockingtosh had still to appear and the original prospector, Thomas Howarth, was still panning for gold with his doctoral thesis on an unknown Glasgow architect. This turned into a seminal book – *Charles Rennie Mackintosh and the Modern Movement* in 1952 and made his name and fortune. From Dr Howarth's solitary trek, the road to Mackintosh has broadened into a mighty highway, and I, for one, relish now being on the path he first mapped out. Generally speaking, however, in terms of the dramatic, Mackintosh has not a long pedigree.

Murray Grigor, another genuine Mackintosh pioneer, was first in the field in 1967 with his documentary film for Films of Scotland, and this may have precipitated the initial Mackintosh interest. There was also a centenary tribute paid in 1968 in the radio documentary on June 7 of that year compiled by George Bruce from material supplied by McLaren Young. Dr Lorn Macintyre adapted the letters as a playreading for John Shedden and Anne Lannan at the Tron Theatre, Glasgow in 1985. In 1987, Alistair Moffat, himself a Mackintosh author, produced Tom Conti and Kara Wilson in a television feature based on the Mackintoshes for Channel Four in London, and ten years later, Wigwam Digital from Bellshill in Strathclyde, produced a compact disc entitled *Charles Rennie Mackintosh – Art, Architecture and Design,* a multimedia documentary on the life and work. More recently, in July of 2003, a radio play, *The Chronicle,* by John Hancox, was broadcast featuring Alex Heggie and Juliet Cadzow. If one also includes a Japanese comic strip about him, that is the complete summary of Mackintosh in performance.

It hardly amounts to a theatrical tradition, yet, 30 years ago I was as intrigued by the prospect of playing him in front of an audience as I am now pleased to present him to the reader as the central character in his own biography. For what a character he was.

A strange, solitary boy, a wickedly handsome youth, despite a drooping left eye, a volatile man, who always resented that he was born with a twisted left foot that gave him a life-long limp. An ostensible failure in his chosen profession, he yet matured into a considerable painter. This was a soul's journey of enormous intensity and he showed himself at every stage to have the courage and humour to survive it all. He was no saint, and was undoubtedly his own worst enemy, yet he achieved a final serenity that was as full as it was unexpected. His tragedy was that he could have done so much more in his life, but his triumph was that he did just enough to be rated by many as a genius and others as a hero.

Today, however, Mackintosh has become an icon and the study of his work has become an industry. Tom Howarth's book has been reprinted, and there has even been a book *about* Tom Howarth and Mackintosh. The letters are now in the public domain and to date there must be a hundred books on the market about Mackintosh, the Architect, – Mackintosh, the Artist, – Mackintosh, the Designer – but none, as far as I could find, based solely on Mackintosh, the Man. So there was obviously a niche – hence this book.

According to friends, Mackintosh was not a tall man, but he had presence. It is this presence I have sought throughout. I want to identify with this ordinary Glasgow man with the extraordinary artistic talent, here shorn of the myths that have enshrouded him since his lifetime, and free, at last, to be himself. In this way, he will be appropriately returned to his roots. And in Glasgow, at first, he was not without honour – as we shall see.

For this book, I have made heavy recourse into the the scripts I have already written and performed on Mackintosh but only as basic research and as a narrative guidline. As far as possible, I have taken every advantage of contemporary Mackintosh scholarship and have fully acknowledged this fact wherever possible. Where I have inadvertently failed to do so, I should be glad to have the omission pointed out for any future editions.

Finally, let us bear in mind what Professor Nikolaus Pevsner, the architectural historian, and one of the first to write about Mackintosh, said of him: 'I never knew Mackintosh personally but all of those who knew him, and I approached many of his friends and contemporaries, spoke of him with light in their eyes'.[1]

Let us hope then, that the light will never go out on the man that was Charles Rennie Mackintosh.

Introduction

Our workmen are grown generallie to such an excellence of
device ... that they sine pass the the finest of the olde.

William Harrison

CHARLIE MACKINTOSH FIRST made an impact on his home town by
having a team of men from his father's bleaching works at St
Rollox go round the Glasgow tenements from close to close and
door to door collecting urine at a penny a gallon. He carefully
supplied the carriers with hydrometers to ensure that they got an
undiluted product from the citizens. This scheme worked so well
that as much as 3,000 gallons was delivered to the factory each
day. Ammonia was distilled from this liquid stock and when this
was added to leftover tar from the Glasgow Gas Company, naptha
was produced, which in turn led to the discovery of rubber and
eventually, by 1823, to the Mackintosh overcoat.

I mention these facts because when the name Mackintosh is
mentioned outside Glasgow, until recently at least, it was always
the raincoat man and not the architect that people first thought of.
There were some, it must be said, who thought at one time of the
latter as nothing more than a piss-artist but that is no more than a
specious connection between the two famous Glasgow namesakes
born almost exactly a hundred years apart.

Charles Rennie Mackintosh is either the greatest-ever Scottish
architect and water-colourist of genius or a capricious interior
designer with a flair for unstable furniture. Or he is all of these
things. Mackintosh is a myth – an almost impenetrable figure in
the history of Scottish art and architecture. So many strands have
gone into its weave that it is difficult to pick out the tartan thread
that links Robert Lorimer to Alexander 'Greek' Thomson or
James Gibb to James Sellars, or all four to the Adam family, father

and sons, and from all of these to the subject now to be considered – Charles Rennie Mackintosh.

The Caledonian connection is something that is pursued in this biography of the Scottish enigma that was CRM. For above everything else, he was Scottish, and a Glasgow Scot at that. This fact will be seen as permeating his every attitude and underlying his every act through the ups and downs of a chequered professional and personal life. For him, the Scottish tradition was not a fixed point of convention but a living reference. A dead past is academic. A living past is NOW.

The first Scottish building was a fortress – it had to be – and it was this stone war-house, gradually domesticated over the centuries, sheathed in its rough coat of harling, that offered the plainest of fronts to the outside world. High walls surrounded a basic tower and this was the basis of the style called Scotch Baronial, that crude cradle that nursed so many of Scotland's great architects and inspired them to their life's work. Mackintosh was no exception. There have been Scots, people not long dead, and known to me, who knew and admired Mackintosh in his lifetime, yet within a decade of his death in 1928 he was virtually a forgotten man. Especially in his own city.

When he died in a London nursing home, he had been living in the South of France for the previous four years of his life, every bit as as much of an exile as that other Victorian Scot, Robert Louis Stevenson, had been in the South Seas nearly 30 years before. Paradoxically, Mackintosh was almost as contented and self-realised as that famous writer was in the end. Stevenson was cut off in his prime at only 44 just as he was coming to a complete understanding of his artistic powers with the written word. Mackintosh lived longer but, to all intents and purposes he too had been cut off in his prime and obliged to leave his chosen profession and native city at almost exactly the same age for a self-imposed exile that was to last till his death.

Nowadays, he is seen not only as an architect, but as a considerable painter, and as a most ingenious innovator of a unique furniture style. More than that, he is the complete artist, and it was his contribution to the 'new art' that gives him his place in the records and accords him a particular kind of genius that one can only describe as Scottish. That is, awkward, uncategorisable and often, self-defeating. It means one who has ostensibly failed but succeeds in the end by a combination of a particular doggedness allied to a kind of application where as much pain is given as taken.

What is not in doubt, however, is that he has been wholly justi-fied by what he left us in his work, whether on paper, canvas, wood or stone, and it is this that is his real testimonial. This is the man whose life and work is remembered in these pages. Recreated from letters, records, lecture notes, anecdotes, sayings, relevant gossip and recollections, in short, from any source, is the fixed impression of a charming taliped who limped awkwardly through his 60 years. Whether in Glasgow, London, the North of England and the South of France – wherever he lay down his drawing board or set up his easel in the last decade of the nineteenth century and for almost the first three decades of the twentieth – the man is there in all that he does. It was a mark of his atypicality that he seemed to grow in stature as an artist in direct ratio to his decline as a pro-fessional man, and, in the end, he emerges as an icon.

To properly understand him we must first appreciate that he had an impediment – literally. He was born with a club foot due to a twisted sinew at birth. In medieval times, this was held to be the mark of the devil, and babies so born were often strangled or drowned immediately. On the other hand, it was also believed that such births were unusually favoured, especially in an uncommon attractiveness of face. Lord Byron had this, and Sir Walter Scott, and the late Dudley Moore in our own day. Mackintosh was the same. Whether good looks compensated for a physical fault at the nether end of their person is a moot point, but there is no denying that, psychologically, the limp must have affected Mackintosh hugely, especially in adolescence, and no amount of swagger with a stick could conceal his awareness of his disability in manhood. Too little account has been taken of this condition when consider-ing his volatile behaviour at points throughout his life. The emotional disturbance caused by this disadvantage in his earlier years could not help affect his mature personality.

In trying to understand him, it will also help by understanding the world he was born into on that summer Sunday in 1868. His Glasgow was then the second city of the British Empire. The 'dear green place' was perhaps not quite so verdant or spacious as it had been for Daniel Defoe in 1725. With its four main streets stretching from the Cathedral down to the River Clyde via the Tolbooth and the Salt Market, it offered the old University on the left and the Merchant City to the right. Defoe recognised even then as – 'a city of business; here is the face of trade ...'. He also noted 'a large distillery for the distilling of spirits from the molasses drawn from the sugars which they call'd Glasgow brandy.' Defoe was also assured that – 'they send near fifty sail of ships every year to Virginia, New England, and other English colonies in America ...' An English engineer officer, Captain Edward Birt, visited Glasgow in 1726 and commented – 'Glasgow is, to outward appearance, the prettiest and most uniform Town that I ever saw; and I believe there is nothing like it in Britain.'[1]

On the other hand the American novelist, Nathaniel Hawthorne, who visited Glasgow just over a hundred years later, walked the same streets with his wife and was horrified by what he saw – 'The High Street and still more the Salt Market, now swarm with the lower orders, to a degree which I have not witnessed elsewhere; so that it is difficult to make one's way among the sallow and unclean crowd and not at all pleasant to breathe in the noisomeness of the atmosphere.' He might agree with Captain Birt that indeed 'there is nothing like it in Britain.' Thomas Carlyle was even more trenchant, calling the great city 'a murky simmering tophet.'[2] For Henry James it was 'a seat of learning' yet for John Stuart Mill it was forever 'tainted with the stench of trade'.

The contrast between these various comments is underscored by the contrast in the buildings then extant. This is true in any large conurbation to some extent but it was especially true of Victorian Glasgow. It was a mean city indeed to the south and east, but to the north and west it was generous and spacious to a fault. The Clyde, winding its way from Lanarkshire through to Greenock, separated both social factions as if they were warring tribes – which in a sense they were. The native poor far outnumbered the new merchant rich. They always do. The comfortable industrialists, safe on the high ground where they lived in Palladian splendour, left the dreadful tenements by the riverside to the rats and cats and their fellow Glaswegians, whose lifestyle owed more to Hogarth than Palladio. However, extensive municipal works by the authorities from mid-century onwards did much to change this. As the dredging of the river brought increased trade right into the city centre so did the provision of parks and green spaces within the municipal boundaries give the overcrowded citizens a chance to breathe. The 'dear green place' was in some sense restored and, to their credit, this is a work that the present City of Glasgow carries on to this day. Who would ever have thought then that Glasgow would one day host a National Garden Festival as it did in June 1988.

In Victorian times, however, it must be admitted, it was difficult to breathe in Glasgow. It was by now a dear green *smokey* place. As Oxford had its spires, so Glasgow had its chimneys. The tallest of these being 'Charlie Tennent's Lum', which at one time was the highest chimney in Europe, belching out its fumes from the St Rollox bleach works far below, and joining, as if in sulphuric chorus, with the hundreds of others to create a lowering canopy that was as toxic as it was dark. Twilight always came early to Glaswegians. The cloak thrown over Defoe's Glasgow was nothing less than a coughing cupola – one is tempted to write 'coffin-cupola' – because its effects were deadly. Small wonder that Glasgow then boasted the highest death rate in Britain.

Gradually, however, improvements were taking place in living standards and in all matters of public health and hygiene. The fresh water supply was one of the first things to be extended by the building of a reservoir to the north of the city at Loch Katrine and ever since this facility has been providing the best drinking water in the country. The new tenements, too, were being built to a much higher quality and architects of the calibre of Alexander

'Greek' Thomson, Robert Rowand Anderson and John James Burnet were engaged to provide housing, which not only accommodated the workforce invading the city from the Scottish Highlands and Ireland, but also stood as visible evidence of Glasgow's betterment in terms of stone. Glasgow was booming and it was not shy about showing it.

In 1866 work had begun on Sir Gilbert Scott's design for Glasgow University. He had begun on this when he was also working on St Pancras Station in London and, frankly, it would have made little difference had the railway station been built on Gilmorehill and the university sited in London as there is much of a muchness about both Gothic designs. The Glasgow City Chambers in George Square date from around the same era but even this edifice, despite its munificent marbled interior, still stands as a bit of everything architecturally.

As a boy born at the Townhead, Mackintosh would have looked down from his tenement eyrie in Parson Street over the Glasgow Necropolis, shadowed as it was by St Mungo's Cathedral. This perhaps laid his lifelong fascination with churchyards and tombstones. He would have hirpled down the same High Street where the old university had now become a marshalling yard, and he would have seen the solitary Tolbooth standing at the Tron Gate as a reminder of the city seen by Defoe. The Salt Market still vomited its cosmopolitan citizenry from crowded closemouths and ships still packed the Clyde at the Broomielaw, except that few now showed sail. Their funnel smoke added to the chimney smoke and this helped create the soot and grime already beginning to work its way into the brand new sandstone rising up at every other street corner.

The young Mackintosh couldn't have failed to notice all this or feel the general excitement pervading the place. One can only suppose that he would have sensed it as he passed the brand new City Chambers on his apprentice's walk to John Hutchison's drawing office and that, observant as he was, he would have taken it all in as he climbed up West Nile Street en route to the School of Art, then housed in Rose Street. Small wonder that this introverted youth with a talent for drawing, later developed a notion of becoming an architect. New building work was going on all around him and one can only assume that all this must have made an enormous impression on an imaginative, solitary boy. He had only ever wanted to be an artist. An artist-architect was only an extension of this first ambition. However, as we shall see, it did not happen all at once.

His boyhood was difficult and he did not make it easy for himself. He might have been called a problem child but his problems were all of his own making and, in his own way, he found his own solution. This is a less-known period of his life but it is a vitally important one. It was at this time that he took the first decisive step on the journey that was to bring him his particular immortality. Many other excellent and perceptive writers have made their comments on all the different Mackintosh aspects since Howarth marked out the original playing field so I do not need to add my stone to their very considerable cairn. Instead, I have gone behind the monument to seek out the man.

Personally, I am like Mackintosh in that I, too, grew up in the East End of Glasgow and have spent most of my professional life outside of Scotland. It is this awareness of common roots which is the dynamic that drives the narrative and gives the subject a particular Celtic energy together, of course, with its concomitant waywardness. These personal links do not, in any way, make this a better book, but simply provide a native insight, which is as good a guess as any about a life that might have been so very different. Mary Newberry Sturrock, a trusted rememberer of the architect through much of his life, commented on his wasted genius – 'He died a forgotten man,' she said.[3]

Perhaps so, but he is well remembered now. Particularly today by those who themselves, are not artists or architects. Thanks to this popular acceptance, he is heading towards a status with the Scottish nation, or at least the Glasgow part of it, that is not unlike that accorded to Burns. We know most everything about Burns but we know relatively little about Mackintosh. What I do know is that Burns survived his mythos. So will Mackintosh, but as John McKean put it in his memorable sentence – 'There are powerful silences in this story'.[4]

CHAPTER ONE

The Limping Boy

1868–1883

Let Glasgow Flourish

This motto of the City of Glasgow sits today beneath the armorial shield that shows a wee bird on top of a tree from which hangs a bell on the right and below, across the base of the tree trunk, a fish balances a ring on the end of its nose. The full wording of the motto should read – *Let Glasgow Flourish by the Preaching of the Word,* but in these more secular times, the injunction to spread the Gospel is omitted. The bird perched on the top is undoubtedly a Glasgow sparrow full of impudent song, sung with a Glasgow accent. The tree represents the builder, or the growing thing that comes up from its roots to touch the sky and the fish is the religion or God-sense that underpins every act of man, whether he likes it or not. And the ring represents the world's reward – because there never has been an artist, except Fra Filipo perhaps, who didn't work for money.

The emblems of course relate to historical myths and legends concerning St Mungo and the beginning of the city but the overall design is also pertinent in that it sums up neatly the various aspects of our man, the enigmatic Mackintosh – builder, artist, man of feeling and Glaswegian. The injunction to 'flourish' is especially apt. If it means 'to bloom', it also means 'to make ornamental strokes with the pen', 'bold strokes to create a showy splendour'. This could be said to apply to the subject at hand. The link from 'bloom' in one sense to flowers as 'bloom' is also easy to understand, for both the beginning and end of his life were marked by his love and enthusiasm for all growing things in Nature – even cabbages.

This was probably due to his father, William McIntosh (*sic* – his son later changed the spelling of his name to Mackintosh, for reasons which will be explained later), who, although in the police all his life, was a passionate gardener. He filled their Dennistoun tenement flat with flowers and vegetables produced from a sooty allotment which he rented in the grounds of Golfhill House nearby. From his father's obsession, young Charlie was to develop a life-long love of flowers as well as a botanical awareness of their structure and an aesthetic appreciation of their beauty. All of which was to inform his adult work in design and form. It is no exaggeration to say that the future artist-architect was born in a Victorian garden allotment and a great deal of credit for this must go to the father, William, the police clerk with the green fingers.

Inspector William McIntosh, as he was then, was a remarkable man by all accounts.[1] He was born in County Cavan, Ireland, of Scottish parents, Hugh McIntosh, a distiller from Paisley and Marjory Morris, a fisherman's daughter from Methil in Fife. The potato famine of 1845 drove them from Ireland, as it did so many others, and the McIntoshes returned to Scotland. Eventually they settled in a tenement flat at 94 Glebe Street in the Townhead district near the centre of Glasgow. After working as a clerk in a city office, William joined the City of Glasgow Police as a constable in 1858 at the age of 22. He was tall and well built and had a good head on his shoulders. He rose up through the ranks and was already on the Promotions List when he married Margaret Rennie from Ayr at McIntosh Street in Dennistoun, the home of one of her relatives. In 1865, Lieutenant McIntosh, now father to a son, William Junior, and two daughters, Isabella and Martha, was appointed Captain, and Clerk to the Chief Constable of Glasgow. The young family was able to afford a higher rent and they moved to a more spacious flat in Parson Street, a street away from the old family house. It was here, on 7 June 1868, at No 70 (now demolished) that their fourth child, and second son, Charles Rennie Mackintosh, first saw the light of day.

It would have been a gloomy view, even from a top flat, as their tenement looked out onto the bulk of the Royal Infirmary, which overlooked the Glasgow Necropolis and also effectively hid Glasgow Cathedral in the High Street. In 1874, Chief Constable Smart promoted Captain McIntosh to Inspector and installed him Chief Clerk in the new Police Headquarters at South Albion Street, where McIntosh was to spend the rest of his police career. He now moved his family a mile or so west along Alexandra Parade (as it is now called) to No 2 Firpark Terrace in Dennistoun and an even better flat in a much better district. And it is here that William found his 'Garden of Eden, as his children called it, in the grounds of Golfhill House.

Golfhill House was the one-time mansion of the estate of that name bought by Mr (later Sir) Alexander Dennistoun in 1856 to form with other estates such as Whitehill, Haghill, Craig Park, Broom Park, Fir Park, Meadow Park and Wester and Easter Craigs, that district between Alexandra Parade and Duke Street which now bears his name. James Salmon, grandfather of James Salmon (the Wee Trout),[2] was instructed to create appropriate properties for the new suburb and in 1864, Dennistoun added Annfield and Bellfield to his domain. As a result whole streets of imposing houses, terraces and tenements were built in the area and still stand to this day proudly bearing all the old estate names. In 1880, Golfhill House and its garden must have been very convenient for William McIntosh at the end of a hard day in the Police office. He spent as much time as he could cultivating his beloved flowers, as well as vegetables for the table. With a house full of children he had plenty of mouths to feed and with so many youngsters running around most of the time, he was probably glad to get out to his garden for a bit.

The McIntosh children were eleven in all but, as with most Victorian families, especially in the towns and cities, only seven survived into adulthood, and of these, one, William Junior (Billy), the first son, ran off to sea and was killed in South America. The others were all either older or younger sisters to Charlie, two above him, Isabella (Bella) and Martha and three below, Margaret (Meg), Ellen and Agnes (Nancy). Small wonder he was spoiled. He grew up as a little prince among all the women in his life, doted on by his quiet mother and virtually waited on by his big sisters. It would appear that Margaret Rennie McIntosh hardly rose from her bed during her 23 years of marriage. When she wasn't pregnant, she was ailing with something or other and was to all intents and purposes a semi-invalid, but her family worshipped her and her quiet influence seems to have made it, for the most part, a happy household.

The bond between her and her only son in the house was deep. Charlie appeared to have inherited her frailty as well as her dark good looks. He was certainly not boyishly robust but there was no question that Charlie was her darling. This may have been because he had been born with the damaged foot. Or did she know the Highland superstition that such a genetic defect only came with every seventh generation bringing with it a gift that is cursed. Or had his merely been a bad delivery? For whatever reason, Charlie was always regarded as special in the family. Even so, apart from a noticeable limp, the foot defect was to give Charlie a decided chip on his shoulder.

In addition, an injury to the muscles of his left eye, supposedly sustained while playing in goal during a schoolboy game of football played in heavy rain, resulted in a severe chill, which developed into rheumatic fever that he was a long time in shaking off. The whole episode left him with a slight droop in the left eye. While it did not affect his vision it gave him as he grew up a slightly malevolent appearance, which some, especially the girls, were later to find attractive.

For these physical reasons no doubt, he was self-conscious outside the family, and even with them often petulant and hot-tempered, and he would fly into loud rages when he didn't get his own way over the most trivial things. This was manifest not only in the house but also when he first went to school at John Reid's Public School in Dennistoun in 1875. Reid had been a former landowner in the area and the school was one of his benefactions, but there is no record of Charlie's having enjoyed it much. Especially wet football matches. Most of us can remember our classmates at primary school but Charlie McIntosh seemed to be an exception. He made few friends as a boy because he didn't need any. Right from the very beginning he was a loner. While he had his mother at home and a ring of sisters around him, and all held together by a strong father, he had no need of anyone else.

His relationship with his father was not as open as it was with his mother, despite the father's natural concern for him. There would always be a slight distance between them if only because of the son's bias towards a delicate mother, but it must also be said that a limping boy, who was remote and aloof, wasn't the ideal son for an active, healthy, sports-loving father. God-fearing and strict as he was in his household, William McIntosh was, nevertheless, gregarious and efficient in the outside world. His exemplary record in the Police was proof of this.

He was a very physical man as his love of, and skill at most sports available to him indicated, yet he was not without sensitivity as his genuine love of gardening also showed. As he tended his garden of an evening, he must have often have mused to himself, on why he had such sons. Billy had left home early to go to sea.

Nothing more was heard of him until he was reported dead after an incident in a South American port. This is just one of the many Mackintosh mysteries. Billy is never mentioned again in the family. Charlie was different and his father knew it. For all their long hours together in the 'Garden of Eden', with Charlie drawing everything from cabbages to crocuses, while his father dug and delved, there is no evidence that they talked much or built up a strong relationship beyond the usual father-and-son deference. William, a keenly intelligent man, must have known early that he had an unusually gifted son – but what to do with him, that was the problem.

His mother was all for letting the boy find his own way in his own time. He wasn't like an ordinary boy. His was a special case in her eyes. To the father, there were many worse cases than Charlie out on the streets earning a living, or at least making a life for themselves, to whom a limp would seem a luxury. The trouble was that all the boy wanted to do was draw. He drew anywhere and everywhere and at all times. He withdrew into a sketchbook and seemed to live only in its pages, so that, at times, nobody could get near him. The sisters accepted that that's what Charlie did – he drew things on paper. That's what worried his father.

William McIntosh deserves some sympathy. He was genuinely concerned about Charlie's often idiosyncratic behaviour. What would it lead to? He couldn't just scribble his way into manhood. William was just as concerned about his wife. She wasn't strong in anything except her trust in God and her upright husband and her supreme confidence in her awkward son. Anyway, whatever was bothering him, she was sure he would soon grow out of it. According to the doctor all the boy needed was long walks in the fresh air. Charlie was only too happy to comply. He got out of town as often as he could and wherever the horse-tram would take him. For any Glasgow boy, plain street spaces were only a penny away but fields and green acres were tuppence coloured at termini like Airdrie or Paisley, Milngavie or Cambuslang. It was only a matter of choice, depending on the weather.

The boy seemed to be a law unto himself. There was no doubt he liked his own company best. He would make his way along the street or the road or the lane, taking it all in. It was as if he were always looking for something. Even on the annual summer trip 'doon the watter' to the Clyde coast in the last two weeks in July when most of Glasgow's working class decanted into Ayrshire, he was always wandering off on his own instead of taking part in the family's normal holiday activities. The McIntoshes, it would seem, did not travel light for the Glasgow Fair Fortnight as it was called. They brought all the family pets, the two cats, a hedgehog, a tortoise – even a goat to provide milk for the younger children.

One year the girls made a great fuss about a pet lamb they adopted from a nearby farm. There were tears when they weren't allowed to bring it back to Glasgow. There weren't many tears in the McIntosh household, and if there were, they were usually brought on by the mother's favourite son. While he may have seemed totally-self-centred, indolent or downright lazy, he was never completely unlikeable. When required, he had all his mother's charm, and even some of his father's out-going nature when the occasion called for it, but, in the last resort, he knew he could always rely on his big sister, Bella, even though she was sometimes embarrassed by his 'arty' ways. There had never been an artist in the family before.

For the most part, however, he was quiet, almost to the point of taciturnity, but he was a boy before he was anything. He bitterly resented his limp and the frustration it caused in him occasionally. At times his feelings would just boil over. The truth of the matter was that as a young male he was more likely holding back an enormous pent-up energy. This would explain the sudden explosions of rage. Recent medical research has shown that there were physical and psychological reasons for this kind of behaviour in young boys, and the noted Mackintosh commentator, John McKean has already pointed this out.[3] He deals with it comprehensively in his book, *Charles Rennie Mackintosh – Architect, Artist and Icon* (2000) and his findings indicate that Mackintosh may have suffered, if only to a lesser degree, from a development disorder which has become known today as Asperger's Syndrome. Dr Hans Asperger was an Austrian who, in 1944, published a paper describing the behaviour pattern of young males of normal intelligence, who also exhibited autistic or dyslexic tendencies to varying degrees, resulting in reading or writing difficulties and a marked lack of social skills. Dr Asperger wrote:

> It seems that for success in science or art, a dash of autism is essential. For success, the necessary ingredient may be the ability to turn away from the everyday world, from the simply practical, an ability to rethink a subject with originality so as to create in new, untrodden ways, with all the abilities canalised into one speciality.[4]

This fitted the young McIntosh exactly for all his boyish interests were fused through the pencil in his hand. Asperger also noted that these same young boys seem to think in pictures. Their retention is visual rather verbal and this can lead to an inventive and creative way of thinking. They tend to live in their own world and see the outside world differently. In Dr Tony Attwood's guide to Asperger's Syndrome, he says of sufferers: 'They are a bright thread in the tapestry of life'. Vincent Van Gogh and Michelangelo were also said to manifest this condition, and it might also be said of Charlie McIntosh that he had similar symptoms.

Later studies have now shown that people with Asperger's Syndrome will never look you in the eye and can be clumsy in general movement. Mackintosh's left eye was inclined to be lazy so he would be reluctant to hold anyone's gaze, and his limp might have made him seem clumsy, but these were physical traits and not due to any emotional deficiency. So the question of any high-functioning autism in his case is one in which the jury is still out.[5]

In 1877, he began at Allan Glen's High School, a private establishment for the sons of tradesmen and artisans. It is hard enough for a new boy at any boys' school but one with a limp and a slight squint doesn't have to look for trouble. Charlie, however, soon learned to take care of himself in his own way. His secure home base gave him the assurance that he was able to carry into the classroom. He was saved by being good at drawing. Schoolboys are always impressed by unexpected skills, and those not good at games soon learn to survive as clowns or entertainers. Charlie's defence was his skill with a pencil and this would have impressed his fellow-pupils even if it were displayed under a desk lid and not on the blackboard. To be known as 'a good drawer' gave him a place, a status and he would have grabbed it – if only in self-defence.

In any case, the Asperger factor could have given him an indifference to superficial popularity and his absolute honesty was a sturdy if awkward shield on every occasion. To his teachers, he must have been a puzzle – outwardly normal but, as we now know, in a ferment inside. To them he must have appeared slow, if not backward, and one of them remembers only his abnormally bad temper. It was no surprise that he did not attain any scholastic heights because he made no great attempt to seek them. He was working his own way out of boyhood, and was travelling by an atypical route.

However, he was also lucky that Allan Glen's was progressive. In addition to the normal subjects, it also ran a Technical Workshop which encouraged pupils like Mackintosh to develop skills in woodwork and metalwork, putting his drawing to good use in learning to set out scientific diagrams and data. The usual leaving age for the boys was fourteen, but for those whose parents could afford it, two more years were offered in more specialised subject. Charlie used these extra years to good effect in the Technical Workshop, and it was here that the seed of an idea about becoming an architect was probably born.

One must bear in mind that he had few conventional outlets open to him at the time. He hadn't the physique for manual work, nor the inclination for academia. He would never make a policeman like his father nor did he want to be a minister of the Kirk – as his religious mother might have hoped. An 'ordinary' job in a shop or an office held no attraction at all. All he could do was draw. So he would wait for a job that would put a pencil in his hand. Architecture would do that but it was a very remote possibility indeed. Where did one of his background start? He did not know anyone who was an architect or anyone who knew anyone who was an architect. All his father's friends were policemen or publicans. There may have been Masonic connections as Freemasonry was a large part of police life then, but Charlie would know nothing of this. All he knew was that he was a McIntosh. McIntosh of Mackintosh, the Clan Chattan, the family of the Cat. His family had two cats. He liked cats. He drew them well. And when did you see a cat that didn't do exactly as it wanted to do – and when it wanted to do it? He empathised with that. In the same way, he knew that a cat had nine lives, and here he was, hardly started on his first. It was 1880, and he was in his third year at Allan Glen's. It was a deciding time for young McIntosh, but he had plenty of time yet. Meantime, he would cover more sheets of paper with his scribbles and wait to see how things turned out.

His birthdate being on June 7, he was born under the sign of Gemini, the twin, an air sign and signifying one given to ideas and self-expression through change. Astronomically, it is the third sign of the zodiac, whose prominent features are the twin stars, Castor and Pollux. If we consider him then as Castor, his Pollux was a young English girl with a Scottish name who had just begun studying art at Stoke-on-Trent in Staffordshire. Margaret Mempes Macdonald was the daughter of John Macdonald, a lawyer turned mining engineer, who had moved from Glasgow to work in England, where he met and married a colleague's sister, an Englishwoman, Frances Grove Hardeman, in Tipton, Warwickshire.

They had five children, three boys and two girls. Margaret came after the son and heir, Charles, on 5 November 1864, making her four years older than Charles McIntosh. Their backgrounds could not have been more different. The McIntoshes were upwardly-mobile working class, the Macdonalds were static, upper-class professionals with several generations of money in the family. They also had continuing roots in Glasgow because of the Macdonald brothers' law practice, which was still maintained there, and the presence of Grandmother White's two maiden daughters, Margaret's great-aunts, Janet and Agnes. This family framework was to be a formidable influence in the years to come. Margaret's younger sister, Frances Macdonald, was born in born at Ravenscliff, near Kidsgrove in 1873, but both girls were brought up at Chesterton Hall, Staffordshire, as young ladies of refinement and leisure, who had no need to prepare for a profession or to look for a husband. They had the luxury of time and well-to-do parents and could more or less do as they liked with their youth. At Orme School for Girls in Staffordshire, both showed an early inclination to the arts and, on leaving to study with JP Bacon at Stoke-on-Trent, Margaret won a First Class Award for Anatomical Drawing. She continued her arts studies in France and Germany over the next few years, becoming, at the same time, fluent in both languages. She also acquired the assuredness she was to need at so many stages in her life. A tall girl, she had poise beyond her years and a striking dress sense. One could not miss Margaret Macdonald. She was an independent woman in every sense. Her sister was smaller, but was no less striking.

Frances was to marry another Scottish artist and designer, James Herbert McNair, who was to become a colleague and close friend of Mackintosh. Thus, these four different young people were already started on the road that would ultimately bring them all together in Glasgow. Bertie, as McNair was always called by the others (just as Mackintosh was always Toshie), was, like Margaret Macdonald, born into money. Of Army stock, the McNairs had land and assets in Ayrshire and Bertie was born in the family home at 'Birchbank', Skelmorlie, where, incidentally, the architect who was to be a big Mackintosh influence, John Honeyman, also had a home. Bertie McNair was educated at the Collegiate School in Greenock with a view to his becoming an engineer but instead, again like Margaret, and around the same time, 1881, took himself off to France to study watercolour painting with a M Haudebert at Rouen.

This is what young Scots artists did in those days – they went Continental, especially if they came from Glasgow. Yet, ironically, the more notable of them came to be known collectively as the

'Glasgow Boys', despite the fact that they included the beautiful
Bessie McNicol on the fringe of this group. Her particular friend,
Edward Hornel, studied in Antwerp, William York Macgregor
went to the Slade in London, Alexander Roche to Paris, as did
James Guthrie, and the future Sir John Lavery (who was technically an Irishman) went to Grez near Fountainbleau, an artists'
colony favoured earlier by Robert Louis Stevenson and his artist-
cousin, Bob. On the other hand, William McTaggart went only as
far as Edinburgh while George Henry of the Glasgow Group, and
some of the younger artists like David Gauld (a later friend of
Toshie's) and Stuart Park, all trained in Glasgow.

There was no doubt that the great majority of this generation
of Victorian Scots looked beyond their own city even though at
the time, Glasgow was indeed flourishing. It was a place that was
more European than British at the time, and its tentacles even
stretched as far east as Japan. In 1882, Christopher Dresser had
published his *Japan, its Art and its Architecture* and this had enormous influence on young Artistic Glasgow. Hornel and Henry
were greatly affected by his work and even went to Japan themselves. Everything oriental was instantly fashionable.

Another profound influence on the group was James McNeil
Whistler, an American artist and wit based in London, who was
proudly Scottish on his famous mother's side. That Belfast-born
Glasgow Boy, John Lavery, made more of a contribution to the
Celtic Revival in the next decade. All these influences, Celtic,
Irish, Chinese, Japanese, would have been absorbed, however subconsciously, by the young Mackintosh, and these imbibed
elements would always be some part of his later design schemes.
Yes, the last two decades of the nineteenth-century was a good
time to be a modernist. Everything on the Clyde seemed to be
looking ahead, and Glasgow was building up a good head of
steam towards the future.

As with any end of the century epoch it was a time of paradox,
of great change. Optimism ran hand in hand with pessimism as
the old order changed giving way, somewhat reluctantly, to the
new prosperity. Not since the Tobacco Lords strutted the plain-

stanes of the Trongate with their high hats and long canes had the dear, green place known such bustling, commercial activity. And there was money around. Tobacco magnate, Stephen Mitchell, left a bequest to found the famous library now boasting his name. Similarly, Baillie Archibald McLellan's cash built the famous Galleries in Sauchiehall Street and William Denny's company made the first ocean-going liner built of steel for the Union Steamship Company of New Zealand, thus laying the keel for the Clydeside's long succession of queenly vessels. Glasgow was glad to leave the law, the church, insurance and banking to Edinburgh, it had other priorities. Auld Reekie may have been the capital but the dear, green place had the capital.

Fortunes were being made in every kind of commerce and these new merchant princes weren't ashamed to display their profits in the palaces they built along the Great Western Road or in the new Park development around the University. Glasgow was discovering its genius for making things and the basis of its later superb craftsmanship in almost every area of industry was being surely developed. Art hoarders like William Burrell sprang up and art dealers such as John Forbes White and Alexander Reid emerged to link Glasgow to the Hague (and discover Van Gogh in the process). Reid also opened the way for many artistic young gentlemen then coming up in the city.

John Keppie, a leading character in the Mackintosh Story to come, and only six years older than Charlie, was one of these. He had been born in Glasgow but he, too, had links with Ayrshire, where his family had property in Prestwick. John had the distinction of training as an architect in Paris, in the year after JJ Burnet, already an established figure in the 'tight little circle of Glasgow architects' as Filipo Alison called them.[6] When Keppie came back to Glasgow in 1883 he was snapped up immediately by James Sellars, one of the leading architects of his day, and soon made his mark. He was unaware then of the role he was to play in the Mackintosh drama that was about to unfold. Neither was his little sister, Jessie (the same age as Charlie), but she was cast as well.

And our leading man, Charlie himself, had made up his mind by this time about what part he was going to play. He was born into the world with Frank Lloyd Wright, Josef Hoffmann, Adolf Loos and Arthur Macmurdo all in the same generation and Pablo Picasso was only a few years after them. The seeds of Modernism were already in the ground and its shoots were sprouting around the 15-year-old McIntosh much as the new building was happening throughout the city. By this time, he knew what he had to do. He had only ever wanted to be an artist, but, as mentioned, the extra two years at Allan Glen's had introduced him to architecture, or at least to technical drawing.

He still needed to draw but now he wanted to draw buildings. He was still going to be an artist but he would be an artist-architect. Meantime, he would make a start at the Art School. He couldn't see himself leaving Glasgow as everybody else seemed to have done. Or going to the École des Beaux Arts like John Keppie. Keppie had done a two-year course in Architecture at the Glasgow School of Art before going on to Paris, but he had his father's tobacco business to back him. The McIntoshes only had William McIntosh's wages – even though they were now a Police Chief Inspector's.

Nevertheless, his mother was delighted at her son's artistic ambitions. His big sister, Bella, thought he was getting above himself and was altogether too stubborn for his own good. Why couldn't he get an ordinary job in an office instead of trying for something away beyond him? His youngest sister, Nancy, thought it was a great idea. She would have liked to become an artist herself, but when she later suggested this to her father, he laughed and told her not to be silly. Yet it was in that same year, 1882, that the Glasgow Society of Lady Artists had been founded by Norah Neilson Gray and Stansmore Dean Stevenson.

It was William McIntosh, however, who came up with the solution to the Charlie situation. He could go the Art School if that's what he wanted – but it would have to be night classes and maybe he could get into an architect's office and train as a draughtsman during the day. At least that would give him a job that would allow him to draw as much as he liked. Then, later on perhaps, if he showed promise, he could move up to become an architect. Thus it was then, that Charles R McIntosh, aged 15, enrolled at the Glasgow School of Art in the Corporation Galleries, Rose Street for Evening Classes in Drawing and Ornamentation, commencing in September 1883, so beginning a part-time studentship that would last until 1893.

Incidentally, he gave his father's profession as 'clerk'. Chief Inspector McIntosh, with the fancy braid on his cap and two sergeants under him, would have understood. After all, under the uniform, that's exactly what he was. He was, however, still a long way yet from understanding his atypical son. The father had doubts about any artist making a living in the world, but, as usual, he put his trust in the Will of God – wondering, at the same time perhaps, how his boss, Chief Constable McCall would react to his Chief Clerk's having an artist son.

What is ironic is that only five years later, in 1888, Mackintosh designed something specifically for Chief Constable McCall – his tombstone. It can still be seen in the Glasgow Necropolis today. It was Mackintosh's first documented architectural work, and it came through his own father.

CHAPTER TWO

The Apprentice Student
1884–1889

'Mackintosh is an enigma.'

Roger Billcliffe

IN 1884, MOST OF the working population of Glasgow walked to work. The weather had to be really bad before they took to the horse-drawn tram. Only the bosses went by private carriage – and the toffs came in by train. It was a different matter when the Corporation put the street rails down for the tram-car, then ordinary Glasgow took to them in droves, but that was a few years off yet and, if it were not to be the horse tram, then, for most, it was a case of Shanks's pony. That was probably how 16-year old Charlie McIntosh would have gone off to start work for the first time.

He would have made his way by one of two ways from Dennistoun – via Duke Street to George Square or by Parliamentary Road into the Cowcaddens and down into the city centre. This would be no problem for a boy who never found any walk boring. Anyway, there was always a lot in the streets for him to see. A new Glasgow was growing up before his very eyes, and, it would seem, at every corner. A whole board of architects with names like Burnet (father and son), Salmon (grandfather and grandson), William Leiper, James Sellars, Campbell Douglas, Charles Wilson and JJ Stevenson (not to mention John Honeyman) were at work with redstone and greystone laying down the Victorian face that Glasgow was to present to the world for the next hundred years. It was, however, an Edinburgh man, Rowand Anderson, who designed the huge Central Railway Hotel at Gordon Street and Hope Street, which was then a year away from completion.

It has been said that if Edinburgh were the 'Athens of the North', Glasgow was its Syracuse. Well, here was direct evidence. There was energy in the atmosphere, despite the smoke, and a confidence exuding from at least half of the citizenry. There was always a half whose only concern was basic survival. The 'better' half had its communal eye fixed on progress and the will to use any available way to carry things forward and turn over an honest shilling, or, better still, a pound. Property was a good bet, even then, and every kind of building, both public and private, was at a different stage of construction and no more so than in the city centre. Here, all along the eastern side of George Square, with its incongruous statue of Walter Scott looking down from its height, the scaffolding was up and the steam-cranes working.

As he crossed the Square on his way to St Vincent Place, Charlie McIntosh might have glanced up to Sir Wattie, wondering how a man with a club foot managed to climb so high in the world – and so far from Abbotsford, too. The boy would also have noticed all the building going on to his left. Glasgow was erecting its City Chambers as a big, fat cake for itself to confirm its status as the Second City in Britain, as well as of the Empire, and one of the leading London architects, William Young from Paisley, was in architectural charge.

The Glasgow City Chambers was a long time building because Glasgow Corporation was determined to get its money's worth in masonry and just about everything that could be built was incorporated into the sprawling design. It impressed by its very size and weight much in the way a sumo wrestler does, but it is not, even today, the most attractive thing to look at. The interiors, however, taking advantage of skilled Italian craftsmen now available in the workforce, are still genuinely impressive in their marble splendour. But it would take a wee while yet to get to that. Meantime, young Charlie would have continued on his way through St Vincent Place (the place of the banks) and its continuation, St Vincent Street, where at No 107, he found the office of John Hutchison, Architect.

This was his starting point for all that was to follow. Everything would stem from this unobtrusive drawing office tucked away at the back of James Hutchison's cabinet-making premises, where furniture was made for the better class of shop in Sauchiehall and Buchanan Streets. Such a conjunction of activity couldn't be better for an artistic boy with a bent for practical design. One wonders how many working hours he spent watching James Hutchison working on wood as opposed to watching John Hutchison working on paper. Either way, it was a valuable pair of learning curves.

Architectural education was a more casual affair in 1884. It had only been twenty years since the Architectural Association had established voluntary examinations for the RIBA and just over ten since the Architectural Master, R Phene Spiers, had given special classes at the Royal Academy. Architecture had not yet become a fully-fledged academic discipline, and boys took up the apprenticeship much as they might have done to become carpenters or watchmakers. But things were always moving forward, and a more regulated entry to the profession was gradually attained, but it was only a couple of years before, in 1882, that the RIBA introduced compulsory examinations.

Hitherto, architectural practices as a whole reflected the style and personality of the senior partner. Burnet showed the ornate influence of his French training, Thomson had a Greek word for it, Sellars looked to Egypt, Wilson to England and John Honeyman had all the restraint of a Christian gentleman in his many churches, although he was not without his own kind of daring, as witness his iron and glass Ca'd'oro building in Union Street. These men were in the Scottish Premier League of architects and were, for the most part, a closed circle to which practitioners like John Hutchison did not belong. This proved no drawback to the first day apprentice. Not being in a large office, he was given more to do sooner and, since the practice had no high prestige projects, the risk was less than if he were a junior in a more high-powered concern.

This did not mean that standards were measurably inferior or conditions so bad that good work could not be done. His articles were drawn up much as they would be for any architectural apprentice of the day. The arrangement was that he would receive no remuneration at all in the first year, five pounds in the second and rise by yearly increments of the same amount until he received 25 pounds on completing his final year – providing, of course, that he 'gave satisfaction'. That he did was proved by the attention given him by Hutchison's chief draughtsman, Andrew Black, a clever and experienced old hand, who saw at once the exceptional quality in this seemingly dour young fellow who kept very much to himself but who, as Black saw, could draw like Raphael.

A bond quickly developed between the two and Black entrusted the novice with schemes that might have appeared too advanced for his apprentice skills. For instance, after only a few weeks, he allowed the boy to work on Ionic capitals for Wylie and Hill's shop front in Buchanan Street. Howarth reports that when it came time to leave Hutchison's in 1889, Mackintosh's place was taken by another apprentice, WJ Blane, who, more than 60 years later, could remember seeing drawings of an Ionic capital to be executed in plaster for Wylie and Hill. He told Tom Howarth that they were 'astonishing in their vividness, vigour and originality'. It was hard to believe that they were the work of a 16-year old boy in the first year of his apprenticeship. Unfortunately, Wylie and Hill's was destroyed by fire some years later and all trace of his architectural juvenilia was lost.[1]

It is not known how the first contact was made with John Hutchison to take the boy on. It could very well have been through the father's contacts once again, but, however it was arranged, he was off to a sound start in his chosen profession. Under the eagle eye of David Black, he progressed speedily from a junior emptying inkwells to an apprentice draughtsman preparing ground plans. Thanks to Black, he was solidly grounded in every aspect of the job and this elementary experience was to stand him in good stead in the years ahead. Since Hutchison did not have the staff to specialise, everyone in the office had to do everything, and even if the work were mostly on shop fronts and store-houses, it was all good experience. Every line set down on paper was a pointer ahead to better things, and young McIntosh revelled in it. So finished and assured was his work becoming that Black soon realised that Hutchison's could not keep the boy for long after his apprenticeship was completed.

In that first year, Charlie worked days at Hutchison's and continued his three nights at the Art School, Tuesday, Wednesday and Thursday and occasional Saturday mornings. The new schedule called for an extraordinary commitment on his part but he does not seem to have hesitated for a moment. It was if he had been preparing for this since Allan Glen's. His father left the decision to work this 'double shift' up to his son. 'As long as he put his mind to it', was all he said to John Hutchison. His mother (who was in decline) worried about the physical strain on him and his sisters were only sorry that they never seemed to see him around the house or in the 'Garden of Eden' as much. Even the two McIntosh cats must have become wary of this part-time stranger as 1884 gave way to 1885 and the week-draining routine continued. But Charlie went forward as if borne up on a great adrenalin surge.

Glasgow wasn't a bad place to get an arts training. It has an unexpectedly long and not unworthy pedigree in that respect. Its Technical College, founded in 1796, most of whose students were also night class attenders, had a strong emphasis on design technology, and the first School of Art (established 1844 in Ingram Street) had a very definite utilitarian bias in its original art course. In a Scottish kind of way, Art was acceptable if it could be shown to be useful. There were more aesthetic intentions shown by the Foulis brothers, Robert and Andrew, when they started their Academy of Fine Arts in the city in 1852 but what they made by selling rare books they lost in buying poor paintings and the project bankrupted both of them.

In 1869, the year after Charlie was born, the Art School moved to premises in Rose Street, adjacent to the Corporation Galleries in Sauchiehall Street. These were no more than several dwelling houses on the site knocked about and together to provide painting space for several hundred students, which was cosy to say the least. It was cramped from the beginning and as it grew more crowded in the decade that was to follow, the need for a new school became increasingly obvious. This fact was to be the turning point in the life of one student, whose double life as an articled apprentice and registered student had just begun.

It is generally forgotten that Mackintosh trained first as a painter and not as an architect. His first year was spent entirely in painting and drawing – painting ornaments from the flat and from the cast. This suited him completely. So much so, that he won the prize for Painting in Monochrome, which was one that carried with it free tuition for the rest of his time at the School. This must have delighted William McIntosh and totally justified Andrew Black's judgement. He went along to the Corporation Galleries to see his favourite apprentice's work hung at the end of the year show with all the other 'proper' art students, who paid twice as much to attend the day course. In Black's opinion, Charlie did not look at all out of his league.

This student showing of work in 1885 marked the first appearance of the new Director of the School of Art, an Englishman, Francis Henry Newbery from Membury in Devon. At only 30 years of age, he had been appointed Director of the Glasgow School of Art and Haldane Academy in succession to the then Headmaster, Thomas Symmonds. Like Mackintosh, Newbery had five sisters and, as the son of a shoemaker, he didn't start with any great advantages either, but when the family moved to Dorset he came under the eye of the local Headmaster of Bridport General School, Mr James Beard. He saw that Francis had artistic talents and recommended him to the local Literary and Scientific Institute. From there he was sent up to London in 1875 to be trained as an art teacher.

When he completed his studies his first job was on the staff of the Art Training School at South Kensington under Sir Edwyn Poynter, and then in 1881, under Thomas Armstrong. The first stressed the primacy of art in the syllabus, the second, the importance of good design and this fell in exactly with Newbery's own thinking and with the contemporary need as expressed in the 1884 Royal Commission on Technical Instruction, which found for more and better design in industry. Art education up till this time had been hidebound in stultified traditionalism and hardly amounted to more than insisting that students copy exactly what was set down before them and reproduce it on canvas or paper to the best of their ability. They might as well have provided them with cameras, which were just coming into fashion at the time.

In 1885, however, Newbery, influenced by John Ruskin, went back to Nature, seeking a looser kind of depiction, so as to free the creative impulse in the learner-artist. At the same time, he realised the basic requirement was to improve the ability to draw, something, incidentally, that the modern artist can't always do. The Kensington regimen had been even more thorough. It had 23 different stages of instruction in drawing, painting, modelling and design, which further broke down into no less than 56 parts where drawing, for instance, would move gradually from flat copy to three-dimensional renderings involving shading in the flat and the round until, at last, the student was free to work from Nature or a living model. It was a long haul in every sense. Except for students of Mackintosh's calibre, who had been drawing ever since they had first been able to hold a pencil. The pencil, as Newbery suggested, 'that was in every student's pocket much as the Marshall's baton that Napoleon declared was in every soldier's knapsack.'[2]

But at the back end of the year of 1885 – Scots always talk about 'the back end' of a year in a solemn tone because that's the time, they say, when a lot of the old folk go – except that Margaret Rennie McIntosh wasn't old. She was only 48 but she died at four o' clock in the afternoon of Wednesday 9 December with her son at the bedside. It was the day before his seventeenth birthday. His was not a happy one. Margaret McIntosh was buried at Sighthill Cemetery on the Saturday. The boy was inconsolable. Half of his very fabric had been torn away. It was noticed that he said very little but he was 'hanging about the doors' again as if waiting for his mother's sympathetic spirit to leave the place.

If Mackintosh himself is an enigma, as Billcliffe suggests, then his mother is a riddle. Little is known of her beginnings. The records show that she was born in Ayr to Martha Spence but it is thought she may have been illegitimate and there was even a rumour she was a Catholic, which in Victorian Glasgow was certainly no advantage. What we do know now, thanks to Iain Paterson's researches,[3] is that she was a 25-year-old muslin darner living in the Calton district when she married the policeman, William McIntosh, on 4 August 1862 at the tenement flat at 54 McIntosh Street, Dennistoun, which was to be their first married home.

So much for the facts. What cannot be recorded is what the loss of what Howarth called this 'unassuming, homely woman of character, greatly loved by her children',[4] meant to her only surviving son. Children generally love their mother but Charlie seemed to have added an extra dimension in the relationship. She was his unwitting Muse as well as his mother. She may have guessed at his inner perturbations without being able to articulate the reasons for them or to suggest any relief. All she could do was offer her all-enveloping mother love and encouragement, and he wrapped his boyhood in its warm folds. Now that protective cover was whipped away and he was on his own. The sisters drew an even closer circle around him but it wasn't the same. He retreated further within himself emotionally. His father said nothing but spent even more time among the flowers and vegetables in his 'Garden of Eden'.

During her last illness, Margaret Rennie had been cared for by her bridesmaid and best friend, Christina McVicar, whose father, Donald, owned a local pub. The McVicars lived at Broompark Drive nearby, and Chrissie, as everyone called her, was the oldest of six children. At 28, she married a widower from Stirling, Tom Forrest, who had come to work in the iron foundry at Cambuslang, where they went to live in 1877. Sadly, Tom died of meningitis after only a few years, and the childless Chrissie came back to Dennistoun to resume her friendship with the McIntoshes.

William wasn't so sure at first – 'A right Madam, that one,' he was heard to remark. Charlie said nothing, but it was a name that was to stick.

In the new session of 1886, his fourth year of nights, Charlie began on his first formal lessons with Thomas Smith on Building and Elementary Architecture. This discipline was new to the School but when he heard it was to be instituted, Andrew Black was insistent that Charlie take the class. He knew the value that such training would have as an addition to the daily practical tuition he could give him at Hutchison's. The night-time artist now had to give place to the day-time craftsman. Yet surely, as Black saw it, the ideal was the integration of both. This was also Newbery's thinking. To him, the great days of art were those when the craftsman was the artist.

In the same year when the student McIntosh began with architecture proper, the new broom, Newbery, made it clear to the city that his intention was 'to provide Glasgow with a race of designers of her own creation'. In his first annual report in 1886, Newbery made it plain where he stood:

> It is for Glasgow to say what is required by her art-loving or manufacturing public... it is for the School of Art without imperilling her fealty to the Department to adapt herself to such requirements. The real problem is how to make the school useful and how to make people use the school ...[5]

The late Sir Harry Barnes, a former Director of the School, took exception to the phrase, 'fealty to the Department' in his *Notes from the Mackintosh Circle* from which this information is derived.[6] He saw such deference to the autocratic attitude of the Central School at South Kensington in London and its rigid National Course of Instruction as nothing more than 'political humbug' and that what Newbery was really about was that the School should be 'true to itself'. This accepted, Newbery did say at a later date (9 February 1893) when the school had won five gold medals, one silver, eleven bronze, four Queen's Prizes and fourteen free studentships, that 'he did not care if he did not win gold medals; he would rather win the golden opinion of Glasgow'.

He wanted the GSA to be 'a distinctive school of art 'and not one that 'required to please the London school'.[7] There was no doubt that Newbery, as an old boy of the London school, was an astute politician in this volatile field and knew what to say and when. He also possessed, as the Glasgow *Evening Times* said pointedly in 1903, 'unusual powers as an organiser'. As we shall see in a later chapter, he was to need every trick he had in his book.

Meantime, a certain Miss Cranston, having enjoyed five years good trading experience at her first tea room in Argyle Street, opened a second one in Ingram Street. Here, she added a lunchroom and placed the whole thing in the charge of Miss Drummond, her manageress. The Cranston empire was on the march. Another important thread in the Mackintosh tapestry was being put in place. An interesting Cranston connection here was that one of Toshie's fellow-students in those first years at the Art School evening classes was PW Davidson.

Peter Davidson was two years younger than Mackintosh, but was to work with him later at Hous'hill, the Cranston/Cochrane home in the north of Glasgow. Peter's first memory of Chas. R McIntosh, however, was the latter's fine brushwork in sepia drawings and that he won prizes right from the start. Davidson ultimately had his own studio and become a tutor in the subject at the School. He also won prizes, but he admits himself that he couldn't match Mackintosh in the glittering swathe that Charlie cut through the prize lists throughout his eventful ten-year part-time studenthood. In his unpublished autobiography, Mr Davidson writes:

> We were both young boys working for our 2nd-grade certificate in freehand, perspective, model drawing and geometry in the Old Art School in Rose Street. We were evening students and all mostly trade apprentices ...[8]

Attendances at these classes was voluntary in the Eighties and most of the young men, tired after the exertions of their day jobs didn't always get to every class every evening. So much did attendances drop that the Glasgow Institute of Architects offered an annual prize hoping to spark off some enthusiasm. Of the first three prizes offered, Mackintosh won two of them – in 1886 and again in 1887. Coincidentally, when Mackintosh went on to win the National Gold Medal in 1891 for his Railway Terminus design, Davidson also won an award for his metalwork.

The thoroughbreds of the artistic racing stable, however, were still the fine artists – especially those who were, as they would say at Allan Glen's, 'good drawers'. At the annual prize-giving address to the Glasgow students in 1886, the Chairman of the School's Committee of Management, Sir James Watson, told them that:

> All our great industries, whether of shipbuilding or housebuilding, whether of engineering or machine-making, whether of pattern drawing or the higher art of painting, must have their first origin in drawing, and without this basis none of them can be established. The builder must first design his model; the architect his structure; the engineer his railway, his docks or his bridges; the painter his sketch; and the designer his ideal, before he can begin his operations.[9]

In 1888, the year Mackintosh won a bronze medal from Kensington for his 'Design for a Mountain Chapel', Director Newbery addressed members of the Philosophical Society on 'The Training of Architectural Students' and also stressed the importance of drawing. He did so in the florid oratory that was this larger-than-life man's style. There was lot of the actor in Fra Newbery:

> With his pencil the architect may command the dull stones of the earth to arrange themselves in ordered masses, and make beauty to live in undying splendour on our walls; may by his proportions lead the thoughts, and by his colours tinge the imagination.[10]

This in fact was a clarion call for the artist-architect, which, thanks to Andy Black, Chas. R McIntosh was now well on the

way to becoming. At Hutchison's, he had been shown the fundamentals of the building trade as far as it related to working
drawings and he had had the extra benefit of close daily contact
with a furniture maker through the wall. Added to this was his
painter's training at the Art School and the further advantage of
Art history and theory. In short, he had within his grasp the full
alphabet of creative expression within the architectural frame, and
this was wholly consistent with Newbery's ideal. 'Wholeness' was
the very word both men embraced from the beginning, and the
view that architecture embraced all the arts. Mackintosh because
of his training, education and natural inclination could take nothing else than a holistic approach to his future trade.

It is significant that in these Glasgow years of his training and
establishment as a professional architect, that is the two decades
between 1883 and 1914, there were no less than three great International Exhibitions mounted in the city – 1888, 1901 and 1912.
He was, therefore, in his most impressionable years exposed to
some of the best work in architecture and design available in his
day even if few of his own contributions featured. Not that that
appeared to bother him unduly. In 1888, he was 20 years of age
and brimming over with promise.

So, too, was John Keppie, only six years older, but also Glas-
gow-born although with a strong allegiance to Ayrshire. In 1883,
after winning a Silver Medal in the RIBA's Tite Competition, he
continued his studies in Paris at the *Atelier Pascal*. He then travelled in Italy, returning with a full sketchbook, which allowed him
to exhibit at the Glasgow Institute of the Fine Arts Exhibition in
1888. Keppie then worked as a draughtsman for Campbell, Douglas and Sellars, and his future with them looked assured when he
was chosen to work closely with James Sellars on the first Glasgow International Exhibition held in Kelvingrove Park in the
summer of 1888. Then Sellars died suddenly, due, it is said, to
overwork on the Exhibition, and Keppie's next job with the firm
was to write an appreciation of his former employer for the
December issue of *The Scottish Art Review*.[11]

He also designed a tomb for Sellars in the Egyptian style with a bronze medallion of the noted architect specially commissioned from Pittendrigh Macgillivray set in Keppie's framework. Having performed this service for his Principal, the other senior partners did not stand in his way when he was invited by a very respected Glasgow architect, John Honeyman, to join him as a junior partner in the following year. Assisted, no doubt, by the proceeds of Mr Keppie's will, young John was delighted to accept and prepared to move offices.

Mackintosh, too, was preparing to clear his desk, and by an odd coincidence, one of the last things he worked on at Hutchison's was a tombstone. As mentioned at the end of the last chapter, this was designed for the late Chief Constable McCall, his father's boss, and it was William McIntosh who had got him the commission. Where Keppie went Egyptian for Sellars, Charlie gave the policeman a Celtic theme. Nothing else but this stone survives from his time at Hutchison's and it can still be seen today at the Glasgow Necropolis behind the Cathedral hardly a tram stop from where he himself had been born.

The firm of John Hutchison no longer exists. It had served its purpose nonetheless in nurturing a genuine and unique architectural talent. Mackintosh never forgot his time there in his youth, especially his warm relationship, rare for him, with Andrew Black. He opened up to the old draughtsman much more than he did to his own father, especially after the death of his mother. Black had obviously been the mainstay of the small firm but now his own time there was nearing its end. However, he knew that he had had a genuine and original talent under his hand for a time and was sure that great things would come from the boy. The only thing that would stop him would be himself.

There was a wilful element in Charlie's make-up that could be a drawback in situations where compromise was required, and his necessary artist's self-assurance had in it a large portion of selfishness. However, these were personal foibles, and it was hoped by all who knew him at this stage, like Black and Newbery, that his professional promise was such that it would far outweigh any private factors. However, as the life of any great artist shows, it is precisely these private and personal elements that drive the engine of their energies forward. A person's personality is often no more than the sum of other people's opinion of that person – and Charlie was to become one who excited immediate opinion – one way or another. Meantime, he was still, as it were, standing in the wings, awaiting his cue.

This came in the offer of his first job as a journeyman. In the strange way that things can work out in the way they were meant to, one of the first things John Keppie did as a partner was to invite Charles McIntosh to join the firm as a junior draughtsman. Keppie had heard about the boy wonder of the night classes, as had most everybody in the little world of Glasgow architecture, and when Toshie won the Queen's Prize for his 'Design for a Presbyterian Church' in addition to a pound note from the Glasgow Architects for 'A Town House in Terrace', he moved to get him. Charlie accepted without any great fuss. He was just pleased to have a job to go to. He could at least look forward to another fiver by the start of the Glasgow Fair Fortnight, and that would pay for another sketching excursion to the Isle of Bute. After all, he was an artist before he was an architectural draughtsman.

CHAPTER THREE

Home and Abroad

1889–1891

Mackintosh certainly was a genius.

Nikolaus Pevsner

JOHN HONEYMAN WAS a Glasgow man of the better sort, who had perhaps the best or worst of both worlds by being educated in Edinburgh. Intended first for the ministry, he went to Glasgow University without taking a degree and after the due apprenticeship with Alexander Munro, he was that architect's assistant by the time he completed his articles. He left soon after to work in London with the President of the RIBA at the time, J McVicar Anderson, before returning to Glasgow to start up on his own at Moore Place, West George Street in 1854.

Appropriately for this Christian gentleman, his first job, won in competition, was for the Greenock West Free Church. A whole liturgy of churches followed in solemn procession, most notably Lansdowne Church in Great Western Road with its distinctive steeple, the highest in Glasgow. These commissions made his professional name and established him as the leading ecclesiastical architect in Scotland. This did not stop him looking beyond Scotland, the Scottish church at Genoa being his. He was also short-listed for the Sydney Houses of Parliament and he may have been the inspiration behind sending a prefabricated cast-iron church from Glasgow to serve as that institution's second chamber. It still stands in that situation today.

This then, was the man that gave Charles McIntosh his first job. Although it was probably Keppie's contacts at the Art School, like the exemplary draughtsman, Sandy McGibbon, who, while working freelance with Glasgow's top architects, occasionally taught there. He would have known about McIntosh. In fact, he was later to teach him penmanship. Word would surely have reached Keppie, in any case, about the brilliant star of the night course, and he would have known of Mackintosh's links with John Hutchison. Keppie, like the good office manager he was, moved to get the best young talent available, so he invited the student to join the firm. He had also, just previously, signed up James Herbert McNair, fresh from a painting year in France, as a junior draughtsman, so Charlie arrived to find a fellow-beginner at the next table. They were friends at once, thanks to the largely outgoing McNair and soon they were being sent off together on measuring trips for the firm to the Abbey on Iona and Achamore House on the island of Ghia. From these expeditions, no doubt undertaken light-heartedly by the two young men, a firm friendship developed. This is important in so many ways, as Bertie McNair was maybe the first real friend the 21-year old McIntosh had made.

The tall, gregarious Bertie, already hinting at the eccentricity that was to gradually overtake him, was exactly the right foil at this time for the introverted Charlie. McNair, who was not without his own design talent, saw that his colleague had that extra something but that did not stop him teasing and cajoling McIntosh out of his studied seriousness. He helped to find that impish quality Bertie saw was in him from the start. In the old Scottish phrase, he just needed 'bringing out of himself'. And bringing out people was what the ebullient Bertie McNair was good at. He was the first to call Charlie 'Tosh' or 'Toshie', in the slang manner of the young bucks of the day, and Toshie he was from then on and remained for many to the end.

They became something of a pair, these two good-looking young men in their white collars and city blacks. They were the same age, of the same aspirations, and had the same sense of humour. They enjoyed each other's company whether in the drawing office or on sketching trips as far afield as Largs and Nairn. Yet to all intents and purposes they were like chalk and cheese, both in character and background. Toshie, as the working-class boy, albeit of a comfortable level, had worked at the Art School with trade-apprentices who shared the same proletarian attitudes. Now, for the first time, he was mixing intimately with the scions of the professional class. People that had money at their backs, as his father would say. People who expected the world to work out for them the way they wanted, and not have to take what came their way as the lesser Glaswegians had to do. Charlie gradually realised that he, too, could make the world work for him, and he was awakened to this first by Bertie McNair. Gradually, he was to let his guard down and embrace this friendship eagerly.

John Keppie was not far behind in being only a few years older than both of them and between the three of them they made for a lively and energetic office. The scholarly Honeyman must have wondered why the drawing office atmosphere at 140 Bath Street (where the firm had moved) was suddenly so charged, but being the good principal he was, he let them have their head. Each of the four men must have acted on the other three, and this showed in the work. While the senior man concentrated on his churches for the most part, Keppie moved between him and the younger pair. He admired John Honeyman, even to extent of dressing like him and copying the older man's cropped hair and beard. They must have seemed liked twins going off to work on the cathedral at Brechin or on many of their other trips on behalf of the now flourishing firm.

At the same time, the two young men, beardless but moustached, also made a pair and both looked to Keppie as their immediate example. He may also have involved them in his own work such as Muir Simpson's warehouse in Sauchiehall Street and the Glasgow Savings Bank at Parkhead Cross in the East End. While their contributions at this stage would have been slight; they were junior draughtsman after all, not designers; it is not too fanciful to think that the Keppie designs had the Mackintosh mark in them somewhere.

It was also thanks to John Keppie that Mackintosh made the next step in his widening contact with the outside world. The big night for artistic Glasgow, and a prominent date in its social calendar was the Grand Costume Ball at the Art Club, where Keppie was a prominent member. That year, 1889, the date was Friday 29 November, and Keppie went as 'The Squire' with his youngest sister, Jessie, as 'Lady Betty'.[1] She was then in her first year at Art School and had recently won a Silver Medal at Kensington for the design for a Persian carpet. (Chas. R McIntosh, incidentally, had won the Queen's Prize at the same competition for a Presbyterian Church.)

John Keppie went to the Ball that night on a very special mission. He was hoping to win the hand of a certain Mrs Helen Law, who had become free to marry again. Unfortunately she turned him down, electing to marry Eddie Walton, the painter, brother of the architect, George. Keppie was devastated and from that time retired from any further nuptial ambitions, remaining a confirmed bachelor, like his painter friend Hornel, for the rest of his life. His partner that night, sister Jessie, was also never to marry and became his housekeeper – but that is a later story.

Jessie was not without talent herself, but in the fashion of the time it was not the custom for genteel young ladies to enter the workforce or seek a profession. They had to aim for the altar or resign themselves to the service of aged parents or unmarried brothers. Jessie's fate was the latter, despite the fact that she made a good attempt to get to the altar with Charlie McIntosh, and for a time it did seem that she might indeed carry him off.

From what one can gather, she had seen him first in a day class on Advanced Design and Ornament, which McIntosh had taken by special arrangement. It was not normal for an evening student to take day classes but as McIntosh went on at the Art School, he was able, with Newbery's permission and Keppie's co-operation, to take special classes and attend visiting lectures as they arose. This again, was an instance of the favour given him by teachers throughout his studenthood. They obviously thought he was worth it. He proved it, in this instance, by getting a First Class Pass in Advanced Design (Jessie got a Second).

Yet even when he gained the prizes, he didn't always please the examiners. As when he won the Silver medal at Kensington, it was awarded with the following note:

> The examiners could wish that his efforts had more relation to the knowledge gained by a greater study of the works of the past; particularly to ancient proportional principles. There is need for a disciplined and codified framework.

Previous to this, in his design for a Town House he was similarly damned by faint praise:

> The design, though not quite satisfactory, is fresh and original, cleverly though roughly drawn and agreeably coloured, the shadows, however, being somewhat overdone.[2]

He was being shown the rules but displayed an increasing tendency to ignore rules. This was partly his youthful arrogance, partly his immaturity and partly his reluctance to be curbed imaginatively. He could not see how concepts could be arrived at freely if they were already inhibited by restrictions and/or academic rules and regulations. He could not see yet that great art is the finding of the vision despite the restrictions. No more so than in architecture where the artist-seeker of the ideal end is bound on all sides by given conditions. The mature Mackintosh was to find this as irksome as the student McIntosh, who prized above everything, a complete freedom of expression. His only rule was that there were no rules. For him, there was a natural order that determined its own rules, and, as long as he could, he would abide by that and his own instinct. He had much to learn yet about being a jobbing architect, and he could have learned from no one better than his immediate superior, John Keppie – who was still hurting from Mrs Law.

Personal rejection must have been hard for Keppie. He had been for so long marked as the coming man, admired in the office, appreciated at the Art Club, and was also noted in sporting circles as the longest hitter of a golf ball in Glasgow. He would have been stunned by Helen Law's refusal. He must indeed have loved her, for he never asked anyone again and something of his creative spark was dimmed from that time too. Or was it only that he was too busy on everything relating to being an architect that he didn't have time to fully practise? He became a company man, seeking out the contracts, soothing the clients, organising the many details. In short, making himself architecturally indispensable – and, gradually, by degrees, dull.

Notwithstanding, work went on as normal. Just before Christmas 1889, his father, James Keppie, died and, early in 1890, John asked his two bright young men, McNair and McIntosh, to come down to the Keppie home in Haddington Park, Prestwick, to help in revising some interiors for the new family needs. It was while involved with this that Toshie met Jessie again – and her four sisters. Appropriately, it was St Valentine's Day.

The Keppie girls were engaged in packing their late father's effects into cardboard boxes when the two young men arrived by the lunch-time train. They immediately retired to the dining room with big brother, John, but their presence had been noted by the sisters, especially Jessie, because it was from around this time that a relationship gradually built up between her and the quiet McIntosh.

As always, everyone else seemed to notice that something was happening before the parties concerned did. With each visit to Prestwick, the fun side of McIntosh came more to the fore and Jessie was soon captivated. Jessie Keppie was no dithering young maiden. She was 22 years old and a promising art student who showed an instinct to teach rather than create and had the Keppie intelligence and good sense. In manner, she was charming and warm-natured and as bonny as any young female in full bloom had a right to be. She would have been a prize for any professional man one would have thought, and at the time, it must be said, Toshie seemed to be of the same opinion. In his way, he allowed matters to drift and Jessie to make the natural assumption that her feelings were reciprocated. This was not callousness on Charlie's part. He was well used to female attentions, because of his sisters, and it may only have been that he was unthinking, being pre-occupied, as he was, with office matters.

Little did he know it, but at this same time, other life-changing, personal Mackintosh influences emerged all at once on the horizon. John Macdonald had decided to come back to Glasgow and he brought his wife and two daughters with him. His son and heir, Charles Macdonald, had gone ahead to Scotland before them, and was already established as a law clerk in the family firm by the time the rest of the family arrived in the spring of 1890. They stayed first with the White aunts at 50 Gibson Street before John Macdonald found an appropriate place at 9 Windsor Terrace in the West End and it was there that the blood-Scots with the English upbringing settled in. It had been decided that the two girls, Margaret and Frances would enrol in the autumn for session 1890/91 at the Glasgow School of Art. Macdonald, McNair and McIntosh. The clans were gathering.

It is only of small interest in the larger scheme of things Mackintosh, but just the year before, Chief Inspector, now Acting-Superintendent McIntosh, and his kilted ten-man team of 'big Highland polis' – as Glasgow policemen invariably were – had won the Tug-o'-War World Championship during the Paris Exhibition, even diverting attention from that specially-built eyesore called the Eiffel Tower. They returned to Glasgow in triumph. Superintendent McIntosh was now confirmed in his new rank and Charlie proudly celebrated with the rest of the family. What he didn't know though, was that another kind of tug o' war was just about to start between two very different kinds of young women, the prize being a slightly damaged if promising architect. And not all the Highland policeman in Glasgow would be able to pull against this kind of life force.

While the Macdonalds were settling in to Glasgow, Toshie was experiencing his first setbacks in competition. He failed in a bid to get a British Institute scholarship, for reasons that were not given, and he also missed out on a scholarship awarded by the RIBA. Apparently, his was the only entry received from the whole of Great Britain, so they withheld the scholarship. Which seemed a bit petty. After all they put it out on offer, he applied for it, he should have got it. He was luckier with his next effort. This was for the Alexander Thomson Travelling Scholarship, which allowed the winning student time on the Continent to study the ancient, classical work at first hand.

It was awarded by the Trustees of the late Alexander 'Greek' Thomson (1817–75), the Scottish architect famous for his Greek temple-like churches with Egyptian additions and Hindu decoration. He was as much an individual stylist as Mackintosh was to become and he had had a considerable vogue in Glasgow just before the grey sandstone gave way to the red. For the competition Toshie gave the judges what they wanted instead of what he might have created. He was learning about competitions. His study for an Ionic-colonnaded public building is now thought pedestrian by some critics but it might have come from Thomson himself, if one allowed for a little touch of Sellars here and there. No matter, it did the trick. He won the competition and 60 pounds that went with it and immediately made his plans to go to Italy in the following year. That would give him time to complete some other projects in hand and also save a bit of extra money for the journey.

Another Silver Medal came his way from Kensington for his design for a Museum of Science and Art. This time the stealing was done from another of his heroes, John James Burnet, as can be seen from the logical Beaux Arts influence, externals reflecting internals. The McGibbon influence is also evident in the striking ink and watercolour presentation he made of this design. And so another prize made its way on to the McIntosh mantelpiece in Dennistoun. With all these trophies and awards, one wonders if there was any room left? Or perhaps they were stored in his own den at Firpark Terrace, which he had now begun to decorate with a frieze of cats.

This may have been inspired by McNair's frieze of mermaids in his Glasgow flat, the mermaid being the McNair family crest just as the cat was the emblem for the McIntoshes. In a letter to Howarth, more than fifty years later, McNair remembered:

> I was in 'digs' at the time, and my frieze was in water-colour, juicily floated on, and on ingrain paper, my landlady allowing me to fix it on the wall with drawing pins. I remember it took an awful lot of both water-colour and drawing pins.[3]

McNair has sometimes been swamped by his Mackintosh association and it is difficult to think of him as an innovator in his own right. The frieze is only a small example but there were other instances at the start of their relationship when Bertie showed a real and original flair, especially in painting. He joined Toshie at the Art School with Keppie's blessing and, like McIntosh, attended selected day classes and heard visiting speakers like William Morris and Walter Crane. Keppie wisely saw this as a good investment in young talents.

Two other talents, in the meantime, were presenting their individual 'outline drawing of a cast' to Francis Newbery, the Director of the Art School, for his inspection. On being favourably received by him, and enjoined 'to give themselves heart and soul to their work and submit to a rigid curriculum and course of study' Margaret and Frances Macdonald were duly enrolled as full-time day pupils. In doing so, they became the fourth set of sisters in the school at that time, the others being Agnes and Lucy Raeburn, Mary and Margaret Gilmour and Jane and Jessie Keppie. It would seem that young ladies went two by two into the Fine Arts. These girls were to get to know each other well later as part of what they called 'The Immortals' – but not yet.

Toshie also took to new studies – books. Pugin, Ruskin, Sedding, Lethaby, Voysey and rest were almost swallowed whole as he made up for the dilatory application of his schooldays. He appeared to have overcome the slight dyslexia as far as his reading was concerned but his spelling remained erratic. Like his punctuation, it always would be. Neither was a worry to him. He was at a stage now where he was a veritable sponge for knowledge of the job and he soaked up everything he could get his hands on. Here John Honeyman, with his bookish approach, was exactly the right mentor at the right time and he complemented the harder drive of Keppie, who concentrated on the practical. One can see now that, with his training at both the Art School and the office, Chas. R McIntosh was getting a first-rate all-round education in architecture. He was riding high and rising all the time. He just had to keep his balance and not get carried away.

What occupied the firm at this time was the entry they made for the design of the new Glasgow Art Galleries intended to be sited in Kelvingrove Park. The Honeyman and Keppie office submitted three designs, and Keppie and McIntosh joined Honeyman himself him in a concerted triple effort entailing three designs – one in Classical form, one in English Renaissance and one in Scotch Baronial. Despite this considerable hedging of bets, none was premiated. One can be sure with Honeyman's sure knowledge, Keppie's diligence and Toshie's flair, aided as it was by Sandy McGibbon's penmanship, these entries would have had quality but they did not win over the Glasgow assessors. Perhaps all of them ought to have combined on one blockbuster entry – or did their different personalities rule that out? At any rate, the work won Toshie promotion to Designer and another five pounds towards the travel fund.

He still continued his boyhood habits of long walks in the countryside at the weekends, sometimes with McNair, but more often alone. He would return to Dennistoun at night with a full sketch-book and, occasionally, with whole branches of trees, bits of bushes, odd flowers, or anything else that had caught his eye during the day. Then, in his den he would carefully copy them, or parts of them, by gaslight and file them away for future action. By these means, the autodidact joined the student and the junior designer in preparing the architect-to-be. He was further helped to this end, again through his father, in being asked to design a new house for an uncle who had built up a successful haulage contractor's business in Dennistoun and wanted to celebrate his marriage in 1890 with a new house of their own instead of the normal tenement flat. So the nephew was called in for what was to be his very first proper, private commission.

It appears that Toshie's first design for what was to be called 'Redclyffe' horrified Mr and Mrs Hamilton by its unorthodoxy but a hurried second set appeased them. A simpler plan for two semidetached homes at 120 and 122 Balgrayhill Road, Springburn, to the north of the city, was set in motion during the summer and completed by the end of the year. This job had all the marks of a 'homer' and little of the later Mackintosh's total control. Yet the houses have a plain dignity that befits their setting in an unpretentious suburb. However, the real truth of the matter might have been that the young trainee-architect allowed two dull people to influence him into building a dull house. As a parting gesture, and as a comment on the Glasgow Colourists, who were enjoying a great success at the time with their vivid canvases, Toshie added his unorthodox touch by having all the interior doors painted in the brightest colours he could find.

With the new Year of 1891, it was time for something entirely different – he agreed to give a lecture. How this came about is uncertain but John Honeyman was President of the Glasgow Architectural Association that year and he also had well-known antiquarian interests. It may have been that Honeyman himself was due to read the paper on 'Scotch Baronial Architecture' but that it occurred to someone at the office that, since young McIntosh had a thing about indigenous architecture, it might be interesting to let him have his head in a lecture and see how he went. At best, it was good experience, at worst, he would be excused because, although he was now 22 years of age, he was, technically, still a student.

Nevertheless, it was with all the confidence of the prodigy that Toshie stood up on the night of Tuesday, 10 February 1891 to address his peers on the subject of *Scotch Baronial Architecture*. He had prepared 36 pages of lecture notes in his own hand complete with drawings, diagrams and photographs and frankly, much of it is ineffably boring – at least to the lay mind. However, one is drawn to the opening paragraph because it touches on love. One wonders why? Was he in love himself at this time? After the usual polite and diffident opening, proper to any lecture, he goes on to say – in his own words – and in his own spelling:

> It may be at first sight imagined that love, of all the human feelings, is best calculated to aid in describing the beauties of its object and in advocating its claims upon the admiration, but it is not so. We can hardly state the reason why we love our parents ... we know that it is a feeling that has grown with our growth, and is part of our very existence. Yet it is probable that an acquaintance who has never shared in these warmer sentiments, might describe their characters and even their virtues more successfully than ourselves. If we seek to investigate them, we find the research all to[o] cold and too methiodical to accord with the tone of our feelings, and like the poet who wished to sing of the Atrides and of Cadmus, the cords of our hearts responded only to love.
>
> So it is with those who have harboured an early affection for the Architecture of their native land ...[4]

His own heart at least is somewhere in there along with all the objectivity of the true artist. Nearly two hours later (Victorians loved long discourses) he concluded, by making an appeal for a return to a national style ('just as much Scotch as we are ourselves – as indigenous to our country as our wild flowers, our family names ... ') and pinpointing the technical difficulty of the style in 'reconciling the internal arrangements with the external uniformity'. This was always to be his cry – 'purpose determines plan – function dictates form'. This is something he may have learned from Voysey and others but it became his own golden rule.

He concluded the lecture by hoping we would regain our Scottish individuality and not 'copy ancient examples without making it conform to modern requirements'. This seemed eminently reasonable. A brief report was printed in *The Architect* on 20 February but it did not include comments from the audience heard afterwards, like – 'This McIntosh is a puzzle. I'm not sure I know what he's trying to say.' Perhaps he wasn't all that sure himself at this time, but he had made his effect and he could now give his mind to the forthcoming trip abroad. It was only a matter of weeks before he had to leave for Italy.

On 21 March he caught the train to London and then, at the docks, boarded the *Cuzco* for Naples. He was required by the Thomson Trust to keep a log of the journey. The following notes are from his diary of his trip which lasted from Sunday 5 April until mid-July.[5] He had wanted to stay on and return via the South of France but since his scholarship money was paid in two parts, one before he left and the next when he returned, he couldn't afford to. He could not persuade the whole amount out of John Shields, the secretary of the Trust, in advance, so he came home, a little huffily, by train via Paris, Brussels, Antwerp and London and so back to Glasgow again.

According to his diary, he did not get off to a good start in Italy. The Italian Customs confiscated his beloved tobacco because he refused to pay the duty, which was more than he had paid for the tobacco in the first place. So it was a disgruntled McIntosh who headed for Pompeii:

> Delighted to get into the Museum for nothing. Next day after a bread and butter breakfast drew first ten pounds from the bank and went to the British Council for permission to sketch in the Museum.

This being given, he got out his sketch-book. And for the next twelve weeks it was hardly to be out of his hand. He laid it down occasionally to 'grapple with maccaroni'. His first letter was written to Herbert McNair on the only day he was rained off from sketching. It was still raining three days later so he decided to leave for Sicily although he:

> thought the price of the boat ticket expensive and resented 'being fleeced on every hand by the beggarly Italians'. It was rough crossing on a 'most miserable of boats – 'just like a Clyde tug ...' Even when the sea was calm it still rolled about as if drunk ... Dread the trip back.

He was glad to get to Palermo and went as quickly as possible to the Cathedral – and was 'disgusted' with its interior ... no relation to the outside' but he sketched it nevertheless. He also discovered a cheap hotel near the entrance and when he found it was only six francs a day he 'closed it at once'. Money was to be his main worry throughout.

The rain followed him wherever he went in those first weeks but he kept on looking and sketching and soon built up quite a folder. On 15 April, while sketching the Campanile Maratano, he:

> gathered such a crowd. About 50 people looking at me as if I was a wild beast. Got very angry then thought I would try the effect of laughing. Laughed at the crowd. They just looked at me as if I was mad. I couldn't see the Campanile ... so I just took up my board & went away ... finished sketch in the hotel ... After dinner had my first Italian lesson from Emile, the proprietor's son.

It was still raining every day. Now he saw why everyone carried umbrellas. Reluctantly, he re-boarded the *Leoni* for the trip back to Naples and the mainland. It was just as bad as before: everybody sick. He was glad to get ashore. This time he made his way up to Cassino and its convent on the top of a snow-capped hill:

> A very nice place. Train [to Rome] disgustingly slow. Went to Hotel d'Europe and went to bed immediately. Quite tired out. Rose about 8 ... went for a turn in Rome ... Along the Corso ... to bankers, drew ten pounds and then to Post Office where I only got three newspapers. Expected some letters ... Went from Hotel d'Europe to Pension Michael – seven francs a day. Very nice hotel. Very nice people ...
>
> Tuesday 21st. Started early for St Peter's. Very, very poor front.
>
> Interior much better. The great attraction to me was the vastness of the fabric ... Went round to the Vatican Museum – entrance one franc. Charmed by the Raphaels but liked the Titians best.

It must have been like a banquet for him – all this great art on every side. What an adventure for a Glasgow boy who'd never been 'abroad' before. He was an accustomed solitary, and although he made casual friends with English and American tourists as he went along, he was quite happy to go through ancient Italy on his own. Now, here he was, unbelievably, standing in the Pantheon. His hand raced over the pages of his sketchbook. Then, on the morning of 23 April he was thrown out of bed by a mighty explosion:

> Good gracious what's that. Most terrific noise then the house starts shaking and all around are females screaming. Got out of bed. windows rattling and breaking on all sides. The shaking lasted for about 2 minutes. Heard after it was magazine explosion 3 miles away.
>
> Went to Arch of Constantine. Took sketch but sun going down I started to home for lunch. Just my luck left colour box in bus. After waiting 1 hour and a half got bus again and also box. Gave conductor four francs. Was mighty glad to get them back. Got an awful fright. Fancy being without colours. Too dreadful to contemplate. Went to Post Office. Got a letter from Herbert and a [news]paper from Father … This explosion will make the glaziers leap with joy. Half the windows in the town are broken. Streets just covered with glass. Most extraordinary occurrence. Must read about it.

On Sunday 26, he went to the Presbyterian Church to hear Professor John Stuart Blackie from Glasgow preach – 'enjoyed it immensely. Went home and wrote letters to Maggie [his sister] and to Mr Keppie in the afternoon.'

Next day he was on his usual round of Catholic churches seeking out the treasure in odd corners and being appalled by the comparative rubbish he saw in prominent places, but it was all grist to his whirling mill and he was getting most of it down on paper. He ended that day strolling through the Forum until dinner time. The rain had stopped but now it got hot – 'dreadfully warm.

Worst I have yet felt. Positively can't do anything. As limp as a herring.' But fore-noon on 2 May found him in the Sistine Chapel:

> most marvellous decoration by M.Angelo. Very much impressed by the Last Judgement. Most beautifully composed picture [but] very much time-worn which is a pity.

It was a pity, too, that he didn't like the Italians more. Perhaps they were just too Catholic for his Presbyterian taste. Pugin might have explained. Whatever the reason he thought them shiftless, lazy, greedy and not fit for much more than loafing about, yet these people were direct descendents of most of the men whose work he was admiring so much and that he was copying so assiduously. The Thomson Trust wanted proof of his study – well, he would give them it and more. His eye was taking everything in and his pencil got it all down on paper. But it was not the only thing he got down on paper. On 3 May he went round his churches as usual, seeing St Agnes' small basilica and St Lorenzo's – 'very good architecture' – and the Scotch Church, which elicited no comment.

Then he adds – 'writing letters all afternoon ...' To whom? His father, any of his sisters, Bertie McNair are all likely correspondents – even George Murray, one of the other young draughtsmen in the office, who had written to him – or John Keppie. Even Jessie Keppie. And why not? After all, they now had what was called 'an understanding' and it is not too much to expect that she might have received a postcard at least to 42, St James Street, Hillhead, but nothing was ever found among Miss Keppie's papers after her death to suggest that he had. It was perhaps another of his little derelictions.

I am sure she would love to have heard of his travels in Italy and his complaints about the wet Italian weather while he sketched in Orvieto. Or of his long, slow train journey to Siena – even these names, which she would know so well, would have interest. Especially when he called Siena's Cathedral a fraud. Then again, his juggling with his finances might have been endearing to one who knew him well. And Jessie Keppie knew him as well as anybody did. But no letter came, even as he continued his tour up through the country seeing everything that was worth seeing in Florence, Pisa, Ravenna, Ferrara, Venice, Padua, Verona, Cremona, Brescia, Bergamo, Como and Pavia before it was time to turn for home.

The litany of these names itself is sufficient to suggest the impact of this overwhelming, exotic experience to an untravelled young man. There is no need to further detail the trip as it consists of little more than a mere recital of architectonic facts garnered on route. All that can be said is that he returned with bulging notebooks and a full folder of watercolours. When he showed these and the drawings at the Art School's Student Exhibition he stole the show. Jessie was particularly evident in the almost proprietal pride she showed in his work and all the McIntosh sisters were one big smile. Mr McIntosh attended with his 'little madame', Chrissie McVicar, and he beamed to one and all. Bertie McNair came in the company of two new girls at the school, Margaret and Frances Macdonald, but Toshie was nowhere to be seen.

He was busy at home in Dennistoun writing yet another letter to John Shields trying to get the rest of the scholarship money out of him. He finally did get it – 30 pounds – but they made him work for it. He had to hang his paintings in a hired room in the Religious Institute ('the drawings will be put on the wall with small drawing pins') and to submit to an oral examination on the day, but he did as he was asked and he got his money.

When Sir James Guthrie, the famous Glasgow Boy but an old boy now, was shown round the Art Students' Exhibition by the School's Director, Fra Newbery, he stopped at the McIntosh Italian watercolours and said – 'But hang it all, Newbery, this man ought to be an artist.'[6] Newbery could not have done anything but agree yet, according to his wife, this was the first time he had been made fully aware of just how powerful a talent had been hiding away among the apprentices in the evening classes for so long. His concern, until that time, had been more with the young ladies and gentlemen of the day courses – but here was a student who could not be ignored.

They say that with the man cometh the hour, but more important is the man who makes it possible for the man to take his chance when his time comes. If Mackintosh was the man of the hour, then Newbery was the man who wound the clock and set it to the right time. It was the start of a very beautiful friendship for both of them. As Jessie Rowat Newbery, recalled:

> My husband remembers little of Mackintosh, until, as a student of the School of Art, he gained the 'Alexander Thomson' Travelling Scholarship. As a result of his journeyings through Europe, he brought home some fine, individual, sensitive drawings of buildings. Since then, he has never been 'out of sight, out of mind'.[7]

The summer of 1891 was spent preparing his entry for the Soane Prize. Sir John Soane was an English architect of the neo-classical school, who had been greatly influence by the Adam Brothers. High prestige attended this award and Toshie took care to prime his design for a Chapter House with appropriate classical detail, which he submitted under the name of 'Griffen', but the offering failed to win approval.

A similar scheme submitted by Honeyman and Keppie also failed but Toshie's original design went on later in the year to win a Gold Medal at Kensington – which says something about the judging. Detail from this drawing was also used by Honeyman and Keppie for the new frontage being proposed for Pettigrew and Stephen's new store in Sauchiehall Street – so it was hardly a wasted summer. What is interesting about this latter client, Sir John Pettigrew, is that, as a boy, he lived round the corner from the McIntoshes in Dennistoun.

A momentous year ended with Jessie and her Charlie becoming officially engaged. It is not known whether a ring was given but at least he had the money to buy one. Ring or not, a definite, and mutual commitment had been made. No date was decided for the wedding. Toshie still had a year to go at the Art School and John Keppie was of the strong opinion that a long engagement would be wiser, hinting that his future brother-in-law might have better prospects at the firm – 'in a year or two perhaps'. Jessie would have married her man the next day, but she agreed to wait. As always, she was willing to abide by her brother's advice. It was to be, for her at least, a sore and long-regretted decision.

Meantime, as they celebrated Christmas 1891 and the New Year of '92 with both the McIntosh and Keppie families, Toshie acknowledged the whole turn of events with the phrase he used when he heard he had lost the Soane with the Chapter House, – 'Ah well, that's the end of the Chapter then.'

CHAPTER FOUR

The Roaring Camps

1892–1895

I always looked upon my friend, Chas. R Mackintosh, as one of the greatest Architects and Artists. His wonderful delight in all things beautiful, large or small, and the charm of his enthusiasm are beyond words.

Herbert McNair

THE 'ROARING CAMP' was the name given to the occasional week-end stay by art students during 1892 on property at Dunure, in Ayrshire, just down the coast from the Keppie family home at Prestwick. Howarth refers to the houses as 'two bungalows' which Keppie rented as required, and put at the disposal of the male and female students so that they might work in relaxed surroundings during the day, and play by night in a congenial environment.[1] One could imagine, with Keppie in charge, that the work would get done and the play, whatever form it took, would have been circumspect and decorous.

Yet this was a combustible and volatile group that took part in these 'camps' by the sea. From the surviving photographs, the men seemed only to comprise Keppie, McIntosh and McNair – although fellow art students of that era included David Gauld, John Quinton Pringle and George Walton (brother of Eddie, who had stolen Helen Law) there is no record of their ever attending. Similarly, female contemporaries were Muriel Boyd, Helen Paxton Brown, Jane Younger, Susan Crawford, Annie Rose Law or the aptly named Ailsa Craig, who surely would have been at home on the Ayrshire coast. On these working trips, the ladies were always in the majority – just as they were at Art School. The photographs, which were formerly in the possession of Jessie Keppie, show the 'Immortals' in all their playfulness and charm – Jessie, of course, and Jane, Agnes Raeburn, Janet Aitken, Katherine Cameron and the Macdonald sisters, Margaret and Frances. The latter, it would seem, along with Bertie McNair, were the ringleaders for all the fun and games that took place on these weekend outings, but Keppie was the mainspring.[2]

It is no surprise that Keppie showed all this energy. The sporting bachelor couldn't take it all out on a poor golf ball. At any rate, thanks to his efforts the gatherings were accounted a great success. Although the surviving photographs show a set of young people looking just a little arch, making the faces and gestures into camera that all young people make while waiting for the photographer to press the button. And in those days one really had to wait. Photography was all the craze in late Victorian times and people posed – and how they posed – for formal photographs at every opportunity.

Except that these photos were anything but formal. They all attempted to be very daring, jokey, however posed. Each made his or her little statement except Margaret Macdonald, who always seemed a little aloof from it all. She is always on the outside and on the edge of the group. Her expression tells all too clearly that she'd rather not be having her photograph taken. Jessie can be seen with her thumbs up – her trademark gesture. It is significant that McIntosh is at the centre of many of these photographs, although he suggests by his expression that he was put there by the others. Yet Jessie said later, in a letter to Howarth, that these were the best likenesses she had seen of him.

I am indebted to George Rawson, the Librarian and Keeper of the Archives at the Glasgow School of Art, for his work in uncovering this find. Apparently, they were in an envelope of memorabilia dating from 1916 kept by Jessie Keppie and only came into the Art School's possession on her death in 1951. They are vital because they give us our first glimpse of the Immortals, that group of women artists-to-be, in large hats and long dresses, who formed themselves into a feminist phalanx during their student days. One feels this was done more in flippancy than from any determined feminist drive. They were all strong personalities in their own right and were not lacking in talent, as their future careers showed. Here, however, they were at play.

Looking at the photographs today, however, it is unnerving, in view of later events, to see Jessie Keppie's almost pleading look to Margaret Macdonald, standing, as usual, at the end of the line, to join in the fun. Margaret seems unconvinced. Toshie, for his part, in another set-up, sits under the arch of girlish arms, happy enough to oblige the camera, but not unduly bothered one way or another. Obviously, he must have got to know Margaret for the first time at Dunure but there is no record of any lightning flash between them. No Wagnerian chords sounded over Dunure harbour. They might not even have noticed each other all that much. After all, he and Jessie were a recognised item and accepted as such by all who were there and were probably left alone to get on with it.

What can be fairly deduced, however, is that Bertie McNair was drawn immediately to Frances. As the youngest girl there, she was full of holiday zest and the atmosphere was conducive to flirtation at least before each set retired to their gender-divided villas. However, since McNair was a natural party person, and Frances a giver to the moment, they would surely have got on well from the start. At any rate, it was from this time on that they began to form a relationship. John Keppie, as far as can be seen, did not follow their example. He was there to work, albeit in a playful atmosphere.

Work, indeed, was done. There were plenty of sketching possibilities all around them and Toshie, fresh from his Italian triumphs, might have felt inspired to put brush rather than pen to paper, but there is no record in McLaren Young, Billcliffe or Robertson of any sketches done at Dunure. This is remarkable in one who was a compulsive sketcher all his life, hardly a line of which didn't make its way one way or another into some architectural scheme. But nothing from the Roaring Camps. What did he do with his time then on these weekends, apart, of course, from submitting to photo sessions? He might have walked out with Jessie, of course. And why not? They were engaged, after all.

Yet one very important Mackintosh work dates from this same year – *The Harvest Moon*. This painting is nothing like anything he had done up until that time. Here the draughtsman's assurance is put to the painter's need. A female figure (an angel?), her draperies swirling round her, stands poised before a yellow moon, which is encircled entirely by her enveloping wings. Her feet seem to stand on a cloud, or is it another figure stretched out below her? Beneath that is an enmeshing pattern of flowers, branches, fruit, twigs and the general density of a confused undergrowth. The whole thing is in a twilit early evening mix of blues and greens with touches of blood red and black dotting the foreground.

It is without doubt an allegorical work although what story it tells is unclear. The presence of cloud adds to the mystery. My reading is that Jessie Keppie and her Charlie are surely intertwined here and the other cloud-like female figure lying across the base of the moon is unidentifiable. Is it really there? Is it a threat – or a promise of things to come? One only says that out of hindsight, of course, but there is a lot to see in this picture if one takes the time to look. Away up top left there is a little chink of yellow light peeping over a long black cloud. What is Toshie trying to tell us here? To my mind, it is a complete manifestation of doubt. Uncertainty is in its every ambiguous line but, then again, that may also be hindsight.

All that we know is that two years later he gave the picture as a gift to John Keppie. Interestingly, Keppie received it via his chief draughtsman, A Graham Robertson, in 1894. Keppie's reaction is not recorded. The picture is signed 'Chas. R McIntosh' and dated 1892. Incidentally, his gift to Jessie Keppie at the same time was a brass casket containing two roses in bud.

Wedding fever was in the air in 1892 and while Toshie and Jessie had been deflected from their own nuptials by her brother, there was no such constraint put on McIntosh Senior. At the age of 56, this sturdy widower màrried his 'wee madame', Chrissie

McVicar, who was by then 37 and a childless widow now known as Mrs Hamilton. She was well-known to the family, having lived nearby and been their mother's best friend.[3]

She and William were more or less thrown at each other by circumstances. He needed a mother for his daughters, she needed a husband for status, and anyway she had always had a sneaking likeness for the upright policeman. So, seven years after the death of his wife and nine years after the death of her husband, William and Chrissie were married. The reception took place in the Windsor Hotel, St Vincent Street, Glasgow. The ceremony was performed by the Reverend Marshal Lang of the Barony Parish Church, Hugh McIntosh, the groom's older brother, was best man and the Chief Constable, John Boyd, acted as witness. Presumably a good time was had by all. There is no mention of Toshie's reaction, although one might also presume he was there with his fiancée and in the company of all his sisters. One wonders how the demure Jessie comported herself among the McIntosh sorority. If they had reservations about the 'wee madame', surely they could have had none about the amiable Jessie. In the way of families, the Keppies and the McIntoshes must have met socially and certainly at a family wedding, but no record or photograph survives to confirm this.

One outcome from the event, at least, was that Toshie gained the name by which he is now known. When McIntosh senior came to sign the wedding certificate, he saw that his name had been spelt 'Mackintosh' instead of 'McIntosh', but he signed it anyway and the Chief Constable duly witnessed it, thus making it legal. This incident became something of a joke in the family and William eventually took steps to have the error rectified and resumed his own name. His son, however, rather liked the change and he chose to keep the new spelling; he was 'Mackintosh' from then on.

It was, therefore, as Charles Rennie Mackintosh that he addressed the Glasgow Architects on 6 September. This time, his subject was 'A Tour in Italy'. Aware of the danger of making it merely a list of dates and place-names, he tried to inject it with some humour to counter the facts, although one is not too confident in a speaker's factual recall when he rises to say that he left Glasgow in February and arrived in Naples in March, when in fact he left in March and arrived in April. That being said, we can accept it as another professional hurdle to be cleared in front of his peers. As in all his 'lectures', the printed excerpts given here boast his own spelling, and there are also stand-out passages of 'fine-writing' to decorate the diary effect of a faithfully-reproduced itinerary. The text contains much cribbing from unspecified authors. This was further evidence of hours spent by him in the Mitchell Library. This time, Pamela Robertson thinks, he may have plundered Ruskin. She also notes:

> Although this is the most personal of the surviving manuscripts, it provides less insight than might be hoped into Mackintosh's professional or private life at this very formative period. It is marked however by a refreshing lack of pomposity, an engaging humour, and Mackintosh's all-consuming enthusiasm for architecture.[4]

He began by saying that everyone would have their own way of giving such a talk and outlined the various alternatives, but he went on to say what he was not going to do:

> I will not even try to give any matter of fact detailed description of any building or object, but will rather endeavour to give a frank & spontaneous expression of the impression left on my mind by seeing each place. For the rest I would refer you to the sketches of the various places ...

He then went on to mention that 'Naples was best seen from a distance,' and that there was more of Pompeii in the Naples Museum than there was at the Pompeii excavations. He also warned his listeners that if they were ever go to Palermo they must never stay at the Albergo Rubecchino, and he noted that all Italians carry umbrellas at all times – for sunshine as well as for rain. What might have been much more interesting if he had told the architects of what he really thought of the 'lazy' Italians, and allowed his latent anti-Catholic bias to show through, but that was not in his remit, nor in his nature. Reviews did say that 'the principal buildings were noted and criticised in a very racy manner':

> I have very little to say of Bologna as we only stayed an afternoon there but what we did see was not calculated to keep us longer.

He admitted, however, that he welcomed the Venetian gondola after the jolting of the train and that his first sight of the Rialto 'took his breath away'. When he 'directed his steps towards the great church of St Marco' he realised that 'a more noble assemblage was never exhibited by Architecture'. However, he could not travel very far without remembering his home town:

> Ancient Rome bore a very striking resemblance to some parts of the east end of Glasgow assuming about two-thirds of the population to be dead of c[h]olera. It is as grimy, as filthy, as tumblesome, as forlorn and is as unpleasantly redolent of old clothes and old women who were washerwomen once and had long foresworn soap ...

That would have had them sitting up. He knew that he was there primarily to inform, and secondarily, to please Mr Honeyman, who might have been interested to hear that Palladio's Theatre in Padua was a 'truly classical structure – so beautiful ... but none of the churches are of any value'. Still, the trip had been done, and the exercise now completed as a public lecture. It was also another way of getting his new name known.

Which is why, probably some time in the same year, he gave his third lecture at a place and to an audience unknown on the subject of 'Elizabethan Architecture'. One gets the feeling that this was another Honeyman operation with Toshie as the front man. It was also a very crucial part of his continuing education in the art of architecture. It forced him once again to extensive reading and then to the discipline of speaking his research aloud. Why Elizabethan? Well, as David Walker has pointed in his introduction to the printed text of this lecture, Tudor and Elizabethan motifs were part of the general Gothic Revival in the first part of the nineteenth century and, in any case, all Mackintosh lectures leaned to the past. It is strange that such a Scottish architect should concentrate on such a very English subject. This is further proof of his eclecticism and his desire to widen his architectural references.

He began by speaking of the Elizabethan Age as a 'period famed in the history of our country'. Did he mean Britain or England alone? To many today, Britain is England. Stands Scotland where she did? Its architecture was not at all significant in Elizabethan times, as his reading of MacGibbon and Ross would have told him. Their publication of 1892 was the Bible of Scottish domestic architecture. However, having so recently talked on Scottish baronial architecture, a change of subject was called for and, besides, there was a fashionable interest by architects in Scotland in the 'English House'. What Mackintosh would have appreciated was that English architecture was 'native' just as his favoured castellated towers and harled walls were native. He was always drawn to any indigenous building style. The great English mansion was true to itself and therefore worth discussion. What struck him as important was that 'the Elizabethan was a fusion between the old and the new in Architecture, and in this character has not been sufficiently considered ...' He now did, and he concluded:

> There was in Eliz. Buildings a care for architectural effect, the construction was generally sound and truthful, and there was an appropriateness in design which rarely fails to please. The style spoke of home life and comfort, and certainly more distinctly national than any that has followed it.

There is no doubt that Mackintosh leaned towards Pugin as his later sketchbooks were to show, and this decorative influence might have started from this lecture. That is about all we need infer from the technical text as much of it is beyond the remit of this present book, except to note that his Elizabethan researches took him to such obviously English locations such as the Old College, Glasgow and Aros House at Rhu. Once again, evidence of these visits was to be glimpsed in much of his own later, much-famed work. Nothing was ever wasted.

It is really remarkable that in the space of a few years, a young man, still technically a student at the Art School and a junior in an architectural office, is invited to give lectures on aspects of architecture about which he had only the most modest of practical experience. It says much for his engaging manner that he was asked, and asked again. During the academic year 1892–3 he was given the rare opportunity of speaking on his much-loved topic, architecture, not once but twice, so much had he to say on this theme. It says much for his rising status in the city that it was felt there was an audience for two separate talks. The first, untitled, paper was given to the Scottish Society of Literature and Art, whose activities would seem to have been short-lived, but we must assume this was in no part due to his lecture. This time he did draw heavily on Ruskin and his *Seven Lamps of Architecture*, and also, at points throughout, he quotes from sources as diverse as Goethe, Madame de Stael, George Elliot and Robert Burns. He was, after all, addressing a literary society.

For those concerned with the specific architectural pulse beating at the heart of both presentations, I can do no better than commend David Walker's splendid introduction to the printed texts as published in Pamela Robertson's edition of *The Architectural Papers*, from which I too have drawn further information. However, for narrative reasons, I have chosen to combine the first lecture with the second one of February 1893 as the second follows on naturally and it makes, for this book's purpose, an acceptable whole in synopsis form. I do so in the hope that the reader will, in Mackintosh's own words, 'make a liberal discount for bias and exaggeration'. In my opinion, the truncation better suggests the impact this persuasive young man must have had on his audience as they sat before him on those two winter nights. He was obviously better heard than read. At least, they were spared his atrocious spelling and wayward punctuation.

What then is Architecture? When Gothe calls it 'a petrified religion' or Madame de Stael 'frozen music' they in common with poets and orators of all times are only considering it as a fine art, but a fairer description is given by Sir Gilbert Scott when he says 'Architecture differs from the sister arts of Painting and Sculpture in this, whereas they arise from the artistic aspirations of our natures apart from practical necessity or utility it arises from the necessity and then from the desire to clothe it with beauty.' ... I am really unacquainted with a definition of Architecture which is quite comprehensive [but] one of Ruskin's aphorisms is as good as any ... 'All Architecture proposes an effect on the human mind not merely a service to the human frame ...' Mr Ruskin is also unprofessional and so presumably better suited to an audience such as this. I would further add that this latter fact is true generally, the greatest writers on Architecture are not architects ...

He then goes on to declare that architecture is not building and castigates the Caledonian & Glasgow and South Western Railways on the bridges they have slung across the Clyde 'with a strict ugliness which a poorer shopkeeper would not be allowed to practise'. He then takes a swipe at architectural critics 'who leave nothing in the inkstand' in their 'frequent sarcasm at the expense of modern architects'. He returns to Ruskin:

The body must be served and the mind pleased but ornamentation added for no use but effect would be to construct the decoration not to decorate the construction. Architecture then must serve the mind and the body. Let us see how it does so when considering the 3 attributes necessary namely ... Stability, Usefulness & Beauty.

Stability
Good sound practical workmanship in all materials. Of course, strength does not mean that a summer house should be built like a fortress ... but the eye is distressed at huge,

lofty tenements resting to all appearances on nothing more stable than plate glass ...

Utility

The highest type of architecture has been the Temple and the Cathedral ... both things of beauty ... and they grew to suit convenience and rarely asthetic wants ... they were truthful to the needs of the building whatever that need was ...

Beauty

There is no final standard of taste to which all might appeal, no code of laws to which every little detail may be submitted – no authoritative committee of taste to decide on disputed points ... The faculty of distinguishing good from bad in design is a faculty which most educated people – and especially ladies – conceive they possess. How it has been acquired few would be able to explain ... the general impression seems to be, that it is the peculiar inheritance of gentle blood, and independent of all training

As he goes on, the general impression grows that the audience is listening to a well-educated young man, and if he is by training an architect, he is also by instinct an artist – an instinct which has obviously survived his training. He acknowledges this himself when he states that 'the architect, with the necessity of giving a prophetic view of a non-existing structure, must have <u>some</u> little artistic skill', and he adds that the practical man is not always the right architect to employ. He also has some words for the then current state of architecture in Scotland.

The history of nations is written in stone, but it certainly would be a difficult task to read a history from the architecture of this nation at the present time. We do not build as the ancients did who in each succeeding building tryed to carry to further perfection the national type. We are a world-related people who show our ill-regulated admiration for foreign beauties. When Burns, in his 'Cotters Saturday Night' after enumerating some of our favourite psalm tunes burst out 'compared wae this Italian trills are tame' as a piece of musical criticism it may not hold true world-wide yet it is a very sufficient reason & obvious truth to Scotsmen

And on that note, here endeth the extracts from the first lecture.

In the second lecture, in February 1893, he was a year older, a little wiser and a lot more confident. This time he was talking mainly to painters and sculptors. The location is not specified but it was likely to have been the premises of the Glasgow Art Club in Bath Street where he and Keppie, a prominent member, were currently engaged in interior renovations. After the usual plea to his audience for indulgence, he offered them no apology for reading a paper on architecture to artists. He began by telling them that:

> Architecture is the world of art as it is everything visable & invisable that makes the world. so it is all the arts & crafts & industries that go to make architecture.

This was always his view of the artist and craftsman: as part of an interdependent artistic partnership working together on every aspect of the project at hand. This view was to influence his life-long attitude to his own profession and to be the cause of misunderstanding and controversy in his later building works. In the meantime, it was a splendid theory and he was, thanks to architectural writers like Lethaby and Sedding, brimful of theories. One has little else when young:

> Behind every style of architecture there is an earlier style in which the germ of every form is to be found … Old architecture lived because it had a purpose. Modern architecture, to be real, must not be a mere envelope without contents … What then will this art of the future be?

> The message will still be of nature & man, of order and beauty … the new, the future is to aid life and train it 'so that beauty may flow into the soul like a breeze'.

78

This is a straight lift from Lethaby. Mackintosh then goes on to quote Sedding:

> We must clothe modern ideas in modern dress – adorn our designs with living fancy. We shall have designs by living men for living men ... of joy in nature in grace of form & gladness of colour.

He also repeats the words of his own mentor and teacher, Fra Newbery: 'If the education of all artists must be conducted on one grand principle all must be educated alike – with one common aim'. But when he speaks for himself, it comes straight from the heart:

> You ask how you are to judge architecture. just as you judge painting or sculpture – form, colour, proportion all visable qualities – and the one great invisable quality in all art, soul.

After renouncing 'wandering fancies' and accepting that an architect's lot is 'apt to represent more survival than revival', his work often 'bound to tradition and precedent', he nonetheless repeats his exhortation to 'look upon all the arts going hand in hand as one – our pencil is our wand'.

And on that lovely image – Mackintosh the Magician, with wand in hand – the lecture ends. He was very much on a high at this stage and every word of each lecture corroborates his enthusiasm and passion, but he still had his day job to think about. Its demands soon brought him down to earth again.

The work being done at the Art Club was a Keppie project and Mackintosh's position was to play the junior. This was Keppie's scene in more than one sense since he, as a very clubbable man, was part of the very fabric of the place. Mackintosh was not at all clubbable and never did become a member. Nor was he encouraged to by Keppie. This was just another quirky aspect of an increasingly quirky relationship.

What he did get from the Art Club job, however, was a close appreciation of Hornel's works, which were hanging there at the time. Eddie Hornel was not unlike Mackintosh in personality in that each was a natural loner, but the former had taken on board all the Japanese influences available at the time thanks to Christopher Dresser, and in 1889 had even gone to Japan himself. In addition, the first of two Japanese ships was being built on Clydeside. Design and ornament had become more and more 'Japaneasy' for Glaswegians, and Mackintosh would have been aware of all this. The Glasgow dealer Alexander Reid imported Japanese prints and drawings and later gave Hornel's work a major showing after that artist's success with the other Glasgow Boys at Munich. Now here was a chance for Mackintosh to study these much-travelled paintings at close hand – and he did. This Japanese influence was to show in his work almost at once, and later to an increasing degree.

Around now, another part of the Mackintosh jigsaw fell into place when Kate Cranston married Major John Cochrane, an engineer from Barrhead with enough money to buy his wife a whole building in Argyle Street as a wedding present. She was able to make these premises into more than a tea room. By adding amenities like billiards and table games, Kate created an amusement centre with tea and scones and customers caught on quickly to the novelty. The Cranston caravanserai was on the move again and it would catch up with Charles Mackintosh before very long.

In October 1892, the senior McIntoshes had moved everything out of Firpark Terrace and flitted to a more commodious house in the South Side of the City. This was the first time Charlie would have gone 'over the water' by crossing the Clyde into Strathbungo, and to a salubrious address at 2 Regent Square. This became Chrissie McIntosh's first home of her new marriage. Her stepson wisely stayed out of the way by going off to Lamlash on the Isle of Arran to sketch while the move was taking place. Moving house was women's work to Victorian men.

It was also a good part of woman's work in that era to find a man, a husband, and for ladies of a certain class it was almost mandatory, since few went out to work. Those middle-strata ladies who did seek professions were thought of as being very 'new'. For the great majority, it was important to secure one's later years and a husband and family generally took care of that. Jessie Keppie wasn't enough of a committed artist to give her all to her art, nor was she sufficiently feminist to stand on her own as a matter of principle. She was an ordinary girl of good family, reasonable looks and talent enough to hold her own at dinner parties. In short, she was the perfect wife for the up-and-coming professional man and, to his credit, Charlie Mackintosh saw that; hence his proposal.

However, when Jessie proposed to him that he might like to stay on at Firpark Terrace, that in fact, they could even marry from there, Toshie seemed to be taken off-guard and took to his heels for Arran. She didn't offer to accompany him. Instead she discussed the matter further with her brother. John was appalled that she should think of moving into the East End – she was a West End girl and she should hang on till Toshie became a West End man. Like many bourgeois Glasgow men, he thought everything east of Glasgow Cross was jungle.[5]

Compliant as ever, Jessie kept her peace. Charlie was still her man and she didn't care who knew it. She realised that he was on a particularly fast track for the moment, and that once he had run out of steam he would make his way back to her and they could quietly resolve their situation. He had been unsettled since his father remarried and it was clear that he was ready to take a wife himself. Jessie was more than ready to take Toshie as she found him, but she soon found that he came in all sorts of moods and phases. From time to time, she wondered if there were other reasons why her brother John kept procrastinating in the matter of her wedding day. Hadn't he agreed to the engagement? Sometimes it must have seemed to Jessie as if Toshie were betrothed to her brother and not to her.

Meantime, he had plenty to occupy him. Going into 1893, a whole line of work with Keppie followed on from the Arts Club with designs for the *Glasgow Herald* building in Mitchell Street (now the Lighthouse Mackintosh Museum), the Queen Margaret Medical College on Hamilton Drive (now Queen Margaret Drive and the BBC's Glasgow studios) and the still-extant Martyrs'

School in Parson Street, Townhead. All this architectural work was to take place for the next couple of years in tandem with increasing involvement, during the evening at the Art School, in painting and graphic projects. He thrived on the activity and appeared to have an endless energy but it was all at a price and would have to be paid at some time.

His philosophy at the time would seem to have been 'live now, pay later'. In other words, as Burns put it, to 'catch the moments as they fly'. He was totally engrossed in the work on hand and would hardly lift his head from the drawing board. Close friends, like McNair, saw the signs before he did but, being friends, they chose to say nothing. Besides, everyone at that stage had their own agenda and who can blame them for minding their own business. His own family feared for him most as he began to show signs again of that manic obsessiveness that he hadn't known since his boyhood and he gave himself to work as if his very life depended on it.

His father moved house again (no doubt at Chrissie's prompting) and to an even better address – a big house called Holmwood on Langside Avenue in the smart Queen's Park district. Toshie might never even have noticed. Bertie McNair protested jocularly in the office that Toshie was going too fast for them all and he wasn't leaving anything for anyone else to do. John Honeyman made no comment and John Keppie took no action, so Mackintosh carried on at the same pace.

The *Glasgow Herald* building was the first to bear the Mackintosh imprint. One can catch a glimpse of Italy (or James MacLaren?) in its water tower. There are indications that his hand was becoming surer by the day. The next project was the Queen Margaret Medical College, the first medical school for women in the country, which stood next to what was once Northpark House, an ornate building in the Florentine Renaissance style favoured by John Honeyman, who had worked on it as a young man. One of the teachers working at the school, Professor Thomas H Bryce, in a letter to a Glasgow newspaper dated 28 April 1933, said:

I knew Charles Mackintosh and admired the originality of genius. I first met him in 1893 when the Anatomy building at Queen Margaret College was being built. He was then a young apprentice with Mr Keppie who designed the building. A good deal of the detail of the decoration was by Mackintosh, and, as it stands, it is perhaps among the earliest examples of his style, which, after that first acquaintance I followed with interest in its development and efflorescence.

Professor Bryce went on to say that Mackintosh on one visit to the site asked to look down the professor's microscope, under which lay 'the developing eye of a fish'. He at once sketched it and incorporated it into the decorative design.[6]

Mackintosh was now 25 years of age and approaching the height of his powers, or at least the first ridge in the Everest climb to real maturity, and more and more he was following, as it were, his own footsteps. Janet Aitken, one of his roaring camp companions writing in the first issue of *The Magazine* put out by the art students themselves, may have had Charlie in mind when she wrote in her article:

It is a great matter for a man to find his own line, and keep to it. You get along further and faster on your own rail ... and it is not the amount of genius or moral power expended, but concentrated, that makes what the world will call 'A Great Man'.[7]

It was at this time that he had his picture taken by James Craig Annan, not as the architect in dark suit and starched collar, but as the artist with soft collar and flowing velvet tie. It is the picture we all know of Mackintosh today. It is the icon and one we see everywhere on every poster on every item, no matter how faintly connected with the architect. It is to Mackintosh what the Nasmyth portrait is to Robert Burns and is virtually unassailable as the mind's-eye image of the man. In 1893, however, it was new, fresh, exciting and different. It was a statement, and it said that Charles Rennie Mackintosh had finally decided who he was.

Someone who saw this at once was the School's Director, Francis Newbery. It was he who noticed the similarity of style between Mackintosh and McNair and the two Macdonald sisters. Newbery thought it would be interesting to have all four working together. Little did he know what he was doing. Or perhaps he knew exactly what he was doing. At any rate, the Four were now officially acknowledged as from this time. It was from this event, and this alone, that all the trouble started. Not that Newbery thought he was doing anything but good. Wasn't his stated aim 'to provide Glasgow with a race of designers of her own creation'?[8] And here were four of the brightest stars in the School's firmament right at hand. To his mind, they could only flash light off each other.

The astronomical parallel prompts the mention here of the possible Rosicrucian influence on Mackintosh. It is known that Newbery was a member of that order, so was his Head of Painting, M Paul Delville, and a new friend Mackintosh had just met, Talwin Morris, who had just come to Glasgow to work for Blackie's, the publishers, and had now established himself at Dunglass Castle, near Bowling. Rosicrucianism was very much the thing at the time. Only recently, in 1891, there had been an International Rosicrucian Exhibition in Brussels, and now, three years later in Glasgow, the wisps of this mysterious order, purporting to be the privileged proprietors of ancient knowledge passed from one to another down through the centuries, were blowing around Mackintosh. He could hardly avoid them. And now an affiliate of the Rose and Cross, his flamboyant Director at the Art School wanted him to work on 'special projects' with those two odd English girls. Toshie must have been relieved that his old mate, Bertie McNair, was going to be involved.

Bertie had, by now, left Honeyman and Keppie – he partly jumped and was partly pushed – and had set up a studio at 127 Hope Street with the Macdonald sisters. He had continued to pursue Frances and was willing to work with Margaret. Not that they co-operated on any one project. It was rather that they fed off each other's ideas – and they could share a studio. The whole project was based on two small commissions – one from Annan, the photographer, and another from Talwin Morris. Not that the Macdonalds needed the work. They were only rarely to be short of money. Bertie, on the other hand, who had the same moneyed background, was just as rarely to be in funds. Toshie, for his part, was always on the edge financially and needed anything he could get from any source.

It was a salient time in his affairs. He was preparing to wind up ten part-time years at the Glasgow School of Art and was also being given more of a free hand by Keppie. At this time he was was busy on designs for the Martyrs' School, Townhead. The finished drawing for this project is interesting in that it is the only plan where he has drawn people in the scheme. The drawing shows three little girls skipping ropes past the school gates and each is wearing a different dress of the period. Perhaps he is remembering his big sisters who might have skipped on that very same pavement when they were younger – or was he, as William Buchanan has suggested, showing off his skills as a dress designer?

If he had now been given a free hand by John Keppie on the Martyrs' scheme, the other was still in the grasp of Keppie's little sister. This affair seemed to have moved into a kind of limbo. Nobody was taking any action. Was he really being fair to the girl in keeping her waiting? What was he waiting for? Another rise in salary? A partnership, perhaps? That was a little way off yet. Did she by any chance know something he didn't? Was it only that she was John Keppie's sister? Could it really be as simple as that? Whatever the reason, the procrastination persisted.

He was involved, hereabouts, in transferring his cat frieze from his room at *Holmwood* to his new cellar den at 27 Regent Square. It was yet another Chrissie McIntosh flitting – and it was to prove her last. Charlie had asked for and been given the cellar as his own. As he pasted up his favourite cats on the wall (no drawing pins for him) he must have wondered how many lives he himself had left. The next phase would depend entirely on how he worked out the Jessie Keppie situation – or how it was worked out for him.

In the November 1894 issue of the students' do-it-yourself *Magazine*, Jessie Keppie had an article published entitled *A Faerie Story*. It concerned the King's daughter, the beautiful Irene ('her figure was as the willow tree') whose noble lover, the Prince, was bound by the magic of the two wicked witches while they enclosed Irene in a ring of flame but she is rescued just in time by the Prince with the help of the good fairies – 'and soon they were married and lived happy in one another's love till there [sic] days were numbered.'

Whatever construction one puts on all this, it is easy to see that at the basic level it was such a patent *cri de coeur* from Irene/Jessie that everyone at the School must have seen the allegory in the Jessie/Toshie situation and felt for her. Timothy Neat elaborates on this connection in his book, *Part Seen, Part Imagined* (1994), but it is possible to read into it what one will.

Battle lines were being drawn, however, and in the April issue of 1895, the redoubtable Jane Keppie took up the pen on behalf of her young sister. This was in an essay in which the happy Portia of *The Merchant of Venice* is compared to the unhappy Ophelia in *Hamlet*. Where in her own story Jessie had hinted at the Macdonald sisters being the wicked witches who lured her lover away from her, Jane had no hesitation in allegorising Margaret as Portia and Jessie as Ophelia. She also suggested that Ophelia (Jessie) was driven mad by events over which she had no control and that, like the Prince himself, 'a noble mind is here o'erthrown'. It was all superficially innocent but underneath there was a darker layer where deeper passions were rising.

This was pointedly illustrated in the astonishing, possibly apocryphal, incident at the Hyndland Tennis Club on a May evening when a dance was in progress. Jessie, being a member, was there with Charlie, who was never a member of anything. What happened, or was reputed to have happened, was reported to me by the much-respected Allan F Ure, when I was having a meal with him at Windyhill sometime during the mid-Seventies. Mr Ure was not an easy man to get to know but, once you did, he was well worth the trouble. I was working on the Mackintosh television script at the time and sought out Mr Ure as a source. He was to prove wonderful value, especially for his anecdote about the tennis club incident. Allan said it caused an awful stushie at the club but few knew about it outside because it was so embarrassing for everyone.

Mackintosh didn't dance (because of his leg) and he was always being teased about it by the girls. Normally he just shrugged it off but this night for some reason he got so riled that he retired to the lavatory more often that usual. Most young men then carried hip flasks to these functions and between dances they used to retire to the gentlemen's room to refresh themselves. Now since Charlie didn't dance he was doing more refreshing than the rest. He wasn't a drinker at all then and everyone thought it very funny to see him stumble about like a clown. But then when the fiddle and accordion began to play for a scottische or a reel or whatever, Charlie suddenly grabbed Jessie's hand and pulled her to the centre of the floor.

He paid no attention to her protests but just stood imperiously in the centre of the floor until the music started. Then, taking Jessie on his arm, he began to whirl her around him in a circle getting faster and faster as the music itself got faster. The rest of the dancers stopped to watch, clapping their hands in time, calling out to Jessie and laughing. Then, when it seemed they could go no faster, he suddenly – whether accidentally or not – let her go and the poor girl went crashing centrifugally into the watching dancers pushing them back so that they knocked over some chairs behind them. Their screams and shouts stopped the band at once. There was an awful silence. Then a man's voice called out: 'Mackintosh, you're a cad.'

Toshie just stood in the middle of the empty dance space, head bowed. Then he drew his flask from his pocket, saying, 'You're quite right, sir – I'll drink to that.'

But the flask was empty and he threw it to the floor then staggered out. The fiddle and accordion then started up again but nobody got up to dance.

And that, according to Allan Ure, was how the Charlie Mack-intosh/Jessie Keppie affair ended. The only comment Mr Ure made on it was:

If it was true, it was sad for the lassie. I know it's heresy to say, these days, but Jessie would have made him a cracker of a wife. Aye. It would have been a different story then, eh?

CHAPTER FIVE

Towards a Masterwork

1895–1899

If one were to go through the lists of really original artists ... the name of Charles Rennie Mackintosh would certainly be included.

Hermann Muthesius

UNTOWARD EVENTS AT the Hyndland tennis club had little effect on the drawing office at 140 Bath Street or the crowded painting cells at the little art school on the corner of Rose and Sauchiehall – or even in the shed that Mackintosh had now rented to experiment with the design and making of original furniture for friends like former fellow student, David Gauld. He also designed posters after the style of Aubrey Beardsley for the Glasgow Institute of Fine Arts. The *Yellow Book* had just come out so he was well up on the play. He had had his watercolours published in the *Glasgow Architectural Sketchbook* and on the work front he went down to Govan to work with an understandably chillier Keppie on designs for the Fairfield Shipping offices on the Clyde. Here, Mackintosh would have seen at first hand the very best of Clydeside's craftsmen – and he would remember.

John Macdonald had died but not before he had seen his two artistic daughters established in their Hope Street studio. Here, the 'brilliant sisters Macdonald' as Lucy Raeburn had called them in 1893,[1] were doing very original work in various media together and individually. So was Bertie, who was creating wonderfully weird things on canvas. It was apparent that he and the sisters had the same odd thing going for them, and now Toshie joined to make up the four, as it were. Puppet-master Newbery had already pulled the strings to this effect and now the quartet began to dance to their own very individual tune. They had all shown together at the Student Show in the previous November to what can only be called a mixed reaction. There had never been heard such a buzz of derision at a hanging before – shouts of disgust and even worse, laughter – but the most telling was the comment of one young girl who was heard to say, 'I think it's spooky.'[2] That did it. A new Glasgow style had been found. The 'Spook School' was born.

What was much more important to Mackintosh, however, was that it was only now, in 1895, that he really began to know Margaret Macdonald. After Hyndland, he saw less of Jessie, but things were not totally broken off between them. It was just that nothing was said. It was at this time, that Margaret came more into his work scene (or he into hers) and Miss Macdonald could hardly be described as inactive. It was this brisk, no-nonsense energy that first drew Mackintosh – and her accent.

Only a Glasgow male of the lesser sort (of which I am one) can vouch for how much of an aphrodisiac a good English accent, especially a posh one, can be to a young, impressionable East-ender. Despite our political bias, ingrained chauvinism and idiot bigotry that keeps everything English at a distance, let a young female loose among a gaping of young Scots males, and let her lilt in tones that suggest tea on the lawn, and we are at her mercy. This question of accent may not have had everything to do with Charlie being very gradually drawn to Margaret during this period but, I can assure the reader, her voice-tone was no deterrent.

Her manner, too, was different. Almost man-like in its decisive-ness, there was no pliant, female submissiveness about Margaret. She was a woman already into her thirties who knew what she wanted and went to work to get it. Not that she went after Toshie. Not at all. It was five years before they married and it took every day of those years for both of them to arrive at that decision. What must be stressed was that Margaret was not the main factor in the gradual dissolution of the Jessie/Toshie relationship. Frances was better known to him because Frances was the more outgoing, as was seen at Dunure, and, as was thought at the time, she was the more promising artist of the two sisters. She and Bertie continued strongly as a pairing, so it was almost by default that Margaret and Toshie were thrown together.

Meantime, the Macdonald sisters were busy on all sorts of things: metalwork, arts and crafts, some serious painting of long ladies and some not-so-serious posters like the one for Joseph Wright's Umbrella Company. They cleverly incorporated the umbellifer plant and suggested that plant's dangerous properties in the forbidding aspect of a typically 'spooky', long-limbed woman. If anyone was going to depict them as witches, nobody could do it better than the Macdonalds themselves. What gave the design wit was their incorporation of the word Drooko, and not only that but Royal Drooko, in the advertising, for every Glaswegian knew that 'drookit' meant being absolutely sopping wet from being caught in the rain. What better advertisement for an umbrella? These women obviously had brains, and the poster got them off to a good start as full-time professional artists. Several Glasgow women, asked by a newspaper reporter their reaction to this and like posters on display in an exhibition, all replied with the same single word – 'Awful!' And one woman added, 'Horrid!'[3] Newbery's answer to such criticism was to send three crates of their work to Liege in Belgium where they were received with acclaim in an international exhibition of students' work. He made sure the Glasgow newspapers printed a full report. He also made sure that London saw it too. Newbery was a PR man of the first order before the world knew of such a thing, and he knew that he had genuine product in these four young people and raw genius in one of them.

This was the time of the Celtic Revival and the emergence of the Pre-Raphaelite Brotherhood in London and the air between there and Dublin and Glasgow hung heavy with mysticism and symbolic meaning. The fake Ossian was having his second wind because the new aestheticism called for a 'new art' to acknowledge the meeting of the nineteenth and twentieth centuries. The end of any century has its in-built mystery where a lament for the old makes its own music with a hymn to hope. It was an exciting time for ideas and the Four were on to all of them.

It was exactly the time for contradiction, for paradox. Death dominated but Life kept peeping in from the side. Propriety was all, but sex couldn't be kept off the page or the canvas. Purity went hand in hand with eroticism and their dance was a celebration not only of survival but of rebirth. Chastity was always shown as modestly dressed, but on occasions her bodice slipped. More than anything, art showed that it could be fun too, and everything that came from the Hope Street Studio seemed to have a smile on it. Didn't Gleeson White, then editor of the *Studio* magazine, describe the Macdonalds when he met them as – 'two laughing girls, scarce out of their teens'? He added that they did not 'advance any theory'. What he did not or could not see was that their theories were already fully worked out in all that they did.

The same applied to Mackintosh. At first he seemed to stand on the edge of the group much as Margaret had done at Dunure, and he only gradually came into things. They had so much in common, these four, as Newbery had seen, but they were really more two pairs than a quartet, and now Mackintosh was beginning to stand back from McNair. Only in the work sense, of course, but it was as if he, Mackintosh, were waiting for something to happen. He carried on his Honeyman and Keppie duties almost automatically. Nothing he did taxed him and he did not yet have the status in the office to demand greater responsibility. Besides, he and John Keppie were barely on speaking terms. Jessie was probably never mentioned by either of them.

He did help out his old friend, George Walton, on stencil designs for Miss Cranston's enlarged tea rooms at Buchanan Street, but he didn't think anything much would come from that, although he enjoyed meeting the larger-than-life Mrs Cochrane. He liked the fact that she dressed in the fashion of her youth and wore the clothes as if they were the latest in *chic*, but to this Glasgow lady, they were just *cheeky*. And she would laugh her husky Glasgow laugh. Yes, he liked Kate Cranston from the start and he was to get to like her even more, but he was still waiting for that big architectural breakthrough. He did not have long to wait.

The Glasgow School of Art may be said to have started around 1844 with the founding of the Government School of Design, which was intended to raise the level of design in all manufactured goods made in and around Glasgow. When, in 1869, the school moved to Ingram Street it became the Government School of Art and, as such, moved to the Corporation Buildings in Rose Street where, by 1896, under Newbery's direction, it had trained virtually everyone mentioned the Mackintosh story so far. However, it wasn't the only art training centre in the city.

In 1881, Robert Brydall, a teacher at the school resigned to form his own St George's School of Art at 147 St George's Road and, in 1889, on Mr Brydall's retirement to London, it moved to 8 Newton Terrace, near Charing Cross under its new director, Robert Greenless. It remained there until 1905. Women at the Queen Margaret College had had Drawing and Painting Instruction since 1885 from a certain G Albert Laundy, who also undertook to 'accompany students to the Art Exhibitions, Annual and Permanent and give critical and explanatory instruction on the works exhibited'. And at the Athenaeum School of Music, a School of Art was established within it under Charles G Kennaway and staff and the Curriculum covered 'the whole course of Art Instruction from Elementary Drawing to Painting from Life and there will be classes for Modelling, Woodcarving, etc. The rooms have been specially fitted up for the purpose, and will be lighted by electricity on the newest method adapted in the Continental Art Schools'.[4] They must have had a lot of students through those famous portals, and some of them might indeed have been artists, because thousands of them were by now earning a living in art and design in all parts of the world. This fully justified Newbery's hopes for Glasgow and, at the same time, it ensured that the general standard of the label 'Made in Glasgow' was maintained at its now-expected high level.

More and more students wanted to attend lectures and courses at Newbery's establishment at Rose Street. So much so that many had to be turned away because there was simply no room for them. This prompted some long discussion among the governors of the School many of whom were artists who had become successful businessmen or businessmen who wished they were artists or those who were neither but became governors anyway. These last were the 'moles', as Newbery called them, because all they could do was find holes in everything.

It was not a mole, but the Chairman of the Board of Governors, Sir James Fleming, who rose on the morning of Saturday 7 March 1896, to propose to his fellow governors that a new building be erected on a site which had now become available in Renfrew Street and that building should be called the Glasgow School of Art and Haldane Academy. It was not a pretty site for such a majestic title. It was cramped in on all sides and fell away southwards down a precipice to Sauchiehall Street but – and it was a big 'but' – it was cheap. Ideally, they wanted a building that was just as cheap. The first thing they did, as any good governors would, was to appoint a committee, a building committee. It is worth recording their names, because it is to these men we owe a world-acknowledged architectural masterpiece.

They are, in addition to Sir James, Sir Francis Powell LLD, Sir William Bilsland Bart, LLD, DL, Col RJ Bennett VD, Dr JJ Burnet RSA, FRIBA, John Henderson MA, H Reid DL, D Barclay FRIBA, JM Munro FRIBA, Councillor J Mollinson MINA, JM Groundwater (Secretary), Patrick S Dunn (Chairman) and the current director of the School, Francis Newbery. This last appointee was to prove crucial. Not that the Committee lacked big guns. There were several captains of industry there and no less than four architects, one of whom was one of Mackintosh's early heroes, John James Burnet. There was of course the nominal Corporation representative but who the moles were could only be a matter of choice. Among the interesting omissions, however, were JS Templeton, the carpet and curtain man who had commissioned William Leiper to recreate the Doge's Palace on Glasgow Green, and W Forrest Salmon, the middle Salmon, whose father had built most of Dennistoun and whose son was one of Toshie's few real friends.

Otherwise it was as good a jury selection as might be found in any great city to bring a prize project home.

The first thing priority was to find the starting money. This was got from the Bellahouston Bequest Fund which was willing to offer a one-off grant of £10,000 towards 'a plain building affording accommodation equal to that in service', on condition that the governors would raise £6,000 themselves. Glasgow Corporation added £5,600, and the Education Department £1,500 and when the governors chipped in with their personal contributions and some Glasgow firms made at least token financial gestures, the Building Committee had the grand total of £14,000 to play with after the site had been paid for.

It was decided that a competition would be announced for which no prize would be offered but the winner would receive 5% of the building costs. Newbery drew up the rules and made a block plan whose constraints would make for a tight brief on a narrow site. Assessors, Sir James King and Sir Renny Watson were appointed, with powers to co-opt if necessary, and only the approval of Thomas Armstrong at South Kensington was needed to get the ball rolling. This was received in May and in June the competition was publicly announced calling for the submission of plans by 1 October.

The general feeling of the twelve architectural firms invited to compete was that even the plainest of buildings was hardly possible on such a budget and it would take nearer £40,000 to build an appropriate building for the number of students involved. Since the Governors kept insisting 'it is but a plain building that is required', a compromise was reached in deciding that the project should be completed in two phases. It was agreed that 153 feet of frontage could be built as Phase One for the money in hand and plans were revised accordingly. The idea was to start at the east and go west along Renfrew Street until the money ran out.

While all this was going on, the relationship between Margaret Macdonald and Toshie was inching towards a degree of mutual acceptability. It had all started when he exhibited with Bertie and the Macdonalds at the School of Art Club and there had been a bit of a noise about some of their work – especially the girls' paintings but Newbery didn't seem at all put out by the outcry. Spooks didn't appear to bother him. He was more concerned that art should make an impact even if the initial reaction was hostile. His 'How are they to learn to appreciate new work if they don't see new work?' seemed logical enough.

The relationship between Margaret and Toshie was further extended during the Fancy Dress Ball held at the Glasgow Institute Galleries to raise funds for the Ladies' Arts Club. Mackintosh didn't trust himself on the dance-floor on this occasion, or was not trusted to be so, as he spent the entire evening on what can only be termed 'stage-management' activities backstage. So did Margaret Macdonald. This threw them further together. Similarly, they both worked on exhibits for the first Arts and Crafts Exhibition held to raise money for the new Maryhill Barracks. The Four had now split into two and two again but this time not by default, but by mutual inclination. Indeed Bertie and Frances were getting to be quite serious and marriage was being talked about. It was not on the agenda of either Margaret or Toshie, but neither was it an impossibility.

In April 1896 he had made her a present of his original water-colour, *Part Seen-Imagined Part* and it was not too difficult to imagine what others saw in the gesture. It was the nearest thing he had got to an actual portrait of Margaret and, although a full statuesque figure is suggested, it really amounts to only head and shoulders, the rest of the 'body' being wreathed in a protective foliage of tendrils and twigs. He obviously had not 'known' Margaret as yet and by the look of things it was going to take time for him to get through to her. Meantime, in another part of the city ...

Jessie Keppie was sitting for her portrait by an old friend, Bessie McNicol, who was on a visit back to Glasgow from Kirkcudbright. More accurately, Bessie was using her friend as a model for a fancy painting (meaning no likeness of the sitter is necessary) to be entitled *Tritomas,* which is the old botanical name for the flowers we now call red-hot pokers. The picture might well have been called *Summer,* because that's when it was done. What comes over so strongly in this painting of a kindly-faced, fair-haired, comely Jessie, now thirty years of age, is a shy lady set among the fiery flowers. The painting itself has disappeared but photographs show that if she has been hurt, she is hiding it well.

There is a resemblance between this face and that of the *Girl in Blue with Parasol,* also by Bess McNicol, which Jessie treasured in her autograph book. In addition, a McNicol painting, *In the Orchard,* showing a romantic Jessie in bonnet, scarf and long cloak was once in the possession of Hugh Hopkins and might well have been commissioned by him. All of which shows that Jessie had her own circle of friends and Bessie McNicol was certainly one of them.

Bessie had been at the old Art School with her sister Minnie the year after Mackintosh. They were yet another Art School sister act. She completed the course, though Minnie did not, but she did not take a diploma. Instead, she went to Paris between 1891 and 1894 when other Scots like Peploe and Yule were also studying there, as was John Duncan Fergusson, who was to be a later Mackintosh friend in London. Bessie was a striking girl, as good a singer and musician as she was an artist, so it was no surprise that she too caught the eye of Fra Newbery and also became a good friend of his after graduation. She saw him regularly when she was in Glasgow and often went with the Newberys and others, like the painter, David Gould, to spend summers at Lundin Links in Fife.

She was more than a good friend to Hugh Hopkins, who had a book shop in Exchange Square which served as a meeting place for all the young book-lovers in Glasgow who had interests other than books. For instance, Bessie loved bicycling and so did Hugh Hopkins and his cousin John Keppie, and all three often went out on the road together at weekends. It might have been on one of these outings that she told Hugh she was going to marry Alexander Frew. Hugh remained a good friend all the same, but it did seem that the Keppie connections were unlucky in love. Sandy Frew was a tall, good-looking man, who gave up obstetrics to paint; when he met Bessie, he became a doctor again and ended up as a consultant gynaecologist at 12 St James Terrace (now Ruskin Terrace) in Hillhead.

Frew had bought the house from David Young Cameron, the painter, who, inspired by Mackintosh, as he freely admitted, built himself a 'Mackintosh-style' studio in the garden – and it was here, sometime in the summer of 1898 that Bessie painted her old friend, Jessie Keppie. It was often Bessie's custom to write in dialogue when corresponding with friends, and she did this in correspondence with her friend and 'soul-mate', Edward Hornel. A small example is given here from Ailsa Tanner's book on Bessie (*New Woman*, 1998). It recounts a conversation Bessie had with Newbery. By the way, it should be mentioned that Hornel may have had a mild form of Tourette's syndrome. Bessie reported:

> He asked me how I got on with you.
> 'Oh, splendidly!! I admire him immensely, & there was nothing antagonistic in our natures.'
> 'Did he ever say naughty words?'
> 'Oh, sometimes he said naughty cuss words, but I always tried to get one better.'
> He opened his eyes at my lie – or at your powers![5]

Bess never wrote to anyone about her session with Jessie in 1898 but the two women were good friends and they had so much in common: friends like the painters Annie Rose Low and David Gauld, the etcher Susan Crawford and others like Harry Spence, nicknamed 'The Josser'. No doubt the two young women had talked freely over a glass of sherry in the back room of Hugh Hopkins' shop and no doubt they talked as freely during the painting session. Had Bessie reported it, in her dialogue fashion, to Hornel – to whom she told everything – it might have read as other similar 'epistles' of hers did:

> *She asked me how I got on with you?*
> *'Oh, splendidly!! I admire him tremendously, & we do enjoy our somnambulating walks and what he calls our "gay festivities" '.*

*She wondered if it had been wise for me to go to Kirkcud-
bright to work with you.*

'I did not go alone, I had my sister with me and he always
had Minnie [his sister] with him [yet] I have not done hearing of my terrible misdemeanors in working in your studio,
Ned. If the people chaffed me I could take it but it comes
to pure scandal, or I should rather say not pure. One vile
brute said he had the best authority for what he insinuated.
In any case whenever I hear any man or any woman has
said anything ... on my next meeting they are met with a
strong British stare ... You see I do not care who knows
the absolute truth but garbled accounts & added-on stories
are the devil's own work to combat'.[7]

*I then asked dear Jessie if she had got over the Mackintosh
business. She only smiled and said,*
'Is that everybody's business, too, Bessie?'

*She didn't get angry with me. I have never seen Jess angry
but she seemed to withdraw a little.*

'I said nothing', she said eventually, 'and Charlie said noth-
ing, so nothing happened. Things just drifted off, you know.
I have tried to forget about it. (She paused for a moment)
Yes, drifted off is about right.'

*For a long time we said nothing than suddenly she was up
on her feet from the stool and was off by the time I took my
head from the canvas. As she put on her bonnet at the door
all she said was 'I'm sorry, Bessie, I hadn't noticed the time
till I heard the clock chime. I'll have to run. John will be
expecting his tea on the table.'*

*Then she was gone. Away to make her brother's tea, when
she might have been – oh dear, who knows what any of us
might have been – if only. Isn't that right Ned?[6]*

When Jessie Keppie hurried out of Bessie McNicol's studio that afternoon she also took herself effectively out of Mackintosh's life and out of our story.

On 13 January 1897 the Chairman of the Building Committee, Patrick S Dunn, opened the envelope from the Assessors, marked with the three wishbones announcing the winner of the competition for the design of the new Glasgow School of Art, and he drew out Honeyman and Keppie. John Keppie graciously accepted the commission on behalf of the firm and the work was put in hand, or more exactly, *into* the hands of one CR Mackintosh

All the competition designs went on view at the Corporation Galleries and since these included the doyen of Glasgow architects, John James Burnet, interest was great. So was the reaction to the winning entry where the main worry was about the placing of the door. Of course, the public did not realise that this was a building of two halves and the whole thing wouldn't make real sense until the second half was completed. Mackintosh had given them half of a plain building, which is exactly what they had paid for.

There could have been no better architect than he was at the time to design such a building. It hadn't been long since he had been a student himself and he knew from first hand the whole range of student needs – space, light, and room to make a mess in. The director can have his office, the governors their boardroom, the scholars their library but for the most part art students only wanted a workspace. The occasional decoration would not go amiss, as long as it had a relevance and, more importantly, some wit. An art school should be for the young, looking forward, and not for the old, looking back. Let the universities do that. An art school is a kindergarten for gifted children who have no desire to grow up.

They're not childish, however. They are wise enough to recognise how much they need the best of the past to implement their future utopias, and Mackintosh had that Janus ability of looking the best of both ways. He was a Modernist-Revivalist seeking the best of both worlds and he made this manifest in his work on the new School of Art. At first, John Keppie was the man ostensibly in charge and was seen to be so as the Very Important Persons met on Wednesday 25 May to watch Sir Renny Martin wield his solid silver trowel over the foundation stone, which was then lowered between two large windows on the first floor and was never seen again.

Never mind: Sir David Richmond, the Lord Provost of Glasgow had made his speech, and Sir James Fleming had thanked him. The deed was done. After the watching crowd in the street had given three hearty cheers, the invited guests went off to the Corporation Galleries for a champagne lunch, the cost of which might have taken the building a few more feet to the west. As the crowd in the street dispersed, one man stood leaning against the railings on the other side of the street. He was the undesignated designer of the project but he had not been invited to the fancy lunch. Not that he minded: it gave him time to stand there on his own and feast his mind's eye on what he knew was soon to rise up before them all. In his own phrase, he could 'prophesy about what was still unexisting'.

William Buchanan, in his comprehensive article on the School in *Mackintosh's Masterwork,* quotes a letter written to Hermann Muthesius which exactly sums up the architect's attitude at this time. Mackintosh writes:

> You must understand that for the time being I am under a cloud – as it were – although the building in Mitchell Street here was designed by me the architects are or were Messrs Honeyman and Keppie – who employ me as <u>assistant</u>. So if you reproduce any photographs of the building you must give the architect's name – not mine. You will see that it is very unfortunate for me, but I hope when brighter days come, I shall be able to work for myself entirely and claim my work as mine.[7]

The Mitchell Street building was the *Glasgow Herald* building with its distinctive tower, which ought to have told the most casual observer that it was the work of an architect with a very individual eye who was only 30 years of age. However much he may have bemoaned his status to Muthesius, he was still very inexperienced professionally and it makes it all the more incredible that he pulled off the Art School as he did – but he hadn't finished yet. As Gleeson White had said about him previously in *The Studio*, 'When a man has something to say and knows how to say it, the conversion of others is usually only a matter of time'.

In the meantime, his salary had been increased to twelve pounds monthly and he had begun work on St Matthew's Church at Queen's Cross for the Springburn Mission and had made some furniture designs for Miss Cranston's tea rooms in Argyle Street. He had to earn that new salary. Gleeson White, an avowed admirer, published an article in *The Studio* making the Four known on the continent for the first time. Bertie had an unexpectedly successful one-man show at the Gutekünst Gallery in London and it led to an offer of a job in Applied Arts in Liverpool. He took it. He wanted to take Frances with him, but the family, perhaps wisely, persuaded her to wait and see how he did in the new job first. The Macdonalds were not as vulnerable to the McNair charm as Frances was.

Talwin Morris wrote an appreciation of the Four, which was never printed but was very flattering, especially to the work of 'Charles Mackintosh'. The tide was gradually beginning to swell and his name was inexorably coming forward. It was at this tide in his affairs, in early 1898, after a brief holiday with the Newberys in Walberswick, Suffolk, that he tackled what ought to have been his second masterpiece – a concert hall.

This was a competition project undertaken by Honeyman and Keppie in preparation for the International Exhibition to be held in the Kelvingrove Park, Glasgow in 1901. The site was magnificent, gazed down on by the Gothic mass of Gilbert Scott's University and set in grounds laid out by Sir Joseph Paxton beside the winding River Kelvin. The proposal called for a Grand Hall to stand adjacent to the existing Art Gallery and Museum and a Concert Hall to be linked to the scheme. Mackintosh, Keppie and Honeyman each submitted a plan for the Grand Hall and, although two were short-listed (one being Mackintosh's), none was selected.

Mackintosh had also submitted a design for the concert hall, but considering that the Corporation of Glasgow was still reeling from the effects of his ultra-modern Art School now rising in Renfrew Street, it was unlikely that Mackintosh would be given another bite at the apple from the tree from which hung the bell and the fish with the ring in its mouth. So it was no surprise, when the results were published in the *British Architect* on 16 September, that his easily-recognisable design was not among the prize-winners. And yet it was undeniably a winner on the page.

His auditorium would have accommodated more than four thousand seated spectators in the round and would have been ideal today for pop concerts. It had, like most Victorian places of public assembly, an immense platform containing an organ case and an encircling gallery, which also provided an exterior gallery, and all of which was contained under a flat saucer dome which might have been designed by Martians. In fact, as Howarth points out, the whole thing anticipates Ralph Tubbs design for the Festival of Britain's Dome of Discovery in 1951.[8] The Mackintosh Concert Hall was an enormous, uncompromising piece of Glasgow impudence, and deserved to be built if only because of that same thrilling impertinence.

It is also, like everything he ever touched, a thing of beauty. Here is no fussy ornamentation – it is its own ornament and would have weathered beautifully in Kelvingrove Park to this very day. It might even have pre-empted the St Andrew's Halls as Glasgow's cultural and performance centre and thousands would have flocked to hear the great choral works of the Victorian era just as modern crowds would have milled to hear Frank Sinatra or the Beatles – but it was not to be. As Howarth reminds us, 'Glasgow was entertained by a jolly outburst of sugar-cake architecture in the Spanish renaissance manner' offered by local architect, James Miller.[9] Mackintosh shrugged and returned to finishing off the Art School – Part One.

The Concert Hall, however, has not been forgotten by Glaswegians. In the mid-Eighties, Dr Lorn Macintyre wrote an article in the weekend section of the *Glasgow Herald* advocating the building of a scaled-down version of the Mackintosh Hall in the Park, especially as Sir Leslie Martin's concert hall complex was about to dwarf the Buchanan Street bus station. *Herald r*eaders, like Andrew Pinkerton and Mrs Mary M Barrie of Bearsden, wrote to the paper to approve Dr Macintyre's idea, but nothing was done. Perhaps it is still not too late. After all, a large circular building housing the National Panorama once sat snugly behind the western extension to the Art School, as can be seen from early photographs of the extension in construction.

Why not a large circular Concert Hall in the same position today? And while we're about it, we could have the Chelsea Studios on to Sauchiehall Street and perhaps his Margaret Morris Theatre on the other boundary if there's room. Of course this is dream stuff, but if I may paraphrase Hermann Muthesius in his comment about the Mackintosh rooms in 1904:

> There is no hope that our aesthetic cultural sense will prevail to allow such schemes to be accepted ... But they are milestones erected in anticipation, in anticipation, by a genius, to demonstrate to Mankind the higher and sublime.[10]

At least such a dream-scheme, say by the 2018 anniversary, would make a grand, emphatic apology to the architect for the way his city ignored him shamefully in his own time and has traduced him to their profit since.

Queen's Cross Church ('a treasury of detail' as Alan Crawford called it) was completed in May 1899 and Mackintosh now took time off to attend Bertie's wedding to Frances at St Augustine's, Dumbarton, and afterwards wave the newlyweds off to Liverpool. Bertie had replaced Robert Anning Bell as Director of Applied Arts at the University College and prospects looked good for him there. He had also come into some McNair money so the Macdonalds gave the young couple their smiling approval. Nobody, however, suggested that they make the wedding ceremony a foursome.

It was a wet Monday in Glasgow when the first part of the new Art School opened on 20 December, ten days after Mackintosh's 31st birthday. Mary Sturrock remembers standing in the rain holding the special silver key (designed by Mackintosh) which lay on a pearly silk cushion with a silver fringe (designed by Margaret Macdonald and made by Jessie Newbery) while the speeches droned on under the umbrellas, until the gloved hand of Sir James King took it up and formally opened the door to 167 Renfrew Street and everyone hurried in – just to get out of the rain. Once inside, there were more speeches – nine in all – including one by John Keppie who was introduced as the *architect*. Mackintosh was nowhere to be seen and his name was not even mentioned.

Yet he was there – in every ingenious nook and cranny of the place, in everything that met the glazed eyes of the usual, glass-holding, finger-feeding, municipal dignitaries that afternoon in 1899. Yes, he was there. Especially in the interior woodwork which, as the *Evening Times* noted was painted in 'an artistic shade of green'. Mackintosh was there alright.

And still is.

CHAPTER SIX

A Scotch Dwelling House

1899–1904

It is a wonder to see how divers men, being bent on
buildage, and having delyte in the spending of their goodes,
by virtue of that trade do daily imagine new devices of their
owne, to guide their workmen withal. So that these workmen are growne generallie to such an excellence that their
new buildage passeth even the finest of the olde.

William Harrison

WHEN THE FIRST SOD was cut by Mrs William Davidson on the
site of Windyhill, the house to be built on a high ridge in Kilmacolm, near Glasgow, Mackintosh fell flat on his face and the three
Davidson children thought it was very funny. Champagne had
marked the ceremony, drunk from a goblet specially designed by
the architect, but he insisted that it was his 'gammy leg' on the
uneven turf. Nobody disbelieved him. It was a happy occasion. He
had known the family in their previous house, *Gladsmuir*, and
had designed some furniture for them, but here he was, with half
an Art School built, and now with a whole house to play with on
its own site on Houston Street. It was a heady moment for him.
He had no need of the Davidson champagne. William Davidson
had given him a completely free hand but Mackintosh was determined to use both of his own.

William Davidson was that rare type, a businessman with aesthetic tastes. In the same way that he had built up his provisions
business in Glasgow he had built up a collection of the Glasgow
Boys' work and had assembled a fine collection of paintings by the

time Mackintosh came to know him. This contact may have been through John Quentin Pringle, the eccentric watchmaker-painter from Glasgow's Saltmarket, who was at the Art School when Mackintosh was there. Pringle was much admired by Newbery who thought he was a genius but he couldn't persuade him to be anything but a part-time painter and a full-time watchmaker. Nevertheless, Pringle did visit Windyhill with Mackintosh and a photograph exists with the two of them and two of the three Davidson boys, Cameron and Hamish. Hamish remembered the sensation that their new house caused among the neighbours, especially with his father's fellow commuters. As he told Alistair Moffat:

> When Windyhill was built my father put up with a fair amount of well-meant but mostly very uninformed banter from his companions on the daily train ride to Glasgow. It was likened by them to a barracks or a prison. I don't think these comments caused him any loss of sleep.[1]

The house was Scottish in every aspect and amounted to a tribute in stone to Robert Lorimer and the Scottish vernacular. It was a clever use of the Free Style which allowed him to select what he wanted of the old and apply it to the new. This was to be increasingly the Mackintosh method, but since architectural appraisal of the works is not within the remit of this book, nor my competence, it is sufficient to say that plans for the slightly forbidding exterior were not submitted until every interior detail had been settled. That was also the Mackintosh way. And in the spring, when the danger of frost had passed, the whole was covered in a grey harling. Here, amenity was sacrificed for the sake of overall effect and it is this which gave Windyhill its particular look.

This aspect did not endear it to everyone, nor its proximity to houses on either side. It did not impress my former wife when I had the opportunity to purchase Windyhill from my friend Allan Ure in 1975 but she could not be persuaded to leave the security of a specially restored, centrally heated, double-glazed sixteenth-century lodging in Fife for a windy hill at Kilmacolm. Not that it mattered, for Allan suddenly sold up in 1979 and retired to Bournemouth where he died soon after.

He and I had had many happy hours in the L-shaped house shifting the pails to catch the rain that was always leaking from the roof and trying to keep the heating going. Mr Ure had some choice words to say about Mackintosh at these times. I was sorry not to have bought such a house. Ironically, when I came to buy Kellie Lodging in Pittenweem at a later date, it was through the National Trust in Scotland, and one of its advisors then was Mr Hew Lorimer of Kellie Castle in Fife, who was the son of Robert Lorimer, the architect who had part-inspired Windyhill.

Mackintosh, this prototypical nineteenth-century man, came into the new twentieth-century on a high and he kept flying. At 32, he gained his maturity with Windyhill and his other project, on which he worked simultaneously, did nothing to diminish his growing confidence. The *Daily Record* building in Renfield Lane must be considered as one of his most underrated buildings. His perspective drawing of it is an art-work in itself and its startling modernity would convince anyone that it is a design dating from the Thirties, at the earliest, yet it was conceived in the first months of 1900. It is a mini-masterpiece in glazed white brick shot through with red and green glazed brick in a kind of tree effect. It sounds awful but looks terrific. Yet it is hidden down a lane off a busy street. This little 'fantasia', as Alan Crawford aptly calls it, vividly represents Mackintosh's increasing technical sophistication.[2] Coming across it today is like finding an earring in the gutter.

On 18 June 1900, Frances McNair gave birth to a son in Liverpool and Bertie brought Sylvan McNair back to Scotland to show him off to the families. He did so by cycling from house to house towing a wicker basket containing mother and luggage, the child being carried in a smaller basket on the handlebars. He was a powerful man was Bertie. His favourite party trick, which was of his own devising, was the 'Kangaroo Dance' in which he jumped with great agility among the furniture. It was a dance which did not catch on with the Liverpudlians. Despite this terpsichorean diversion, their home at 54 Oxford Street became a centre for every kind of artist and those who had artistic aspirations. Bertie repeated his Mermaids frieze around the house and covered the staircase in sheets of lead. There were candles everywhere and symbolic paintings on the walls and the 18-inch knocker on the front door gave great delight to the local small boys.

The McNairs (or MacNairs as Frances preferred) had had a good start in Liverpool. Bertie was a popular instructor of Design and Stained Glass at the University College (later to become the University of Liverpool) and it may be said that he introduced Art Nouveau to the city – or perhaps it was the Glasgow Style as the Four had seen it. He taught in a clutter of old buildings down by the railway cuttings known as the Art Sheds.[3] Discipline was very relaxed and in the evenings everyone took part in rehearsals for Greek drama for which the McNairs did the sets and costumes. On every vacation they pointed the tricycle towards Luss, on Loch Lomond, where hilarious holidays were spent, often with McNair's students, such as Enid Jackson or 'Bee' Phillips and her sister. Or with Margaret and Toshie when she could get away from Bowling (where her brother had bought Dunglass Castle for the family) and he could get away from working on their flat at 120 Mains Street (later Blythswood Street on the corner of Bath Street). He was now a man of rented property, who still lived at home with his father and sisters but soon he would have his own door and someone to carry over it.

Margaret and he were married at St Dunstane's Episcopal Church, Dumbarton on Wednesday 22 August 1900, and the McNairs came up to officially witness the event along with the Macdonald brothers, with their wives, the Newberys and the Talwin Morrises. Superintendent and 'Madame' McIntosh may have attended out of respect but it certainly wasn't a grand family gathering. It is known that the McIntosh sisters were not totally at ease with Margaret, nor she with them. Margaret Rennie Dingwall, a daughter of Mackintosh's older sister Bella, moved to Tynemouth when her McIntosh grandfather remarried but she remembered the Christmas visits to Glasgow. As she told Alistair Moffat:

When Uncle Tosh got married we all went to his house for a tea party ... It was the first time I ever had meringues. I didn't know how to eat them and I remember Aunt Margaret watching me. She seemed very superior and she certainly took no interest in her nephews and nieces. When she did talk to me, thinking about it now, she was condescending and aloof. When Uncle Tosh came to visit us in Tynemouth, Margaret never came with him. And I don't remember her being with the rest of the McIntosh family at Regent Park Square at New Year. We never met any of her family, her sister Frances or her parents, or any of her and Uncle Tosh's friends. But I remember thinking that they must love each other. I don't know why but I just thought that.[4]

The honeymoon, or 'Honeyman' as Toshie called it, was spent sketching on Holy Island in Northumberland, not all that far from Tynemouth. Holy Island was to become a very favourite place of theirs. It was here, that they started initialing drawings together but there was no denying the identity of the artist who made the superb drawing of the monastery on the rock. It anticipated the rock paintings that were to be the later masterpieces of Port Vendres.

They returned to Glasgow to collect Margaret's two Persian cats and together they moved into their new home in Mains Street. And what a place he had made of it. It was less of a home than an artefact. To all intents and purposes, No 120 was another first-floor two-room and kitchen flat reached by two flights of stone stairs from a close leading directly out to the pavement, but in reality it was much more than that. It was a living, three-dimensional work of art, a breathtaking space within four square walls. The door on the landing opened into a Mackintosh world – a world of white and violet dominated by a full-size grey carpet which defied you not to wipe your feet on the mat. Ideally, one should remove one's shoes before entering. It was really quite unbelievable the transformation the two of them had made out of a very ordinary domestic situation.

They had created an all-white room before, at Dunglass Castle for the Macdonalds and at Westdel in Dowanhill, Glasgow for the publisher, Robert MacLehose. It was also in Glasgow, at 34 Kingborough Gardens, that he experimented with another white room for the Rowat family, whose daughter Jessie, a fellow student, was to marry Fra Newbery. In this scheme, Mackintosh made a special effect of the first-floor fireplace which carried on from where he had left off at Dunglass Castle and Mains Street. Unfortunately, nothing of this charming restoration remains. In 1943, it was broken up for firewood because the upholstery on the surrounding seating had grown a little threadbare. Only the white fireplace survived – under several coats of heavy, brown paint.

At Mains Street, however, in 1902, they had the whole apartment to work on and the result was a honeymoon home of quite unique distinction. The three rooms had been made into a drawing room/studio (taking advantage of large windows to the front), a dining room and a bedroom graced by a four-poster bed. The former kitchen range had been boxed in to create an extraordinary fireplace with a raised box at either side, to hold a grey cushion, one for each cat. The gas mantle over the old fireplace had been transformed into an elegant corner light served by an intricate arrangement of slim pipes.

Altogether the almost theatrical arrangement of new furniture in a series of contrived spaces amply bore out William Morris's adage – 'Have nothing in your house you do not know to be useful or believe to be beautiful'. He held the view that 'art was anything well done'. Well, one can only say that 120 Mains Street was artistic. One wonders though where Margaret did the cooking, and whether the lavatory was still on the outside stair! This was the practice in most tenements, except the very swankiest, right up to recent times in Glasgow and it was a facility shared by landing neighbours. And what did the neighbours think of the strange young man who limped up the stairs and the foreign woman he lived with? To Glaswegians, an English accent was 'foreign'. We have no idea of what they thought of the decor because the neighbours were never invited in. Which must have been galling for them, for neighbours everywhere are nosy.

But if no one called from across the landing, visitors did come from across the Channel, especially from France, Austria and Germany, and when they came, they saw – and were conquered. The French critic EB Kalas was enchanted by its 'virginal beauty' – the work of 'two visionary souls in ecstatic communion ... wafted aloft to the heavenly regions of creation.' If his prose is too much, then we can be sure it was not caused by any excess in the decor. If anything, the rooms had an austerity which I am sure the cosy homes across the landing did not have, but it was the cleanness, not the spareness, which attracted. It was probably the first minimalist decoration scheme in a home. It was also, to the professional eye, a domestic oasis in a cultural desert, and as such had the same first impression as a mirage. People could hardly believe what they saw. The same Kalas was to write later of it:

> On the second floor of a modest building in the great, industrial, smoky town of Glasgow there is a drawing room amazingly white ... Went there, as on a pilgrimage to meet ... the occupants of this house of white and violet. A gentleman, thirty five years old, dressed all in black, with long, dark hair parted in the middle; the eyes slumber in their setting of bushy eyebrows but flame up from their gloom in occasional flashes of varicoloured sparks; the mouth betrays caution, perhaps timidity – probably mockery. The general appearance is of a clean-shaven American clergyman who is still pulsing with the emotion and travail of his last metaphysical discourse but has succeeded, by powers of restraint, in preserving an impassivity and unnatural silence – Charles Rennie Mackintosh.[5]

He did not mention Margaret. Perhaps he saw them as already joined at the hip, although Ecclesiasticus, Chapter 42, Verse 44, does state that 'all things go in pairs, by opposites'. There is no doubt that in their differences they complemented each other. Their marriage was reflected in the union that now took place in the work they did together. It was a fusing of form and structure underlaid with symbolism. The rose vied with the fish eye as their constant *leitmotif*. It was an ideal partnership, a unity created by the blending of the utilitarian and the artistic. Working hand in glove, as it were, although she kept her gloves on while painting while he, on the other hand, was covered in paint while he worked. No doubt he was sustained by the Mackintosh clan motto – 'Touch not the cat but the glove', which simply meant that a Mackintosh should be handled with care.

From the very beginning Margaret handled her husband with compelling care and skill and the reckless, wayward Toshie gave way for a time to the restrained Tosh. Not that he seemed to mind and he gave himself over entirely to the pairing, but close friends like Hamish Davidson noticed:

> After his marriage there is a change. He no longer called himself Uncle Tosh – though we continued to do so. [In the Christmas presents to my brothers and myself], the inscription was no longer drawn freehand in a box but is more formal – 'From Margaret Macdonald Mackintosh and Charles Rennie Mackintosh'. It had been Mackintosh whom we first knew but it was Margaret's name always came first. And it was always in her handwriting.[6]

Nevertheless, it was Margaret who hosted the parties for the various McIntosh nephews and nieces from time to time and had to watch while meringues were trodden into the pale grey carpet and sticky fingers smeared the muslin curtains. She dealt with these little disasters just as she managed the coals that might fall occasionally from the fire and the ash that fell constantly from her husband's ever-present pipe. One just had to cope with these things although she must have been tested. Like when Uncle Tosh organised rowdy games for his screaming and whooping young relatives in and out of the famous furniture. He would have made a wonderful father but what kind of mother would Margaret gave been? Sex exuded from every line she put on a canvas and there was passion in every one of her tortuous design schemes but would she have coped with the ordinary, day-to-day mess and smells of child-bearing matrimony? One wonders. She was four years older than Toshie but that gap would appear to get greater as the years went on.

It cannot be denied, however, that at this time they were very happy indeed. He was sufficiently excited by their life together to design in that same year a pair of ideal homes that they one day might build, one in town and another in the country. The latter was in fact actually constructed, but nearly a hundred years later in 1992, at Farr, near Inverness, for Mr and Mrs Tovell. The architect involved, Mr Robert MacIntyre, said only that he was 'fortunate enough to be available to serve as Mr Mackintosh's job architect'.[7] One can only hope that someone will build the town house one day, and where better than in his home town of Glasgow.

By this time, reports of his work by Gleeson White in *The Studio* magazine and rumours about the impact of the School of Art had led to growing interest in his work on the Continent. The Austrian architect Josef Hoffmann, his fellow architect Joseph Maria Olbrich and their mentor Otto Wagner were known in Austria as the *Die Jungen*. They had seceded from the staid Künstlerhaus to develop the *jugendstil*, the young style, and they recognised in Mackintosh's work a fellow Modernist. Like him, they wanted to create a new holistic architecture, which would blend all the modern technologies available to a truer effect, where function would dictate the form and the outside of any building would be determined by its interior

Fired by their enthusiasm for these ideas they sent Fritz Wärndorfer to seek out Mackintosh in Glasgow and he arrived during 1900 with his wife. He insisted on being shown everything they had done to date. He was extremely impressed. Wäerndorfer was a scholar and his English was exemplary so he was able to make himself and his ideas well understood. The two couples got on very well indeed, and Mrs Wärndorfer was especially taken with the Mains Street flat. Herr Wärndorfer was equally taken with Margaret. He said: 'I have become acquainted with one distinguished lady in my whole life – Mrs Mackintosh'.[8] So intrigued was he that he commissioned Mackintosh there and then to design a Music Salon for the Wärndorfer home in the Carl-Lud-wigstrasse, 45, Vienna. This was duly done and when completed in the following year it caused a sensation in artistic circles there. It was the first Mackintosh work to be seen in Europe and it made his name at once. Really it was just Mains Street again with Maeterlinck panels done in gesso by Margaret and the addition of a massive, rectangular grand piano. Despite this, *The Studio's* Vienna representative said of the room:

> The composition forms an organic whole, each part fitting into the rest with the same concord as do the passages of a grand symphony; each thought resolves itself as do the chords in music, till the orchestration is perfect, the effect of sweet repose filling the soul.[9]

And this for one room? What would he have said about a Mackintosh palace? With this interest established, he and Margaret were asked to design a 'Scottish Room' for the Eighth Secession Exhibition in Vienna in November 1900. They accepted at once and an area was put at their disposal. This was their last hurrah and they were determined that the Viennese should see the new Glasgow Style at its best. The Art Editor of the *Viener Rundschau* reported:

> There is a Christ-like mood in this interior: This chair might have belonged to St Francis of Assisi. The decorative element is not proscribed, but is worked out with a spiritual appeal.[10]

Despite the fact that the Mackintoshes were announced as 'Mr and Mrs Herr Macdonald' a great time was had by all in Vienna. Margaret's flaming red hair got as much attention as their pale Scottish room. According to Howarth, the art students dragged both in a flower-bedecked carriage to the station.[11]

There were a few raised voices against – 'a hellish room … with furniture as fetishes' but otherwise it was a Scottish triumph. The

Mackintoshes were on their way to becoming, as John McKean puts it, 'public property in German-speaking Europe.'

In addition, a new and vital contact was made in the imposing presence of Hermann Muthesius, a German architect and art historian who wrote his first article on the Mackintoshes in *Dekorative Künst*. He was to have a great influence in spreading the Mackintosh name throughout Europe. After the Exhibition, he wrote to *Die Künst*, a German arts periodical, defending the distortion of the human figure in the Four's work:

> Hitherto, with each ornamental application the fundamental proportions of the human figure have been preserved, the figures have neither been drawn out into lines like baker's dough, nor compressed. But in Art there are no laws, the decisive factor is the artistic deed.[12]

Mackintosh could not have agreed more with that final sentence.

Just as that letter was published, early in the new year of 1901, John Honeyman retired because of increasing eye failure and John Keppie moved the practice to new premises at 4 Blythswood Square. He also restructured the partnership, reluctantly offering Mackintosh a junior partnership on graded but very negligible terms. It was a gesture more than any real advancement but it was one Mackintosh fully deserved and Keppie had to acknowledge the younger man's accelerating development since the Art School project. Work was increasingly divided, in that Keppie kept all the commissioned work as office projects, and Mackintosh had to rely on competition prizes and his Cranston connection. He had been busy re-designing George Walton's interiors at the Ingram Street tea rooms – the first in which he was allowed to make his own statement and Miss Cranston was delighted. A firm working relationship was established and four more schemes were to be developed at these premises over the next decade.

While discussing plans for Scotland Street School with the Glasgow School Board he was also on the look-out for new competitions and his next effort in this area was *Ein Haus Eines Künstfreundes* – 'a house for an art-lover' – organised by Alexander Koch at Darmstadt for his design publication *Zeitscrift fur Innerdekoration*. Mackintosh submitted his entry under the pen-name *Der Vogel* ('the Bird') but, for some reason, it arrived late and was also missing the required number of interior perspectives. This is where Toshie missed the Keppie efficiency and he was repeatedly careless in matters of administration, much to his later cost. However, the entry itself, a Scottish castle with ornamentations, took the competition by storm and its stunning originality won approval all round. He had managed to combine bits of Windyhill with Art School detail and Mains Street effect and in so doing created a magnificent edifice. It was the nearest he ever got to his fantasy of building an ocean liner on land. He wasn't a Clydesider for nothing.

Unfortunately, although he got all the attention, he didn't win the first prize. In fact, no prize was offered but first place went by default to a first-rate English architect, Baillie Scott, for his orthodox mock-medieval castle. Mackintosh's design was anything but orthodox but it could be said that Mackintosh lost by a technical knock-out. The judges added a note to their report:

> Among several works that could not be considered with the finalists owing to violations of the rules of the programme, the design with the motto, 'Der Vogel' ... especially stands out because of its pronounced personal quality, its novel and austere form and the unified configurations of its interior and exterior.

It was a winner in all but name. As a consolation, and as a practical acknowledgment by the assessors of the quality of the entry, he got 600 marks as a special 'purchase prize' and, more importantly won a lot of Viennese attention, which was to pay fruit in the not-so-distant future.

At a much later date, a far-seeing Glasgow civil engineer, Graham Roxburgh, fought hard and long to have the Art Lover's House built and in 1996 this was attained with the help of Andrew MacMillan, the Professor of Architecture at the Mackintosh School of Architecture and his team, and lots of money from various bodies including the Glasgow City Council, who now own it. It was not an easy project. Perhaps they needed those interior perspectives after all, but with ingenuity and not a little skill it was done and it now stands in Bellahouston Park as a cultural and conference centre and a tribute, not only to Mackintosh but also to the faith shown by Graham Roxburgh.

Meantime, Windyhill was completed at last to Mackintosh's satisfaction and the Davidsons moved in. Hamish Davidson continues:

> The move to Windyhill took place in July 1901. I remember a Christmas party in the house at which there was, as it appeared to us as children, a very large Christmas tree. It was covered with presents for everyone and with candles in holders clipped to the branches – a most dangerous arrangement. Uncle Tosh was chosen as Santa Claus and when the time came he proceeded to pick off each parcel and hand it to its recipient. He was clothed in a voluminous red gown copiously adorned with cotton wool. Unfortunately in stretching up to get a parcel he touched or pulled one of the candles which set the cotton wool alight. When the blaze could not be put out and showed signs of spreading there was a moment of emergency which was dealt with by my father pushing Mackintosh hurriedly out of the house and into the little square pond by the front door …[13]

And Mary Sturrock remembers:

> Mackintosh arranged the garden to absolute perfection because it was just little green lawns beautifully shaped and arranged with grey stone walls. It's one of his best things … Contractors are liable to chew up the garden and level it flat [but] he very carefully arranged things around the house to look just right. There's a little square pool as well.[14]

In 1901, Augustus John had just arrived in Liverpool to take the place of a man who had volunteered for the Boer War. He and his wife Ida got to know the McNairs quite well and John wrote to John Rothenstein:

> We dined with two artistic people called McNair, who, between them have produced one baby and a multitude of spooks – their drawing room is very creepy and the dinner table was illuminated by two rows of nightlights in the McNair pattern ... However, the McNairs have a homely way of conversing which immediately sets people at their ease.[14]

John doesn't mention if he were asked to perform the Kangaroo Dance but it is on record that he was not overwhelmed by McNair's artistic talent – although, or perhaps because of, the fact that Bertie had designed an interior for the men's lavatory at the Sandon Studios, which indicated a dressing table with a gentle curve, on which no hairbrush could be at ease, always sliding to the floor. This, I am sure, was the impish sense of humour that Bertie shared with Toshie, without the latter's vast talent to support it. Bisson always referred to Bertie's work as 'the refined melancholy of McNair'. How true this must have been for a very underrated designer who hid his disappointment in extrovert behaviour and increasing eccentricity. The pity is that nothing of his better work from this time has survived to show his real quality, which had nothing to do with Art Nouveau.

In 1902, his class was moved out of the Sheds to a site in Myrtle Street and with this movement the gradual but steady spiral downwards of James Herbert McNair, artist and designer, may be said to begin. Typically, he used a Mrs Ryan as a model for his stained glass work because she had beautiful feet – 'due to her barefoot childhood in Ireland'.[15]

If McNair was continuing his 'missionary' work in England, Mackintosh was also keeping up with his 'foreign' contacts. In early January of 1902, on the invitation of a Mr Edgar Wood, he went down to Manchester to give a talk there to the Northern Art Workers' Guild on his attitude to architecture. Wood, like Henry Wilson, Sedding and Shaw, shared Mackintosh's desire to be free of fashion in architecture. After the usual, disclamatory opening, he made a typically candid start:

I have chosen as my theme 'Seemliness' but the theme will often be lost in my wanderings, will sometimes be only faintly heard in the variations ...

That being established, he continued:

I want to speak to you only as artists, and on the possible improvement in the education and work of the architect and craftsmen as artists. If anything I say has already been said by any of you, I sincerely hope it will not lose anything in the transaction ...We have all heard about ... the vulgarity of the public, of the ordinary man in the street, but I do not think it will do any of us any harm to turn our attention for one night ... to the qualities of our presumably highly-educated artists and designers ... The architect must become the art worker and be content to forego the questionable distinction and pleasure of being respected as the head (perhaps the founder) of a large and successful business – the art worker must become the architect. Architecture must no longer begin and end with the mechanical possibilities of the tee square, set square, pencil bows and dividers ... The man with no convictions – no ideals in art – no desire to do something personal, something his own, something that will leave the world richer ... is no artist. The artist who sinks his personal convictions is no man ... All artists know that the pleasure derivable from their work is their life's pleasure – the very spirit and soul of their existance. But you must be independant – independant, independant. Don't talk so much – go your own way and let your neighbour go his. Don't medle with other peoples ideas when you have all your work cut out of you in trying to express our own – Shake off all the props ... and go alone crawl – stumble – stagger – but go alone.

The Mancunians must have wondered why they were being hectored by this vehement Scotsman who appeared to care so much for the state of his art. He then went on to stress further the place of the individual and the quality of work the artist produces, especially in relation to the use of the imagination:

> The artist cannot attain to mastery in his art unless he is endowed in the highest degree with the faculty of imagination. In analizing the work of today, it will be found that this essential faculty is most conspicuous by its absence ... What one misses ... is the large rythm that undulates through that of the great masters ancient and modern ...

'Ancient and modern' is a phrase that could not be more apt in this context, for this lecture, probably because it was delivered on a Sunday evening, has all the feeling of a religious sermon, and doubtless, it was delivered with the same fervour. He concludes in poetic vein:

> Art is the flower – life is the green leaf. Let every artist strive to make his flower a beautiful living thing – something that will convince the world there may be – there are things more precious – more beautiful more lasting than life ...

His patent sincerity, and good sense, must surely have impressed his audience of northern art workers. It would have been as uplifting to them as any Methodist meeting. The only thing missing was the harmonium. Now that the job was done, there was only one thing on Mackintosh's mind however – the Liverpool Cathedral competition. It is known that he stayed with the McNairs in Liverpool on his way home and would have checked out the intended site. No doubt he and Bertie had a jar or two at the Philharmonic Hotel and compared notes on wives and work, and the competition committee, before Toshie had to return to Glasgow and begin work on his cathedral.

Arguably, the Liverpool Anglican Cathedral project ought to have been another Art School for him. He gave them what they wanted – a Gothic arrangement not unlike Durham Cathedral – but, although highly commended by the assessors, it lost out in 1903 to Gilbert Giles Scott, a third generation of the Scott family who had not even qualified as an architect at the time of his entry.

But he was the son of England's great Victorian architect, Gilbert Scott, and Mackintosh always felt there was something odd about the whole business. He suspected a certain Charles Reilly who had worked in the office of one of the assessors and had much to do with the organisation of the competition. Given Mackintosh's then reputation, he ought at least to have got into the late stages but he was put aside in the first round and fobbed off with 'Highly Commended'.

Some critics say that it might have been due to Toshie's tendency to cover his drawings in a wash of green. He always had a predilection to green – and this might have clouded or obscured the superb penmanship he had learned from Sandy McGibbon all those years before, but there is no evidence for this. All we know is that Mackintosh lost, and also, that he never lost his resentment about losing. This was going to be his cathedral and it was denied him. He, latterly and unashamedly, blamed Reilly. The same man, when he was later appointed as Head of Architecture at the University of Liverpool, was quick to dispense with the services of Herbert McNair. Perhaps he just didn't like Scotsmen.

However Mackintosh was not without friends. Even if most of them were not English. Josef Hoffmann had visited in 1902, and Mackintosh's letter to him on his return showed that they were still very much at one. Hoffmann and his colleagues had now formed what they called the *Werkstätte*, combining the ideas of Ruskin and Morris, and they wanted Mackintosh to join them. They even offered him a studio, but Mackintosh would not, could not, leave Glasgow. He wrote to Hoffmann:

I have the greatest possible sympathy with your idea and consider it absolutely brilliant. If one wants to achieve success with your programme ... every object which you pass from your hand must carry an outspoken mark of individuality, beauty and the most exact execution. From the outset, your aim must be that every object you produce is made for a specific purpose and a specific space ... Many years of hard work, earnest, hard work by the leaders of the modern

movement will be required before all obstacles are removed
... Begin today! If I were in Vienna I would assist you with
a great, strong shovel.[16]

It was just the implement needed at this time because Mr Walter
Blackie, the publisher, had just bought a potato field in Upper
Helensburgh not far from Kilmacolm and Windyhill. On the
advice of his designer, Talwin Morris, Blackie invited Mackintosh
to call at his office to discuss the building of a house on the site.
Mackintosh was there the next morning. Blackie had imagined
that the architect responsible for the new School of Art wouldn't
stoop to design a dwelling-house. What he didn't know was that
Mackintosh would have given, as he said himself, 'the same care
to the design of a pepper-pot as he would to the conception of
a cathedral'.

When they first met at Blackie's office, the publisher was
'astonished at the youthfulness of the distinguished architect'. As
he wrote in his memoir of 1943:

I myself wasn't terribly old in 1902 but here was a truly
great man, who, by comparison with myself, I esteemed to
be a mere boy. I soon found that the 'mere boy' was a thor-
oughly well-trained, experienced architect, fully alive to the
requirements of the villa dweller as to those of a school of
art. The conference didn't last long ... I told him that I
didn't like red-tiled roofs, brick and plaster with wooden
beams – I preferred roughcast for the walls and slates for
the roof ... He suggested I should see Windyhill at Kilmacolm. An appointment was arranged and my wife and I
were shown around the house by Mrs Davidson and left
convinced that Mackintosh was the man for us. Thus we
got started.[17]

A good omen for the project was that when Mackintosh went to
Dunblane, to see 'what manner of folk he was designing for', he
spotted an oak wardrobe in the entrance hall which he had
designed for Guthrie and Wells in his student days. His first
designs were not approved by the family but the second set of

plans was, and soon the spade was out again and the first sod cut – being careful first to take in all the potatoes. Once again, the site was on a hill, so the new house was given the rather obvious title, Hill House. Soon work on another masterpiece was under way.

During that summer of 1902 an International Exhibition of Modern Decorative Art was held at Turin under the patronage of the royal house of Italy and once again the Mackintoshes were invited to create a display; this time the whole Glasgow team was involved. Marshalled by Newbery himself, he fielded his strongest side – the Mackintoshes, the McNairs, Peter Davidson (metal work), Mrs Jessie Rowat Newbery and Ann Macbeth (embroidery), Jessie M King (book covers) and James Craig Annan (photograpy) – the last two winning gold medals. Mackintosh had to be satisfied with a Diploma of Honour for his and Margaret's Rose Boudoir. As he wrote to Muthesius:

> I am afraid there is little chance for us getting a grand prix at Turino, but when you say we should have it we feel we've got something we value much more.[18]

Fra Newbery was knighted personally by the King of Italy, and Newbery would have certainly enjoyed that. Mackintosh even joined in the social scene. Joseph Maria Olbrich, his architect friend from Vienna, was there and he remembers a night out in Turin:

> In the evening I got together the Misters Berlepsch, Walter Crane, Mackintosh etc for a fine meal at the Restaurant Cambio. Afterwards, we were joined by the Grand Duke and we chatted till quarter to eleven ... I thanked Mackintosh without great feeling but politely. I said – 'Dear Mackintosh, you are the worthy one'.[19]

Olbrich had been one of the judges for the Art Lover's House and had admired Mackintosh ever since, although he always teased him about throwing away the competition through carelessness and haste. One feels that Olbrich had a lot to do with no formal prize being offered. If Mackintosh couldn't win, then no one would. The extent of his feelings for the Scot was shown in the following year. He was going to be married and he wanted to travel to Glasgow and be married there so that he could meet Mackintosh again, but his future wife wouldn't let him. Poor Olbrich, a brilliant designer himself, and just a year older than Mackintosh, was to die of leukemia in 1908.

The Grand Duke mentioned above was possibly Ernst Ludwig of Hesse who founded the artists' colony at Darmstadt. He was so taken by Mackintosh's work that he invited him to come to Moscow under Imperial patronage. Unfortunately, by the time this was possible (in 1913) things were not so good for the Mackintoshes in Glasgow and they were not able to see their work acclaimed by the Russian public at the Petrovka. But that is to anticipate. Things were very good indeed for the Mackintoshes at this point and Olbrich was only one of the many who showered praise on everything they did. Alexander Koch featured them in the September issue of *Deutsch Künst und Dekoration* and thus 'Der Scottische Secessionist' Mackintosh came back to Glasgow saying 'Vienna was the greatest experience of my life'. He perhaps may have added 'because it was a six-week second honeymoon with everything paid for'.

Before they resumed work in Glasgow, however, the Mackintoshes joined the McNairs and the Macdonalds on a sketching holiday to his favourite Holy Island before coming back to continue with work on Hill House at Helensburgh. Like Frank Lloyd Wright, Mackintosh was often uneasy in the architect-client relationship, although his experience in this area was brief and would remain so. His methods of working did not always endear him to his clients, except the odd few, but there was nothing odd about Walter Blackie. A shrewd businessman, he knew what he wanted – and what he could afford. But Mackintosh was not without his own shrewdness in this respect. He held such a tight grip on every aspect of any scheme that any deviation from it showed up even to the lay person and eventually Toshie got what he wanted. But so did the client. Walter Blackie continues:

Mackintosh took a broad view of his architectural duties. Every detail was seen to by him, practical and aesthetic. He provided cupboards where they would be useful, all fitted up to suit the practical requirements of the house keeper. The napery cupboard for instance, well provided with trays and drawers, has the hot water system hidden behind it to keep the linen warm and dry; the pantry is also well supplied with convenient drawers for cutlery etc, and presses with glass doors for china etc, he gave them minute attention to fit them for practical needs, and always pleasingly designed. With him the practical purpose came first. The pleasing design followed of itself, as it were. Indeed, it has seemed to me that the freshness or newness of Mackintosh's productions sprang from him striving to service the practical needs of the occupants, whether of a school of art, a dwelling house or a tea-shop, and give these pleasing decorative treatment. Every detail, inside as well as outside, received his careful, I might say loving, attention: fireplaces, grates, fenders, fire-irons; inside walls treated with a touch of stencilled ornament delightfully designed and properly placed.[20]

This could not have been better said, and to my mind it should be mandatory reading for every architectural student to this day.

In November 1902 he submitted his designs for the new school in Scotland Street. By this time, the Glasgow School Board were wary of Toshie's extravagant reputation and insisted on detailed plans before a spade was put into the ground. Mackintosh complied but sent a different set of plans to the contractor. This was discovered and he was in hot water before he had even started. Mackintosh was called in to face the Board and by all accounts gave as good as he got. This resulted in a stiff letter to Honeyman and Keppie:

I am directed to state the Board have no desire for controversy, but the attitude taken by Mr Mackintosh in his

interview with our committee and his letter, left them no
alternative but to state their position in clear terms ...[21]

Keppie no doubt smoothed things over but probably Mackintosh
was still smouldering over Liverpool Cathedral and couldn't really
be bothered dealing with School Boards. Despite this, a truly
impressive school resulted as still can been seen. It has all of the
characteristic Mackintosh ingenuity evident in every corner. Most
of 1903 was given over to Scotland Street and the several house
schemes that didn't come to anything because it was found that he
was suddenly suffering from acute eye strain and Margaret packed
him off to the Orkney Islands for a complete rest.

He came back to complete the Scotland Street designs and
brood about his lost cathedral. As it was, Liverpool Cathedral
wasn't completed until 1960. What a wonderful life's work it
would have been for his immense talent which was then at the
very summit of its powers. Instead he had to deal with his Glasgow School Board committee members and huffy workmen who
were always walking off the job because of the demands he made
on them. Neither they nor he knew at the time that this was the
last architectural work he would see built. It was almost a relief
near the end of the year to turn to the new tea room Kate
Cranston was planning for Sauchiehall Street but that would
belong to the next phase.

In March 1904 Mackintosh handed over the keys of Hill
House to Walter Blackie, saying:

> Here is the house. It is not an Italian villa, an English man-
> sion house, a Swiss chalet or a Scotch castle – it is a dwelling
> house.[22]

And what a dwelling house. With its masculine exterior and
feminine interior, part fortress, part wonderland, it is a kind of
grand relation to Windyhill and is possibly one of the most beautiful domestic buildings in Britain – and Mackintosh managed to
bring it in under budget too. Ruth Hedderwick, one of the Blackie
daughters, remembers that a little girl friend of theirs thought it
was a monastery. The famous white bedroom certainly has a kind

of artistic sanctity and reminds one of what George Fuchs wrote about the Music Salon in Vienna: 'We feel ourselves among the poets when entering the rooms of Mackintosh. It often seems as if the dream were a personal aim.'

And what other architect would have the consideration to place the nursery at the opposite end of the house to the study but apparently he was much put out when Mrs Blackie put yellow flowers in the hall. It clashed with his colour scheme, so they were quickly removed to the drawing room. The house remained in the Blackie family until Mr T Campbell Lawson, a Glasgow accountant, bought it in the Fifties. In the Seventies, the Royal Incorporation of Architects in Scotland took it over as a Mackintosh memorial and converted the rear portion into flats for rental. It is now owned by National Trust for Scotland who maintain it as an outstanding property for the benefit of visitors who flock to it from all over the world.

He had created another monument to himself but the ghost of a cathedral still haunted him, and always would.

CHAPTER SEVEN

Who's for Tea Rooms?

1904–1906

O ye, all ye that walk in willow wood,
That walk with hollow faces burning white
What fathom depths of soul-struck widowhood,
What long, and longer hours one lifelong night,
Ere ye again, who, so in vain have woo'd,
Your last hope lost, who, so in vain invite
Your lips to that, their unforgotten food,
Ere ye, ere ye again shall see the light?

IT IS FITTING that these lines of Dante Gabriel Rossetti's should introduce what Robert Macleod called Mackintosh's Alhambra, the Willow Tea Rooms at 217 Sauchiehall Street, Glasgow's long, most famous, if undistinguished thoroughfare. 'Sauchiehall' derives from the Gaelic meaning 'the way of the willows' and the willow was also the *motif* in Margaret's plaster frieze in a willow tree design which she called *Willow Wood*. It is just as important to acknowledge that this particular project was very much a co-production between the Mackintoshes, architect man and artist wife. She was never to work again with him to this degree and it is true that the longer they were together the less Margaret worked, so that she ended up not working at all. At this stage, however, she was his equal and working partner in every sense.

His, of course, was the overall creation but her design input was crucial to the result. Their collaboration delivered a strictly commercial undertaking, which succeeded in touching the edge of an art work in itself, as much as it touched the busy city pavement before it. And inside, it was an Alhambra indeed. Not far from the site – just turn right on leaving, take a sharp right again at Renfield Street (which the old trams managed and no more) – and tea room patrons would have come to the Alhambra Theatre, a most beautiful playhouse of its time, both outside and in. With its welcoming foyer, its candelabra, its velvet draperies and plush seats in crimson, it was a haven of colour and romance and a welcome escape from the grey streets. It still hurts to realise that it was criminally demolished not so very long ago to make way for yet another anonymous commercial square box. Well, there was nothing square box about that other Alhambra, the Willow Tea Rooms, except perhaps its frontage, which was largely determined by the uncompromising neighbours either side, and consequently stands out unabashedly from their dullness. Even here a statement is made, and the facade shouts to passers-by that 'here be wonders within'. The all-white facing must have caused a sensation in October 1904 when it opened just in time for Halloween. Glaswegians flocked to it as if it were a theatre. Which in a way it was.

It was on three floors – a tea room and general lunch room at ground-floor level, a ladies' tea room on the first floor and a gentlemen's smoking room and billiard room on the third. It sounds prosaic when thus described, but to walk the long entry and see it all open up before your eyes must have been an experience. The Salon de Luke on the second floor featured Margaret's gesso panel and much else to take the eye and distract the senses. Everything seemed to merge into everything. Things curved and curled in all directions and the new ladder-backed chairs, especially made for the room, stood like guards round every table. Colours were unexpected and outrageous. The whole thing was meant to shock – and it did.

Glasgow had never seen anything like it and that was exactly what the client, Miss Catherine Cranston, wanted. Kate Cranston, as she was commonly called, was a formidable Glasgow girl who was born to business, and over a long life succeeded in making herself precisely in her own image. She persisted in wearing the fashions of her mid-Victorian youth right into her old age – large hats and crinolines – and was still wearing them when she died an old woman in the North British Hotel, in George Square, the very hotel where she was born.

Her father, George Cranston, had opened the first tea house in Glasgow more than thirty years before in that same hotel – then called the Crown – in George Square, but he drank most of the profits away which is why his children became strictly Temperance. Kate and her brother Stuart bought the old Aitken's Hotel in Argyle Street and opened their first tea room there. A Mr Barclay was their architect – but really Kate was her own architect. She knew what she wanted from the start. When she got a chance of premises in Buchanan Street, she got George Walton to redesign them, and it was he who called in Mackintosh to help him out and that's where it all started for Kate Cranston and Mackintosh. He hadn't much to do, but she liked what he did and she wanted to use him again, despite the reputation he already had for being 'difficult'. Not that that bothered Kate Cranston. She had the view that if you are talked about in business you must be doing something right. She was talked about in Glasgow all the time.

Now she wanted to give Glasgow something to really talk about. In fact, she wanted to give her patrons the fright of their lives, and she wanted Mackintosh to do it. In her view, they needed to be shaken up a bit and the best way to do that was to give them style and quality and beauty. She thought they didn't have enough of any of those in their lives. They needed colour to counter the soot and, most of all, something to take their minds off alcohol and open their eyes to things other than the bottom of a glass. She saw drinking as the working man's chief occupation in the city and was convinced it was the death of him and the ruin of his family. In short, she was offering an alternative.

Tea and scones were hardly tempting but she was sure if they were offered in tempting surroundings by pretty, well-dressed waitresses she would winkle the working man out of the pub and the businessman out of his club – and sell a lot of tea and scones. She had class, Kate Cranston, and she wanted her places to have class. She spotted class in Charlie Mackintosh and, to her mind, it was good business on her part to hire him. She gave him complete *carte blanche* in all matters of design – her only stipulation was that the places should work. She had been in business all her life and knew that the pleasanter the place of work, the better the work got done. That being said, she left him to it.

I think it could be said that he did not let her down. For two whole decades he was as faithful to her as she was loyal to him. For an architect of his standing, the opportunities may have seemed limited but the various schemes allowed the artist in him to join forces with the architect so that something magical resulted in what were technically only interior renovations and decorations. This is what delighted Nikolaus Pevsner, who was of the opinion that:

> Mackintosh was audacious, even in comparison with Frank Lloyd Wright and Le Corbusier, in interpreting interior space to the determined and specific requisites of a particular situation. In the Cranston tea-rooms extraordinary effects were created in surroundings with no intrinsic allure: none of the tea-rooms was built as such.[1]

This last is a good point – all of them were conversions. From Argyle Street to Buchanan Street, and then to Ingram Street, now finally, to Sauchiehall Street, the tea-cup quadrilateral was to contain a remarkable aggregate of art work in terms of colour, lighting and, as Pevsner has mentioned, space control. The rooms drew the crowds, not for the tea and home-baking, or even the billiards, but for the astonishing vistas the interiors provided. Kate Cranston proved something that is only gradually being realised today: good art is good business. She gave Mackintosh the free hand she had promised him and, like the artistic magician he was, he waved it like a wand. He was like a little boy again. He played with light as if it were a new toy and took an impish delight in more functional considerations. The bucket-shaped recesses in some of the armchairs required a posterior commitment of unreasonable accuracy. He even selected and arranged the flowers, delivered every day by a green-uniformed boy driving a donkey cart. All was class, and style and good taste – in every sense.

The tea-room craze developed to such an extent that Glasgow became almost synonymous with the phenomenon. To this day, Mackintosh is remembered by some more as the designer of the tea rooms than as the creator of the Art School. It was certainly so in his own day. Glasgow was then, as one writer put it at the time, 'a very Tokio [*sic*] for tea rooms':

> Now he who loves aesthetic cheer
> And does not mind the damp
> May come and read Rossetti here
> By a Japanesey lamp'[2]

As has already been noted in a previous chapter, the Japanese influence was everywhere in Glasgow at the turn of the century and it pervaded so much of what was designed and crafted in this period. As Neil Munro remarked, 'Japanese art was the hobby of those in Glasgow ... who could not afford Whistlers.'[3] The same Munro, in his alias as 'Hugh Foulis' wrote some very funny pieces dealing with the ordinary, cloth-capped Glasgow man wandering out of curiosity into the strange world of the Mackintosh/ Cranston tea room. David Daiches gives an example in his book, *Glasgow* (1977):

> (Erchie, the waiter, has met his friend, Duffy, the coalman, who had been into Glasgow in his Sunday clothes to collect the 'three-pound-ten' insurance money on his dead horse. Erchie persuades him to try the new tea-room 'wi' the comic windows'.)

> 'It'll cost ye nae mair than the Mull o' Kintyre Vaults [Duffy's favourite pub],' I tellt him, and we began sclimmin' the stairs. Between every rail there was a piece o' gless like the bottom o' a soda-water bottle, hangin' on a wire; Duffy touched every yin o' them for luck.

> 'Whit do ye think o' that noo?' I asked him.

> 'It's gey fancy,' says Duffy; 'will we be lang?'

'This wey for the threepenny cups and the guid bargains,' I says to Duffy, and I lands him in whit they ca' the Room de Looks. Maybe ye havena see the Room de Looks; it's the colour o' a goon Jinnet used to hae afore we mairried: there's whit Jinnet ca's insertion on the table cloths, and wee beads stitched a' ower the wa's the same as if somebody had done it themsel's. The chairs is no' like ony ither chairs I ever clapped eyes on, but you could easy guess they were chairs; and a' roond the place there's a lump o' lookin'-gless wi' purple leeks pent onit every noo and then. The gaselier in the middle was the thing that stunned me. It's hung a' roond wi' hunners o' big gless bools, the size o' yer nief – but we din't get pappin' onything at them.

Duffy could only speak in whispers.

'My jove!' says he, 'ye'll no' get smokin' here, I'll bate.'

'Smokin'!' says I, 'ye micht as well talk o' gowfin'.'

'I never in a' my life saw the like o' t afore. This cows a'!' says he, quite nervous and frichtened-looking.'[4]

At this point we shall exit the tea rooms with Erchie and his friend. These lovely places, alas, were left to fall into their inevitable desuetude when they would disintegrate into the heaps of old timber that men like Duffy, working for the Glasgow Corporation in the Sixties, burned in the basement of the City Chambers to keep the boiler going. 'We didnae ken,' was all they said at the time. Well, they ken noo.

The fruitful Cranston/Mackintosh relationship, however, did not end with the tea rooms. In tandem with some of the Cranston schemes he had begun working on other conversions at a mansion in the Barrhead Road, Nitshill for Mrs John Cochrane, who was Kate with her private hat on. She and her husband, the Major, who was an ironfounder in Barrhead, had bought a very old eighteenth-century mansion house, which had had some frontage work done on it by the early nineteenth-century architect, David

Hamilton. Mr Hamilton had been known to complain that he was only given frontages to do instead of whole buildings. At this stage, Mackintosh could well have sympathised with him. There were architectural murmurings about various house projects but nothing to shout about, so he was glad to pick up the wand again to try it on House'hill, or Hous'll, as the locals called it.

The most successful feature was undoubtedly the Music Room to which Mackintosh gave a daring curved partition screen affording the room two distinct areas without any loss of light He worked on this house project more in the manner of a set designer in the theatre than an architect. He did nothing to alter the main fabric but everything he could do with the interior he did, and the end result was a most striking domestic environment. There was dramatic lighting in the entrance hall and the stairs boasted horse-hair carpet. He designed special chairs while Margaret made special curtains and the fireplace in the card-room had a surround of thick plate glass. One has the feeling that the Mackintoshes would have made a fortune today designing for celebrities or talking design on chic television programmes. At any rate, the Cochranes were delighted and the Mackintoshes were paid.

It is known that Mackintosh did most of this work on the drawing boards of the old Honeyman and Keppie office at 140 Bath Street. Perhaps he and Keppie were keeping a polite distance from each other, or was it merely a viable *modus operandum* in order to keep their areas of work separate and accountable in terms of fees. Perhaps it was at Bath Street then that Mackintosh met up once more with his old friend from night school days, Peter Wylie Davidson. Mackintosh had contacted him to see if he would make candlesticks for the card tables at Hous'hill. Mr Davidson was only too willing to oblige and remembers that when the work was done, the candlesticks were to be delivered to the house – personally. Mackintosh had sent him a message telling him to be at St Enoch Station on a certain day at 3 o'clock to accompany to accompany him and Miss Cranston to Nitshill.

Mr Davidson goes on:

Miss Cranston was at the appointed place first, then I arrived, and some minutes later Mackintosh appeared saying he had been detained by a previous appointment. He wore a great Highland cape, fashionable during that period and with a characteristic swing of his stick he greeted me with,

'Well, Davidson, how are we travelling?'

'First or third,' was my ready reply, to the great amusement of Miss Cranston. Of course I realised it would be First Class.

When we arrived at Nitshill Station a horse-drawn cab was waiting for us, and with another flourish of his cape and a swing of his stick, he exclaimed again to me –

'Well, where is it to be, Davidson – inside or out?'

'Up on the dicky,' I replied, and the lady did enjoy the joke …

The entire turn-out was so like Mackintosh, and Miss Cranston seemed to be delighted with it all.

On arriving at her house, we were met by a large peacock in full feather strutting about the garden in the full sunshine as if he owned it. A large wrought-iron grille protected the entrance of the doorway…

The fireplace in the card-room was a centre of great beauty, and had to be seen to be appreciated. When the sun shone on it the mixed colourings of green, gold and violet were reflected from parallel rods of plate glass … The wallpaper was hand coloured and the candle sconces on the walls were in beaten aluminium with sprays of silver behind to ensure the imagination of perfect harmony of colour … I was shown the card tables so set to work immediately in placing the candlesticks in their sockets. The finished work seemed to give them complete satisfaction … A cup of the well-known blend of Cranston tea was handed round before my departure and my interesting visit came to an end.[5]

It is good to see Mackintosh in this light – a confident, ebullient, almost swaggering figure on top of his form. He could have done anything at this time. The pity was that he wasn't fully extended. Peter Davidson goes on with a further recollection:

> My next encounter with Mr Mackintosh was at a dinner in Mr Newbery's home in Buckingham Street, Hillhead ... The entire staff of the Art School had been invited ... I was there too. Mr Herbert McNair was also there. [He] had quite a reputation ... having a responsible position at Liverpool University. He designed the Newbery Medal and I executed the pattern for casting. I became very friendly with him ... and he presented me with one of his unique book plates in a little black-edged frame ... His wife, Mrs Frances McNair, [later] helped in the needle-work department of the Art School under Miss Ann Macbeth, so I knew her very well too. It was amusing to see them sitting side by side on a tandem tricycle when they rode off ...[6]

Bertie returned to Liverpool to find that he had been made redundant following the new Head of Department Reilly's re-structuring of the Architecture Department at the University in 1905. With another victim of the changes, Gerald Chowne, he set up the Sandon Studios as a teaching and creative centre and Frances gave embroidery classes from home, but, sadly, there were still a few twists in their story to come.

Mention in the Davidson account of the Art School's entire staff being present at the Newbery Sunday *salon* prompts the question of whether proceedings were conducted in French. According to Margaret's letter to Frau Anna Muthesius at the time, most of teaching staff at the School were French – Delville for Painting, Artot for the Antique, Giraldon for design and Bourdon was its first Professor of Architecture. Eugene Bourdon initiated *Vista,* the School's architectural magazine. He was killed in action during the Great War.

Mackintosh's many German connections led to an invitation to show at an exhibition sponsored by AS Ball in Berlin but, because of the outbreak of war in 1914 this was to prove his last major exhibition in Europe. Peter Davidson, in his *Memories of Mackintosh*, also makes mention of the unfortunate impact the war made on architecture as a whole, and on the Mackintoshes in particular, because of his German friends as will be seen in a later chapter. Still in this European connection, Mr Davidson's article continued:

> It is interesting to relate, that while I am writing this, I read on the *Glasgow Herald* of 9th Nov, 1960 that samples of [Mackintosh's] work, such as furniture and various objects of applied art, with drawings and photographs are displayed in the 'Council of Europe' Exhibition in Paris ... Mackintosh was indeed the genius of the Newbery Period ... had he been permitted to rebuild Sauchiehall Street from the Art School to Charing Cross, the world would have come to see it.[7]

This commendation is all the stronger because it comes from a man who knew Mackintosh in his own day and who survived until ours. Peter Davidson died in 1963.

Meantime, in 1906 everything was on the move in Glasgow. John James Burnet transferred to London to even greater success, as did George Walton to build the Kodak show-room, and the Mackintoshes moved house. With the Cranston money in his pocket, Toshie bought a whole house at 6 Florentine Terrace, Hillhead for £950 and moved in on Monday 6 March, minus two Persian cats. They had committed *felo de chat* by swallowing their own fur. Nevertheless, the Mackintoshes were going up in the world – literally – as their move was uphill. Across Sauchiehall Street, up to Charing Cross, then up Woodlands Road to Gibson Street (past the Macdonalds) to Florentine Terrace (later renamed Southpark Avenue). Here, at No 6 (later to be 78), they set up their new home.

If they had made a fairytale kingdom out of Mains Street, they now proceeded to create a whole new world out of Florentine Terrace. Mackintosh had plenty of time to think about it. Work still came in, but apart from the Kingsborough Gardens scheme, it was uninspiring stuff. In the past year all he had to show for his hours at the drawing board was a fireplace for Miss Rowat at Paisley, a gravestone for Rev Johnson at East Wemyss, some alterations at Cloak and a conventional 'boss's house' in mock-Tudor for FJ Shand at Auchenibert. He poured out all his pent-up creativity into the new house at Florentine Terrace. Mary Sturrock remembered it well:

> The room at 78 Southpark Avenue was always very tidy. Magazines were never just left on a table. They were piled up square with the sides of the table. And Mackintosh was a smoker, as most men were in those days, and he always knocked out his pipe very carefully … If there was a mark on the white furniture … the maid cleaned it with tepid water and a soft cloth, and if it didn't come off Margaret herself went to clean it with warm olive oil. I saw her do that myself. But Mackintosh's furniture used to get six coats of eggshell paint and it lasted virtually forever. But mostly I do remember a group of chairs around the fire, burning bright red with very good quality coal, the sort you can't get nowadays. A formal room but a cheerful, friendly atmosphere …[8]

Margaret Dingwall felt the same:

> I liked his house. I remember the carpet in the drawing room very well and the studio in the attic. The dining room had, it seemed to me, splashes of colour on the grey walls. He never spoke about his work to me but I do remember him helping my sister Katherine with her drawing. She enjoyed that because he could draw things so quickly with a pencil.[9]

Major Desmond Chapman-Huston also tells us about what he called 'the little house at Hillhead':

[It] was a unity, perfect from top to bottom. I frequently stayed there in after years, occupying the small, unique guest quarters made out of two attics in the roof with a little door leading out to a small flower-filled balcony ... Lady Alix Egerton used to declare that the tiny, attic suite ... was the loveliest lodging in the world ... in the Mackintosh household everything was in keeping; the wine, the food and service being exquisite rather than lavish.[10]

Chapman-Huston also tells us something about what it was like visiting Mackintosh 'at home'. This well-born Irishman with connections was a professional actor at this time (before he became a highly successful professional biographer) and he was playing in *Hamlet* for the Frank Benson Company at the Theatre Royal in Hope Street. Benson was a famous actor manager of the day and rather eccentric but he was loved by his company, who called him 'Pa'. Chapman-Huston writes:

Having somehow got 'Pa' safely on to the ramparts of Elsinore, and knowing that for a solid three hours he would be continuously occupied with the state of Denmark, I left the theatre and made my way westward along that endless dreary highway with the lovely name – Sauchiehall Street ... Climbing out of the foggy valley into Hillhead I eventually reached a row of high, narrow, late Victorian stucco houses then known, only God knows why, as Florentine Terrace. It was dark. Going up the narrow, flagged approach, I climbed six steps and stood expectantly before an arresting doorway and fanlight ... A neat Scottish maid opened it. I was in a long, narrow hall and facing a flight of not undignified stairs, hall and stairs being softly lit and covered all over in a rich, plain pile carpet, as soft and browny-grey as the ruff of a Siamese cat. The feeling of restful space in that narrow hall was extraordinary. Following the maid to the first floor I was shown into a large, L-shaped room with two fireplaces. Studio? No drawing-room, in the conventional sense, certainly not. My host, smoking a fate-filled pipe, rose to greet me, placed me in a very large box arm-chair on one side of the principal fireplace and took a similar chair opposite. I was, I instinctively realised, talking to a great man; soon I was to know that he was also a great architect. There is something at once humbling and exhilarating about true greatness of any kind; moreover the surroundings were, in the full meaning of the word, unique. Mackintosh's two primary colours were black and white, his constant motives (in the musical sense) squares, oblongs, perpendicular and horizontal lines. His supreme skill as an architect was his masterly handling of space. This room was the shrine he had made with love for his artist-wife, Margaret, and himself – the nest to which they fled for rest and refreshment from the bitter horrors of commercial Glasgow. To me, but recently escaped from the Irish plethora of Victorian furniture and decoration, the room was an oasis, a revelation, a delight ...

The Mackintosh room was all ivory white relieved with pieces of dark wood hand-made furniture and skilfully selected patches of vivid colour. The all-over carpet, then unusual, was the same browny-grey as covered the rest of the house; the window curtains were carefully designed to keep the windows in the room. The two fire-grates, very simple in design, around one of which we sat, were of hand-wrought iron well raised from the hearth, and, rightly, prominent, but the dominating feature of the room was the splendid window at one end facing south-west made, as my host told me: 'for my wife, Mistress Margaret, so that she can watch the sunsets.' Mistress Margaret, as it happened, was away and, after that first meeting, I spent every evening I could escape from the theatre with 'Toshie', as I soon came to call him. He had recently completed his masterpiece, the Glasgow School of Art, after, as he told me, 'a daily fight for over three years' with the Corporation Committee responsible for the work. From the effects of that three years' continuous, heart-breaking struggle Mackintosh never fully recovered. Discerning people have for years been drawn to Glasgow from all over the world only to see Mackintosh's School of Art, as they go to Stockholm to see Ostberg's Town Hall ... Acclaimed in Europe as he was ignored at home, much of what has since passed in English architecture as 'modern' is merely Mackintosh and water.[11]

The Scotland Street School was finally completed at a cost of £15,000 to everyone's complete satisfaction – even the architect's. As they admired it through the railings and across the playgrounds no one realised it was his last statement in stone. How fitting though that it should be called 'Scotland Street' – hadn't he said that 'our architecture should be as Scottish as ourselves? And here was this redstone glass and steel castle with the thistle featured on its railings, standing four-square in Kingston as his unwitting valediction. Significantly, perhaps, on 1 December of this year, 1906, he became CR Mackintosh FRIBA – officially.

However, there remained one mighty thing yet to do – the School of Art extension – if Honeyman and Keppie could secure the contract. It was not a foregone conclusion. The Building Committee had been sitting since the previous September to approve Mackintosh's plans for the extension. Thanks to Newbery's skilful advocacy, though not entirely due to it, they were impressive drawings, the plans were eventually approved on 22 April 1907. It took until 14 November to get them through the Dean of Court and work began on the extension the very next day. Mackintosh wanted to be on the job daily as supervising architect but he was trammeled by all the other bits and pieces that had come up while they waited for all the other permissions.

There was the boardroom at the School, a Dutch kitchen and an Oak Room for the Ingram Street tea rooms, a pulpit for the Abbey Close Church in Paisley, not to mention Scotland Street School – no wonder he pleaded 'pressure of work' to Keppie. However, by the new year of 1908, on the recommendation of John Keppie no less, he became a Fellow of the Incorporation of

Architects in Scotland and was ready to give all his attention to his masterwork. Then his father died.

William McIntosh had been ill with bronchitis at home at Regent Square. His condition was aggravated by a heart complaint and he died, aged 70, on the early morning of Monday 10 February 1908. Did he have a chance to talk to Charlie? Did he ever mention Billy, killed in South America? We shall never know. All we know is that the much-respected ex-Superintendent, and now popular lawn bowler, went to join his two wives in the family lair at Sighthill Cemetery and, for better or worse, Chas. R Mackintosh, the clerk's son, was his own man now.

This was borne out when Patrick Dunn, Chairman of the Building Committee, asked Mackintosh for a copy of the plans, the architect replied on behalf of Honeyman, Keppie and Mackintosh – 'We think it undesirable to commit ourselves to any elevational treatment until the general scheme of internal arrangements is approved.' It was still his old cry to let the inside determine the outside. However, a thousand pounds set aside for the carving and placement of three statues, to Cellini, Palladio, and St Francis, on the West Wing Wall was not approved by the Committee. A letter sent to Mackintosh, as his father was dying made the official position clear:

> Referring to my informal conversation with your Mr Keppie in the Art Club today it is right that the views of the Governors should be put before you formally. Six of the Governors inspected the newly-erected sub-basement Porch and Entrance in Scott Street and were surprised to find that the work was carried out in an extravagant manner and not in accordance with the plans and estimate which were submitted and signed. I beg to intimate that we must decline all liability for any increase of cost.[12]

In reply, Mackintosh told them he would simply save in other areas but they were not satisfied. He was dealing with the kind of safety-first, self-preserving mind that always says 'it's more than my job's worth' in any situation that threatens normal procedure

– or worse, adds to cost. Mackintosh's reaction was that of any artist dealing with officialdom and that was to press on regardless. Thanks solely to his drive and initiative building progressed and the second part of the Art School pushed its way east along Renfrew Street much at his whim. This is what made it a work of genius.

One has to bear in mind that the architect who created the first part of the school was not the same one who resumed on the second. He had done a lot of good work in the intervening years and was all the better for it. He stood on the rungs of Windyhill and Hill House to get further up that architectural ladder. Every trick devised for the tea rooms was used again here, every idea that worked in the Art Lover's House and Hous'hill was reworked for this project. Nothing he had ever done was wasted for it was done again here – only better. Some of the best effects were due to the very restrictions imposed upon him.

He embarked on the completion with his team of craftsmen, some of whom had learned their trades on Clyde-built ships, like a master-shipwright about to build an ocean-going liner, or a medieval master builder commencing a cathedral. This building would be his fantasy liner on land, his cathedral on the hill. He was to think of it as 'a daily fight for three years' but he would bring it on budget, including the £110 for electricity, making it £22,753 for the most important building of its day and give the governors, not the 'plain building' they wanted but Glasgow's first architectural Mecca. Where he had copied the first phase, he created the second. It was a bridge between ancient and modern and a hymn to one man's singular vision.

Not only did he know what he wanted, he knew now how to get it. Everything in his life had led up to this time, and he was well aware of its significance. He brought to it the confidence of instinct and experience. Murray Grigor tells the story of the 'Great Carpenter of Auchendinney', who told him he'd never seen an architect on the job like 'Cherlie'. That's what the carpenter said they were to call him. Apparently, he came on to the site with his hand proferred to every tradesman. 'What's your name?' he asked, and when told, he nodded and said, 'Call me Charlie'. Murray was also told that if any workman couldn't manage a particular job, Mackintosh would off with his jacket and do it himself. It seems that, on one occasion, he took the adze off the carpenter who was having a problem with a beam – 'an' wi' wan scud the beam was cut. Oh ay, there wis nae palaver wi' Cherlie.'[13] This was by no means the norm in working relations.

He virtually improvised much of the closing design, going off the blueprint as the inspiration took him, settling strikes, soothing officials yet ignoring their memos, doing what Lloyd Wright was to do in Chicago and the American desert and doing it with the same panache. Going over budget, over everybody's head, or behind their backs, but going ahead anyway in a white heat of creativity that gave Glasgow the first modern building in Europe and something that is still one of the wonders of the architectural world.

In May the contractor was off the job, in September the painters were in and at the end of November Mackintosh reported that the extension had been completed. And so the building that the world was to know as the Glasgow School of Art was formally opened on Wednesday 15 December at 2.30 pm by Sir John Stirling-Maxwell. In his somewhat guarded speech he said that Mackintosh 'should deserve well of his generation were it only because he made them think'. This was a nice case of fence-sitting as reaction was by no means unanimously positive. This time, however, Mackintosh was recognised by all present as the architect. He even made a speech, and presented the casket which he had designed, and Peter Davidson had made, to Sir James Fleming, the Chairman of the Board of Governors. The official party then descended to the ground floor where Sir James threw aside the curtain that divided the two parts and the Art School became one. Then the real party began.

Newbery came into his own as Concert Master and Master of the Revels and organised a three-day celebration to mark the event. There was a reception in the Museum where works by former students like Sir John Lavery, George Henry and 'Watchmaker' Pringle were hung. A symbolic masque, written by

Newbery, was performed in the Architectural School by the students, containing such deathless lines as:

Fall! Good St Mungo's Blessing's on this School
Its work make prosper and its fame let spread.[14]

The governors, in their report for the Session 1908–9, formally noted that 'The Glasgow School of Art is now a completed structure' and at the end mentioned that the architects were Honeyman, Keppie and Mackintosh. *Who's Who* for 1909 went one better by announcing that the architect for the new Art School was one John Keppie, but had the grace to add – 'with assistance from Charles R Mackintosh.' Director Francis Newbery, however, in his own way, set things graphically to rights five years later. Page 98 of the Minute Book, detailing the gubernatorial meetings at the School, has the following entry:

Friday, February 13th, 1914 at 12–30 pm

The Director asked permission to be allowed to present to the School, his portrait group representing the members of the Building Committee (1906–1909) in Session. The gift was accepted and it was decided, on a day to be fixed, that it be formally unveiled by the Chairman.

So, with smiles all round, Newbery took away his very dignified painting of the Committee, and on the fixed day, 18 May, he returned with it for the official unveiling. The Director invited Sir John Struthers to unveil the painting and to the general consternation of the meeting, the Governors saw that Newbery had added the standing figure of Mackintosh at the left margin, and there was nothing the Governors could do about it. Sir John, after a few words, handed the painting over to the Chairman. Mr Dunn, trying to put a brave face on it, expressed his gratification that these gentlemen, who had done so much for the School, should have their work thus acknowledged by art. The proceedings closed by Mr John Henderson proposing a Vote of Thanks to Mr Dunn for presiding.[15]

No mention was made of Mackintosh at the unveiling. Officially, he did not exist. The painting still hangs in the Board Room of the Art School to this day, and the wry expression on Toshie's 45-year old face as painted, firmly clutching the building plans in his hand, tells it all. Thanks to Newbury, Charlie Mackintosh is still in the picture – despite them all.

CHAPTER EIGHT

Before the Fall

1909–1914

No artist owes less to tradition than does Charles Rennie
Mackintosh: as an originator, he is supreme.

J Taylor, *The Studio*, 1906

EVERYTHING THAT HAS to be said about the finished Glasgow
School of Art has been said and every qualifying adjective available has been brought into service in its praise. Not that there
weren't detractors. The *Building Industry News,* for instance,
reported that the South Elevation, as seen from Sauchiehall Street,
caused 'wayfarers to stop and marvel that the authorities have
permitted the running up of a house of correction or poor house
on such a site'. More outspoken gentlemen were of the opinion
that Mackintosh 'should be horse-whipped for showing his bare
arse to the face of Glasgow'. Office workers took time to gape at
the strange picture it presented in construction but in the end all
agreed that the new building was 'something'.

Herbert Honeyman, then an architectural student at the GSA,
wrote an article in *Vista,* the student magazine, deploring the rep-
etition of ornament and saying, that 'an office boy or a trained
cat' could do it as well. Did this critic know that he was dealing
with Clan Chattan? Not that this opinion counted for much. One
can see in it the quite forgettable architect he became. What was
much more hurting was the comment made by Eugene Bourdon,
the Head of Architecture at the Art School at the time, who:

> wondered if Mr Mackintosh felt forlorn or relieved at hav-
> ing this child of his imagination off his hands. Of course

that would depend on whether it was a child of joy or sor-
row to him – a prodigy or a freak. In our opinion – but
silence is the better part of discretion.[1]

What an impertinence from a supposedly responsible teacher, but
then small minds are apt to make big statements – or rather not
make them in this case, which was merely cowardly. It is fitting,
perhaps, that the 'plain' box containing the present-day Mackintosh School of Architecture almost adjacent to the Art School is
named after him. It is quite unbelievable that this concrete cube
could be set so near the famous North Facade, which, as late as
1945, Robert Venturi was to call 'one of the greatest achievements
of all time, comparable in scale to Michaelangelo'.[2]

This may be going a bit far, but it is true of this building, that
the more one looks the more one sees and every new visit is
rewarded by yet another pleasing detail missed the previous time.
It worked at once for the Victorians as it did for the neo-Geor-
gians of my generation and it works now for the new Elizabethans
of today. To define it aesthetically one would have to say that the
entire design serves that moment when pencil touches paper, paint
meets canvas and the chisel strikes stone.

The Art School has been described as Mackintosh's self-por-
trait. Well, it now seems as if it has been defaced by municipal
graffiti. What needs to be urgently addressed is the state of its
frontage. What can be seen, despite the perpetually-parked cars, is
shadowed by an edifice they have named the Newbery Tower,
which is so sited that the north light, for which the large studio
windows were designed, is now denied it.

Ironically, the offending construction was designed by Keppie,
Henderson and Partners, the descendants of the very firm that created the building it now over-shadows. The situation is just as
Mackintosh himself saw in one of his lectures – the needs of Mam-
mon, or what is now called market forces, prevail. It brings to
mind something an anonymous writer in *Dekorative Künst* said,
writing about Mackintosh in 1906. This writer noted:

> It is indeed a great delight to oppose an all-powerful enemy,
> and this is precisely the reason why Charles Mackintosh is
> working in Glasgow.[3]

Nothing has changed in a hundred years. Just add unthinking
insensitivity and historical unawareness and you have a formidable enemy indeed. However, what is also true is a saying much
older than Mackintosh – *Ars longa vita brevis*. We can wait. Not
for too long, I understand. Even as I write, plans are being put in
hand for a £20-million facelift to the building as part of a 'new
concept campus' – whatever that may mean. Any gesture of caring
would be enough.

I am not the first to complain about the gradual dereliction,
not to say desecration of the Art School environment. In 1970,
film-maker, Murray Grigor, one of the first to raise the Mackintosh banner in the city, wrote:

> But what of Glasgow, the city he made famous? The place
> with the permanent outdoor exhibition of his buildings.
> Well, there was a rumour that Glasgow might mark the cen-
> tenary [of his birth] by knocking down a Mackintosh
> building or two. They didn't quite do that. Though the
> decline of all Mackintosh's buildings in the city continued.
> No help was given to clean and restore the fabric of the
> Glasgow School of Art. And those tram-pole lights and
> cables still criss-crossed one of the most famous facades in
> modern architecture. Visitors to Glasgow even found it
> hard to photograph … But now the site is sealed. An intim-
> idating block has arisen to dwarf the school. In its towering
> arrogance it symbolizes the regard in which Mackintosh is
> held in Glasgow by the Governors of the School of Art who
> commissioned it, and by Mackintosh's old firm, Honeyman
> and Keppie, who designed it. But the cruellest irony of all
> they are going to call it [the] Newbery Tower …[4]

Just as cruel an irony was evident in the treatment of Bertie
McNair when he returned to Scotland in 1907 after the failure of
the Sandon Studios in Liverpool. He was never to live perma-

nently in Merseyside again, yet today, Liverpool boasts the McNair Hall of Residence. Bertie would have loved that. In the following year, 1908, he was turned down when he applied for a job at the Art School, where only a decade before he had been one of its heroes. Even worse, less than a year after that he could not even get a job as an Art Teacher at Clydebank Academy. Here was a genuinely talented original being victimised for a superficial oddness, although some would have phrased that more strongly. No, it was not a good phase for James Herbert McNair.

It was only marginally better for she whom he dubbed his 'little France'. One can only assume that their toddler, Sylvan, was thriving. Newbery got Mrs McNair a job assisting Ann Macbeth in the Embroidery Class, but the latter's preoccupation with the 'Machine Art' of the day did not accord with Mrs McNair's more Symbolist style and relations were soon strained to a point where Frances had no option but to resign. While Bertie was trying to find work, he, his wife and child were encamped in the McNair family home at Birchbank, near Skelmorlie, the Macdonalds being unwilling to take in Bertie because of his less than abstemious social habits. George McNair was just as disapproving and he packed his son off alone to the Isle of Man to dry out.

By 1910, there were still lingering bits and pieces for Mackintosh to do at the Art School and also the making of furniture for its various rooms but, otherwise, to all intents and purposes, work for both Charlie and Margaret completely dried up. The only new commission that came his way in the next two years was for a hairdressing salon in Union Street, but this was 'tea room' stuff again, and hardly the kind of thing to get his creative juices flowing, although his latest work at Ingram Street showed the benefit of his Art School experience. It was unbelievable that the man who had created what was possibly the first truly modern building in Europe was sitting at home twiddling idle fingers. Those same fingers that had woven such magic for Miss Cranston and delighted two successful and intelligent house-owners now drummed the table at Florentine Terrace waiting for something to turn up.

There is no record of it, but it is also hard to believe that Margaret didn't see Frances through this vacuum time for both sisters. And if sister saw sister it is quite reasonable to suppose that brother-in-law met brother-in-law, and if they did, it was unlikely to be in a tea-shop. Bertie had returned from the Isle of Man to find himself disinherited by his family. He and Frances were taken in by the Mackintoshes while they looked for their own place. It must have been very odd for them all to be sitting round that elegant fireplace – the four of them together again – but so very different now. Where were the perpetrators of the Glasgow Style now? The Famous Four had now reduced to a middle-aged quartet staring into the fire wondering where the flame had gone. Their lovely world of symbols and hidden meanings seemed to be melting all around them. Spooky indeed.

Bertie had not dried out and was off the wagon whenever he had the chance. Mackintosh was not in the same drinking class, but he was growing ominously quieter during this period. Clouds were gathering around his head and it seemed that before long, the storm would break. It didn't help that he had an idle Bertie on his hands and a disappointed Frances, not to mention their son and heir, Sylvan. The Mackintoshes had a full house and that in itself must have made for tensions.

McNair was Toshie's oldest friend, and it must have puzzled him enormously on his return to Glasgow to see the sudden change in the Mackintosh fortunes. Here he was, scratching around looking for something to build, when he ought to have had Glasgow to play with. More than anyone, Bertie, would have known that Toshie's personal foibles may have had a lot to do with his business problems, but even they could hardly explain away a complete drying-up of opportunities. It was almost as if a tap had been turned off.

It might only have been that, in the Art School, Mackintosh had given Glasgow something bigger than it had bargained for and when this was set beside the tinsel sensation of the tea rooms, people were confused as to where the real Mackintosh was. It was as if Caruso were singing in the music-halls. A public that is con-

Mackintosh 1893
(Photograph courtesy T&R Annan & Sons Ltd, Glasgow)

Glasgow Police Tug-of-War Team 1889, Golfhill House, Dennistoun, Glasgow –
Mackintosh's father, William McIntosh (centre & inset) captained the team which won
outright both the standing and sitting tug-of-war 'open to the world' at the
Paris International Exhibition of 1889
(Reproduced courtesy of Iain Paterson, copied by Derek Maxwell from the original in Strathclyde Police Museum)

John Keppie

John Honeym

Mackintosh's first documented architectural
work, the tombstone of Chief Constable
Alexander McCall in Glasgow Necropolis
(Photograph courtesy Iain Paterson)

Mackintosh with Hamish R Davidson 1898
(Photograph courtesy T&R Annan & Sons Ltd, Glasgow)

Miss Catherine (Kate) Cranston 1900
(Photograph courtesy T&R Annan & Sons Ltd, Glasgow)

Margaret Macdonald Mackintosh 1902
(Photograph courtesy T&R Annan & Sons Ltd, Glasgow)

Margaret Macdonald Mackintosh c. 1903
(Photograph courtesy T&R Annan & Sons Ltd, Glasgow)

The Immortals at Dunure, Ayrshire c. 1893-5
L-R Katherine Cameron, Mackintosh, Janet Aitken, John Keppie, Agnes Raeburn,
Jessie Keppie, Frances Macdonald, Herbert McNair, Margaret Macdonald
(Reproduced courtesy Glasgow School of Art)

The Immortals at Dunure, Ayrshire c. 1893-5
Top: Frances Macdonald
Middle: L-R John Keppie, Jessie Keppie, Agnes Raeburn, Janet Aitken,
Katherine Cameron, Margaret Macdonald
Front: L-R Mackintosh, Herbert McNair
(Reproduced courtesy Glasgow School of Art)

Jessie and Fra Newbery dressed for a Costume Ball c. 1900

The Immortals at Dunure, Ayrshire c. 1893-5
L-R Frances Macdonald, Agnes Raeburn, Janet Aitken, Mackintosh,
Katherine Cameron, Jessie Keppie, Margaret Macdonald
(Reproduced courtesy Glasgow School of Art)

The Immortals at Dunure, Ayrshire c. 1893-5
(Reproduced courtesy Glasgow School of Art)

Quai du Commerce,
Port Vendres c. 1900
(Reproduced courtesy Robin Crichton)

Quai de la Ville
Port Vendres c. 1900
(Reproduced courtesy
Robin Crichton)

The Building Committee of the Board of Governors of the Glasgow School of Art 1914
Mr Chas. R. Mackintosh FRIBA – The Architect/Col. R.J. Bennett V.D./ Mr David Barclay FRIBA/
Sir Francis Powell, LLD, PRSW/Mr John Munro FRIBA/Mr Patrick S. Dunn – Convenor/
Councillor J. Mollison, MINA/Mr Hugh Reid DL/Sir Wm. Bilsland, Bart. LLD, DL/
Sir John J. Burnett, RSA, FRIBA, LLD/Mr John Henderson MA/
Sir James Fleming – Chairman of Governors/Mr John M. Groundwater – Secretary/
Mr Fra. H. Newbery CAV OFF, INT.SOC, SPG, ARCA – Director, pinxit
(Oil on canvas by Fra Newbery, reproduced courtesy Glasgow School of Art)

Mackintosh c.1920
(Photograph by EO Hoppé, reproduced courtesy
Glasgow School of Art)

Mackintosh c.1920
(Photograph by EO Hoppé, reproduced courtesy
Glasgow School of Art)

Margaret Macdonald Mackintosh passport photograph c.1929
(Photograph reproduced courtesy Hunterian Art Gallery, University of Glasgow, Mackintosh Collection)

Mackintosh c.1920
(Photograph by W Ransford, reproduced courtesy
Glasgow School of Art)

Mackintosh c.1920
Photograph by EO Hoppé, reproduced courtesy
Glasgow School of Art

fused is a public that loses interest – and it seemed that many were starting to lose interest in Charles Rennie Mackintosh. Yet he saw no reason to change. He had done all that he was asked to do and had done it well. He saw no reason that things should not go on as they had done. This did not apply to his domestic situation. Bertie's drinking did not please Margaret, and before long she had found a flat for her sister only a street away and she and Toshie resumed their steady, even breast stroke through the sea of despondency.

Mackintosh had been in a white heat when he forged the Art School extension and now the fear was that the anvil would be allowed to cool and eventually grow cold. In no way could he give up architecture but Newbery's fear was that architecture would give him up. 'It would be a national calamity,' he said to his wife. Neither Mackintosh took up his offer to teach at the school – he would survive as long as he had her. As Jessie Newbery said, 'Margaret's gifts were a great asset to Toshie – as adviser, appreciator, collaborateur.' Some recommended Mackintosh try America, but he didn't want to leave home. He wanted to work in Glasgow – and for Glasgow.

His two allies at the office, draughtsmen William Moyes and Robert Frame, had left and Mr A Graham Henderson, FRIBA, Keppie's office chief, was now in charge of commissions, as Keppie took on more responsibilities at the Art School where he was now a governor. Henderson and Charlie had never got on and now this dullard was virtually in charge of day-to-day activities. He kept his eye on Mackintosh:

> Mr Keppie's partnership was with Dr John Honeyman. This was an association of a young man with a mature and able practitioner, but it is clear that they worked as individuals rather than as a team ... Keppie and Mackintosh worked almost entirely in an architectural sense as individuals – Mackintosh blazing the trail for the 'modernist' and Keppie upholding the traditional outlook. This, I need scarcely say, was a highly stimulating and provocative situation for

members of the staff who at times were called upon to work for either partner.[5]

William Moyes, on the other hand, had his own version of the 'junior' partner:

> I worked for each of the partners and was very interested in the work of Mr Mackintosh ... I drafted out his scheme for Scotland Street School in pencil but he add the masterly touches in ink ... His heart was in his work and 'in the beauty of the flowers he rejoiced'. He had no hobby as far as I knew and he limped when he walked. I remember him being much amused in the office by a reply given to him by the contractor on the site after being chided for being behind on work at Queen's Cross Church – 'I'm building for eternity'.[6]

Mackintosh would have liked that. He considered endurance the crowning quality of building. It was a quality, however, that he did not have in abundance in himself. His fuse was very short indeed and the resulting explosions did him more harm than anyone. At this period, he could not be described as likeable.

And it appeared that the same applied to Bertie McNair who went from crisis to crisis like a pinball machine. He and Frances made trips to Liverpool from Glasgow but Bertie was becoming increasingly difficult. His honorary membership of the Sandon Society was revoked because he had 'been causing annoyance to members of the club'. Having nothing to do all day, he took to wandering about the club, his jacket buttoned up to the neck like a tunic but still with his old preference for tennis shoes. Members were distressed to notice 'that when he came indoors after a shower of rain that the prints of his wet toes were visible on the floor'.[7] One way or another, the outrageous, but likable Bertie, was determined to make his mark.

Hermann Muthesius had visited the Mackintoshes in Glasgow when he was appointed to the German Embassy in London as Cultural Attache, which meant he was a kind of 'architectural spy' sent to study the English house and learn from it. His visit to

Mackintosh then was in the way of business. However, he and his wife, Anna, became good friends with the two Mackintoshes (Mackintosh was asked to be godfather to their only son, Eckart) and all four became quite close. In 1904, Muthesius had written in *Das Englische Haus*:

> Mackintosh's interiors achieve a level of sophistication which is way beyond the lives of even the artistically educated section of the population. The refinement and austerity of the artistic atmosphere prevailing here does not reflect the ordinariness that fills so much of our lives. A single book with the wrong type of cover lying on the table would spoil the effect; indeed, even an ordinary person, especially an ordinary man, would look out of place wearing his simple working clothes in this fairy-tale world. At least for the time being, it is hard to imagine that aesthetic culture will prevail so much in our lives that interiors like these will become commonplace. They are paragons created by a genius, to show humanity that there is something higher in the distance which transcends reality.

This is German high-mindedness at its height, but there is no denying the architect's genuine and lasting admiration for Mackintosh, which had been evident since around 1898. He was the Scot's vociferous champion in Europe until the First World War blasted their world away for ever. When he visited Glasgow, he saw for himself what he had written so enthusiastically about but did he really believe that the houses were as 'other-world' as he says? I cannot believe that Toshie never spat tobacco juice into the fire, or that Margaret never let her beautiful hair down. These were two real people living in a real world where meals were taken and laundry was done.

The rooms were magnificent but they weren't for Sunday display only. If we only see them as pristine it is only because we only see them in photographs, but we must remember they were deliberately set for such photographs, but the rooms must have had a week-day look at times. It's a tribute to their design that other people lived in both Mains Street (before it became offices) and in Florentine Terrace (before it became Southpark Avenue) and they found the living spaces both congenial and practical. This was directly in line with Muthesius' own thinking, that good design always functions well. The difference was that Mackintosh made it beautiful, too.

It is true enough that the ordinary working fellow, as they said then, might have found the all-white rooms a bit of a strain and he would have been easier in his mind among the usual, comfortable, home-spun muddle of the time, but the Mackintoshes lived by themselves and for themselves and a touch of spartan austerity suited them. They were still, to all intents and purpose, living as they did as students only with a little more girth round their middles. Their work was their life and they made an art of it. The trouble was when there was no work, there was no life and it needed an even greater art to survive this deprivation. Mackintosh's earnings from the office had dropped dramatically although at this stage there was no lack of money, Margaret saw to that. Unfortunately, as she was to find out soon enough, it was a diminishing resource.

Thanks to her contacts, they now moved in University circles. Margaret was very friendly with Lucy Raleigh, wife of Professor Walter Raleigh, and saw her when she 'wasn't having one of her grey days', as Chapman-Huston puts it. Mackintosh kept, or was kept, to the edge of this academic group but it did not detract from the fact that the Mackintoshes were still accepted socially at the best Glasgow levels. Toshie had little to add to the academic chit-chat, however, and increasingly kept to himself. It was hinted that he might go to London and make his fortune there, as John James Burnet had done, and who now was on his way to a knighthood. Mackintosh only wanted to work. Without it he was quite at a loss about what to do with himself.

Talwin Morris died in 1911 and his wife Alice asked Mackintosh to design a tombstone. He gave his friend, with whom he had stayed at Bowling while courting Margaret at Dunglass, a slender memorial stone with appropriate Rosicrucion symbolism and the inscription read:

Life is greater than we conceive
and Death keeper of unknown Redemptions

Alice Morris was to remember Mackintosh as 'a warm-hearted, kindly, genial man, simple in his tastes and pleased with simple things – a tremendous and tireless talker and talks with him would often go far into the night ... to him, the artist's creative idea was the element of absolute and eternal value ...'[8]

Toshie was one of her husband's greatest friends and we must remember that it is to Talwin Morris we owe Hill House, and to some extent architecturally, the School of Art, for one led to another. His death lost Toshie another valuable ally, and he needed all he could get.

He walked off yet another job at Auchenibert. Ostensibly it was because he found the client crass, but really the client had justifiably objected to Mackintosh's viewing the work, another 'dwelling-house', from a bench outside the pub across the road. Things couldn't go on like this. Mackintosh may have made the reputations of Honeyman and Keppie, but Keppie was carrying his junior partner now. The question was how long before he dropped him. Meantime:

at a banquet held in the Kunsterbund, at the Dekorative Exhibition in Breslau in 1913, at which were gathered all the most distinguished architects, decorative artists, sculptors, etc, one of the toasts of the evening was – 'To our Master, Mackintosh, the greatest since the Gothic.'[9]

Other good German friends like Hermann Muthesius had seen the warning signs much earlier:

Herr Mackintosh is a tense and hyper-sensitive person of forcible opinions and high idealism. Capable of immense energy and intense depression. Warm-hearted, yet aloof. Certain yet over-reacts to any criticism. At the height of his powers, but there are reasons for strain. His relentless pursuit of perfection, his meticulous attention to detail, his unreasonable demands on time and skill impose upon him an immense mental and physical strain. If he goes on like this he will crack.[10]

The climax came when Honeyman and Keppie entered the competition for Jordanhill Demonstration School in 1912. Mackintosh was given the project but seemed to show little interest and his first sketches were not encouraging.

His lunchtimes generally extended to tea-times and he often slumped to the floor while at his desk. It was thought at these times that he was drunk and admittedly there was often whisky on his breath, but it is seen now that part of this behaviour pattern was the beginning of severe clinical depression which was to culminate in a bout of pneumonia later in the year which almost killed him.

He took to working nights and was often left alone in the office. Sometimes, he was still there when the clerks came to open up in the morning – fast asleep at his desk. They had to open all the windows to get rid of the whisky fumes and the tobacco fug, but when they helped him off his stool, there on the desk were sheets of immaculate drawings without a blemish or blot on them. Unfortunately, there were little technical omissions here and there and as Howarth tells us, 'some of his corridors terminated in mid-air'.[9] Nevertheless, the grand design was his. The master hand had not lost its touch, and if, as was said, he did that sort of work when drunk, what might he have done if sober?

However, Keppie and Henderson were in no mood for flippancy. Months had passed and they still hadn't the finished plan. Henderson took Mackintosh's work and tidied it up as far as he could. He finished it off just in time to get it in for the closing date. Meantime, Keppie called Mackintosh into his office for yet another 'discussion'. Staff learned to talk loudly so as not to hear, although it was difficult not to. No doubt Mr Henderson kept his ear to the ground. As far as the Jordanhill scheme was concerned, Keppie had no quarrel with the overall plan, it had all of the

Mackintosh hand in it, but it was the amount of minor technical errors in it, like the location of wash-hand basins. Mackintosh countered that these could be easily amended – and they were – but Keppie considered this time-wasting and not up to the standard set by the office. Who, he might have been asked, did most to set that standard? However, whatever was said by either party, it did not help the already strained relations between the two partners since the Jessie incident. That may very well have been at the base of the whole thing. Both were volatile men, used to having their own way, and neither would give to the other on any point. It all depended on who was stronger morally, or at least had the greater emotional control – and this was, without doubt, John Keppie

He knew Mackintosh needed to work again. Here was a man who had made places for poets; now he was being castigated for misplacing the toilet facilities. No wonder he lost his temper at these office 'meetings'. Keppie kept his cool, and when similar faults were found in Mackintosh's drawings for the new 'Dough School' (the Glasgow College of Domestic Science) it was the last straw for Keppie and the last chance for Toshie. Keppie knew that clients are beginning to talk about the state of things at the firm, and for John Keppie, clients were his business. That's why he was an architect. But that was not why Mackintosh was an architect, and that was the difference between them. Unfortunately, that difference could not be reconciled and Keppie knew that Mackintosh had to leave.

Mackintosh only wanted to build – to create: to see the pictures in his mind realised in wood and stone and set in their space with light and beauty. His dreams were about shape and form supplying a need more than mere utility, but Keppie's nightmare was going over budget and losing workmen to Toshie's frequent whims. He only wanted to please the client; Mackintosh wanted them to gasp in wonder. One can easily understand Keppie's position. He had an office to keep up and wages to pay. His was a totally realistic approach in a workaday world. Mackintosh was no fool, he knew this too, but it wasn't his first priority.

Mackintosh was probably the most creative ideas man Keppie had ever met and he was well aware of his status with the continentals, but the senior partner didn't work on the Continent. He worked in Glasgow and had sterling to find every week whatever happened. Architecture was a service he provided for a fee so that he could pay the bills. It was as simple as that. He maintained that Mackintosh had responsibilities to the firm just as much as the firm had to him. It was not unreasonable to expect him to live up to these responsibilities. After all, he was a professional man. The trouble was that Mackintosh thought of himself first as an artist, and John Keppie could not afford to retain an artist. In the end, he had no option but to ask Toshie to go. He went immediately. One can be sure the office got no work done that day. Incidentally, the office won the competition for Jordanhill Training College – despite the wash-hand basins.

Many years before, Toshie's big sister, Bella, had thought him 'too proud and stubborn' in holding out against his father in order to become an architect. Well, here he was again, still holding out to be an architect – but his own kind of architect. He took over the old Keppie and Honeyman premises at 140 Bath Street – the very place where he had designed the Art School. Could he ever be so inspired again or had he shot his bolt? He hung out his script – 'CR Mackintosh FRIBA' and sent out his letters – 'I assure you of my very best professional attention ...' and waited. And waited. Nothing happened. Not a thing. Nothing. Then, one day, Mr Walter Blackie, of Hill House, called to see him:

> I had received a brief note from Mrs Mackintosh asking me to call on her husband at his office ... I found Mackintosh sitting at his desk, evidently in a deeply depressed state of mind. To my enquiry as to how he was keeping and what he was doing he made no response. But presently he began to talk slowly and dolefully. He said how hard he found it to receive no general recognition; only a very few saw merit in his work and the many passed him by. My comment, given without reflection, was that he could not expect to receive

immediate general recognition being, as he was, born some centuries too late; that his place was among the 15th-century lot with Leonardo and the others. He rather gasped at this hasty appraisement but presently began to speak clearly and collectedly. He told me that his partnership in the architectural firm was now dissolved and though that, in itself, did not worry him, it so happened that certain plans for a public building which he had submitted in the name of the firm had that very day been accepted... and now he himself would have no superintendence of the construction which would be seen to by others who might not understand what he had intended in his plans ...'

He had won the battle but he had lost the war. It was time to retreat. Coincidentally, Margaret received her mother's bequest around this time in a tidy lump sum, so they were in funds. Frances had received a similar amount but hers was to be paid in small, regular instalments on condition that Bertie didn't touch a penny of it. He couldn't in any case, he was in Canada. The Macdonald family made him an offer of a one-way fare to Canada, hoping he might make a fresh start and stay there. He finally agreed to go because the Macdonalds promised to look after Frances and Sylvan if he went. Like Captain Oates, he went out into the Canadian snows, knowing 'he might be gone for some time'. Frances and her son went to relatives in Liverpool.

Mackintosh, meantime, had become seriously ill. A bad bout of pneumonia forced him to bed and for a time his condition was quite critical. The pneumonia was a fact but one wonders how much of the illness was pschycosomatic. Did he in fact *want* to be ill? Did he need to escape from it all? Whatever the root of it all, it was enough for Margaret. One of the first things she did was to arrange the transfer of the house to her name and also the complete control of all their financial accounts. He was in no condition to take care of such things, nor had he a mind to. Or so he said.

THE QUEST FOR CHARLES RENNIE MACKINTOSH

Margaret discussed the whole matter with the Newberys (who else?) and Fra suggested that Toshie should get out of Glasgow as soon as he was well enough to travel. He badly needed a holiday, they both did. Newbery recommended they go a place they themselves rented on the Suffolk coast, in a small fishing village called Walberswick. Margaret made arrangements immediately. The house was locked up, their bags were packed and soon they were both on a train going south. They were travelling light and they were travelling light-heartedly. It would be good to get away for a bit. It was July 1914 and the last idyllic Edwardian summer before the twentieth century changed forever, but nobody knew that then.

And what Mackintosh didn't know as the train pulled out of the Central Station that morning was that he would never see Glasgow again. They were going on holiday, yes – but it was to be a holiday that would last for the rest of their lives.

The story goes that around the same time, Sir John Burnet, at home in Glasgow on a visit, called in at the Art Club in Bath Street one evening and asked of the members – 'Any news of Mackintosh?'

There was no reply.

CHAPTER NINE

Walberswick

1914–1915

I don't think you can speak of my work until you see it
exposed side by side with others in some show – my work
is not like these others. I am trying for something else – but
even so it must take its place and hold its own in any
company ...

CRM

WAR DECLARED

AS THE BRITISH PEOPLE returned from the August Bank Holiday,
the headlines screamed at them that a war was on. The date was
Tuesday 4 and it was the end of the old world as they knew it.
Those two fatal pistol shots fired by the 19-year-old Gavrilo
Princip at a harmless and unimportant Habsburg heir in Sarajevo
were to reverberate in what Wilfred Owen called 'the monstrous
rattle of the guns' at Mons, Ypres and the rest of the muddy fields
that were to become the graves of millions, British and German,
Belgian and French. War is bad enough for anyone, but it was bad
luck for the Mackintoshes. They had planned to visit Paris and
perhaps go on to Berlin and Vienna in order to take up continental invitations that were many, sincere and longstanding. Their
'agent', Muthesius, had just such a trip in mind for them, but now
battle lines had been drawn up across Europe and all such projects
were laid aside. In a way, Margaret was relieved. Her husband
was in no great shape for travelling. She was just glad to get him
away for a time, and even if it were only as far as Walberswick, it
would do for the meantime. As she wrote to Anna Geddes:

THE QUEST FOR CHARLES RENNIE MACKINTOSH

We have been here since the middle of July – coming then just for our holiday and I induced Toshie to just stop on and get the real rest-cure that he has so badly needed for the last two years. It struck me as the right thing to do. There will be nothing really doing until the war is over for one thing, and for another, it is too dangerous to go on. When a man is over-worked he must rest or something serious will happen – so it was all arranged. We are going to have a real <u>Wander Jahr</u> – already Toshie is quite a different being and evidently [by] the end of the year will be quite fit again and by that time we hope the war will be over and perhaps we can have a hand in rebuilding the beautiful cities which are lost to us.[1]

Sadly, they were never to be be given that opportunity but they were still the *Künstpaar*, the artist couple, still striving for the mutual dream, still fighting their own war against apathy and indifference, still 'taking delight in opposing the all-powerful enemy' but for the moment at least, one of the partners was 'retired injured' and needed time to lick his wounds.

They had found accommodation at Millside, home of the Nichol family, a semi-detached villa, the other half of which was rented by the Newberys, who always stayed there when they came to Walberswick-on-Blyth. Toshie's first visit with them had been as early as 1897 and he would frequently add it to his itinerary whenever he travelled to sketch on his beloved Holy Island, a bit further up the coast, or when he called on his sister at Tynemouth which was nearer. Altogether, Mackintosh was no stranger to England as his many sketching trips there showed. Apart from Holy Island, he had taken himself off over the years to places as far south as Wareham in Dorset and the Scilly Isles and other very English places in between. It was, however, in Walberswick that the bulk of his new preoccupation, watercolours, was done, and some forty splendid works survive from this period.

Walberswick was, and is to this day, a quiet place. Its few sleepy streets still resent the motorcar. There's no car-park. I think they would prefer if one walked. The village green is still much as it was in Edwardian times and the two pubs are the same, except that the Anchor was moved, brick by brick, to its present spot comparatively recently. The houses that he sketched that first summer still stand, and if the tarmacadam were scraped from the road, the place would still be much as he first found it. And the local people like it that way.

It always was a haven for artists. Arthur Ransome lived nearby. Eddie Walton (he who stole Keppie's only girlfriend) was at Wenhaston, also very near, but they made little contact by all accounts, although they did meet. The Mackintoshes were, wherever they went, always self-sufficient. They didn't go out much socially, not since Newbery's famous Sunday nights in Glasgow. If people wanted to see them, it was the Mackintoshes who were always 'At Home'. Most of all, however, it is the sea, and its long, empty sand dunes that are the attractions of Walberswick. That's what drew the artists just as it drew fishermen and pirates and, in a bad storm, the occasional shipwreck. Being near to Snape and Aldeburgh, of Benjamin Britten fame, it is, literally, 'Albert Herring' country, for the herring girls came down annually from Aberdeen and Stonehaven to help gut the fish that came in at Lowestoft, Southold and Walberswick. They lent another kind of colour to the district for a week or two.

In Mackintosh's time, the area was a botanical paradise and several property-owners in the district had gardens 'famed for plantmanship and beauty'. Whole acres were given over to 'flowers that tell the history of the garden' and this was to have great bearing on Toshie's floral painting over the next few years. Mary Sturrock bears this out in her recollections of that momentous year of 1914:

> The Mackintoshes used to come in the evening to discuss the war. He was very patriotic, Mackintosh ... Mother got them a studio along the riverbank. It was really only a fisherman's shed, very open on one side. They liked the conditions and went on working there. They were doing the decorations for Miss Cranston's [Willow] tea-room ... It

was called 'The Dug-Out' because it was downstairs ... Mackintosh took to serious watercolours ... He told me he started drawing [flowers] when he was eighteen, but had lost the first three books he had done ...[2]

She went on to talk of his working methods and how he preferred the white, tough Whatman paper which he put in the bath then scrubbed off what he didn't like in the big washes 'he was so good at doing'. Mrs Sturrock pointed out in the same recollection that 'Architects are skilled at these because they do them for their set-pieces.'

It was in October, while the two families were together in Walberswick, that Newbery suffered a nervous breakdown, due, as his wife said, to 'years of overstrain and the shock of the war'.[3] After a few weeks in bed, he returned to Glasgow, and on arrival there, was diagnosed by Dr Souttar McKendrick as suffering from neurasthenia and depression. Consequently, on 23 November, he was given six months' leave of absence from the School of Art. Although he didn't officially retire until 1918, Fra Newbery was never really the same man again. His periods of absence became longer and more frequent. It was merely coincidental but it did seem that from the time of Mackintosh's disaffection with Glasgow, Newbery himself seemed to lose heart and was glad to retire to Corfe Castle.

It was strange that these two great friends, and, in their different ways, great artists, both paid with their bodies for their artistic achievements. Newbery's breakdown followed hard on Toshie's and it was impossible not to think they were linked in some way. Perhaps it was another cost to be added to the Art School's building budget. Both men were destined to do their best work when young but in the time of their pairing great things were achieved in Glasgow, and their tandem in terms of the Art School alone was a fortuitous coupling no less important in Mackintosh's life than his marriage to Margaret Macdonald.

Newbery had sold the idea of a new building to the governors of the Art School just as he had sold the idea of Mackintosh as architect. Although the design was won in open competition, Newbery was in Mackintosh's corner throughout the whole slogging match the building process was. Newbery was always there and now, he too, had fallen victim to the after-strain of those heady years. Mackintosh was only now recovering from the very same thing. The links that bound them were strong indeed and as Jessie Newbery was to comment later – 'The Mackintoshes have been friends for forty years and never a rift between us'.

Incidentally, while Newbery was away on sick leave, his place as Director was taken by a Mr Henderson. Surely not AG Henderson from Keppie and Henderson? It was possible. After all, John Keppie was now a governor of the School and had his eye on the Chairmanship. Speaking of Keppie, shortly after Newbery's first breakdown, and possibly prompted by Margaret, Mackintosh had written to the firm about his share of the Jordanhill prize-money. Keppie replied on office stationery from 257 West George Street on 31 December 1914. It could be seen that Mackintosh's name had already been removed from the letterhead. Keppie wrote:

Dear Mackintosh,

I was glad to get your letter of the 28th and find from it you were working at Walberswick. I had almost given up hope of hearing from you and must confess you are not distinguished as a correspondent. I heard from Newbery you were in Suffolk. He has been very unwell with nerves and is not likely to be back at the school for some time yet. I hear however he is improving slightly.

I see from the share account that what you are due is – 397.3.9. and if you concur ...

Here follow details of a small amount still owed by Mackintosh, unfortunately illegible in the original letter to this writer. Which is perhaps why Mackintosh had never paid up. The letter continues:

I am going off to Kirkudbright for the week and will be bringing in the New Year as usual with Hornel. I hope that things will go well with you next year and end with my good wishes for the season to you and Mrs Mackintosh.

Faithfully yours

John Keppie

This is either the letter of a man trying to make the best of a bad situation, or a blatant piece of smug hypocrisy, but either way, John Keppie was nothing if not scrupulous.

The partnership was legally dissolved in 1914 and, as Mackintosh himself had foreseen, AG Henderson was promoted partner in his place. Once again, dullness had won, but then, as every original artist in history has found, dullness always wins because it is always better organised. The only thing Mackintosh could do was to try and put it all out of his mind and make a fresh start in Walberswick.

The idea had been to work towards a book of watercolour paintings to be published in Germany but that was now out of the question. Mackintosh decided to paint flowers anyway. As he had said to Mary Sturrock, he was returning to his youth, back to his 'Garden of Eden' at Golfhill House, and nothing could have pleasanter or more helpful for a quick return to health and peace of mind. When the Newberys went back to Scotland, the Nichol family who owned Millside moved from Walberswick and sold their house. So the Mackintoshes moved to other lodgings in a house called Westwood on Lodge Road. Westwood had a famous garden and it was this supplied Mackintosh with all his floral subjects. One of the earliest was 'Larkspur' from August 1914. Its botanical exactness coupled with gay, artistic fancy is hardly the work of a man suffering from *delerium tremens*.

All the signs of the old, impish Mackintosh are there. For instance, in this particular painting, look closely at the central stem at the highest point and you will see the outline of bird in the shape of the leaf. Is it a repeat of the bird on the finial of the Art School's East Tower? Just under this is another possible bird shape and right at the centre on the right hand side of the main stem one can see plainly another bird's head with beady eye and bill open.

There are bird shapes all over the total design and yet it remains a perfectly defined flower. It's brilliant piece of work, and I'm sure he must have chuckled to himself, or to Margaret, as he was doing it.

This was a Mackintosh game. He even played it on house-fronts. Alan Crawford pointed it out on the facade of Ruchill Street Free Church Hall in Glasgow. As he said:

> I remember the first time I saw a face under the gable on the right. Now I cannot not see it. In 1902, Muthesius likened Mackintosh's furniture to 'primitive forms which stare at us with a mysterious gaze'. Is this another of Mackintosh's games? Are you looking at the building, or is the building looking at you?[4]

Which is why we should always keep our home windows clean because they are the eyes of the house. We use them to see out to others as others use them to see in to us. Mackintosh would have understood that. Now, sixteen years after Ruchill Stree Free Church Hall, here he was saying it with flowers. He was obviously getting better. What is interesting is that while at Walberswick, he never drew or painted the famous windmill (now burned down) or the St Andrew's Church ruins (still standing). He did sketch a couple of houses but the main concentration was on the flowers. Had the architect been dismissed – or merely laid aside for the botanical painter?

At the end of each day, the routine was always the same. He would walk to the Anchor Inn or the Bell Hotel or from the Anchor Inn to the Bell Hotel or *vice versa*. Then, as darkness fell, he would make his way to the long beach and walk by the water. Blucher English, who was a little boy at that time, saw him do this many times. In 1984, he told Alistair Moffat:

> I must have been playing near the ferry and I saw this man coming, dressed like Sherlock Holmes. He had a limp and carried a stick. Once he got past me I started to follow him. He was going towards the beach. Anyway, I kept out of sight beyond the dunes and watched him walking along the

tidemark. He kept stopping and looking back but I'm sure he didn't see me. There was a big moon but it was still too dark ... As I watched him on the beach, he wandered down, right down to the sea. I thought he must be looking for clues. Anyway, he got right to the water's edge, and he stopped and just looked out to sea. For a long time. He didn't seem to notice the waves, washing around his boots. Well I got a bit fed up with this and I went back to the village ... I was playing on the track, and I heard something and looked up. And there he was. Sherlock Holmes. I got a real shock. Frightened the wits out of me, he did, towering above me with that big, black cloak thing.

'Enjoy your walk?' he asked.

Well ... I'll never forget his face. He had a big face, not a fat face, but a big face and really piercing sort of eyes. He really looked at me ... but thinking about it now... I don't think he was angry ... My mother told me he was a bit of a drinker. He used to have one or two. Well, in a village this size, and only two pubs, you can't hide it.[5]

This child's-eye view of Mackintosh might have been more perceptive than he knew. Mackintosh was at the start in what was to be a process of transition, a move away from architecture and towards painting full-time. He was very gradually turning again towards his own beginnings.

In many ways he forgot there was a war on. Armed with his child's paintbox of watercolours, he just went about his daily business, drawing and painting, walking and looking, hardly saying anything, except to himself and being late for Margaret's 'exquisite teas'. At nights he would sit in the pub facing his usual Glasgow tipple – a half-pint of beer with a wee nip of whisky as a chaser. The customers thought him a very rare bird indeed. He never joined in their banter, he just sat there happy in his own company and saying as little as possible. They all knew he was an artist, and artists were queer folk. They also guessed from his name that he was a Scotsman, but he didn't 'talk Scotch' like the herring girls. They were loud and raucous and the villagers thought them quite scandalous with their shouts and loud remarks to the men. But this man kept to himself and only spoke when people spoke to him.

That was it as far as some of the locals were concerned. His Glasgow accent sounded very foreign – more like German than English. And that's how the rumours started. They were a strange couple, Mr and Mrs Mackintosh. The wife was English admittedly, but she was very toffee-nosed and never mixed. She often took the train leaving her husband alone at Westwood. Where did she go? And where did *he* go when he went walking along the beach – and at night, too? It was all very mysterious and was ready fuel to their own Suffolk-village-sized suspicions. It was an artificial time of hysterical jingoism and the bitter truth about what war really meant had not yet hit home. The casualties were still to come. Meantime, one thing led to another and the local policeman was forced to take note that people were talking. Pressure built for him to do something about this silent stranger in their midst. They hadn't had so much excitement in the village since the last shipwreck.

Unfortunately for Toshie, Margaret was in Glasgow when all the trouble started. Frances and Sylvan had moved into Uncle David Macdonald's flat at 50 Gibson Street now that the aunts had gone but Bertie returned unexpectedly from Canada and had moved in as well. He insisted he had come back to help with the war effort. His return had not been part of the plan at all so Margaret had gone up to sort things out. Neither of the McNairs was earning. They were eking out a living on the small allowance paid to Frances each month by her brother, Charles. He and Margaret might do all they like about fiscal and financial arrangements but they could do nothing about the fact that the McNairs loved each other despite everything and were best left to get on with it.

Meantime, back in Walberswick, Toshie was having trouble one night with a flickering lantern, probably an oil-lamp and he was some time in getting it to remain alight. He was not aware that his house was being watched and as far as the locals were concerned this intermittent light through an uncurtained window was definitely a signal going out to a German ship at sea – or even to one of those new underwater boats they call submarines. The military were informed and when Mackintosh returned from his nocturnal constitutional the next night he found an armed British soldier standing guard at the door.

Inside, there were several other soldiers under the command of an older officer, and they seemed to be searching his house, turning over all his paintings and going through all the papers in the bureau. Standing in the doorway watching all this Toshie exploded and in his best Glasgow manner asked his visitors what they thought they were doing. His language and temper got even worse as they ignored him and carried on. Then the pent-up rage of the last decade burst out in Mackintosh. He simply went mad. He grabbed the letters from the officer's hands and when, after a struggle, they fell on to the floor everyone could see that they were in German. It was the full correspondence from Muthesius, Hoffmann, Olbrich and the rest dealing with intended 1914 trip. The shock stilled the room for a moment, and the officer, his dignity still ruffled by Toshie's manhandling of him, promptly ordered his soldiers to take him into custody. Mackintosh was then seized by two of the 'Dad's Army' soldiers. Although taken aback, he gave as good as he got, both physically and audibly, and the soldier on guard had to lay down his rifle and help control this manic, frantic 'German' who was screaming incomprehensible Scottish obscenities at the top of his voice. This was hardly the taciturn, solitary drinker of the Anchor or the Bell.

According to the locals, he spent the night in the nearest police cell which was at Southold, and next morning he was standing before a local magistrate and the captain of a small Royal Navy anchored off Southold Pier, being cross-examined by both of them on suspicion of espionage on behalf of the enemy. It was a nightmare. Surely this couldn't be happening? But it was. He refused to say a single word in answer to the charge and this silent, sullen contempt didn't do much to help his case. The part-time magistrate was at a loss. There was a move to take him up to Lowestoft

for stronger detention and more intensive interrogation but luck-
ily, Margaret, her red hair flaming with indignation, returned at
the last minute from Glasgow and briskly saved the day.

Her county manner impressed officialdom sufficiently to let
her take her husband home, provided he remain there until a full
board of local magistrates could be convened and further advice
taken from the military. Mackintosh still didn't say anything.
They wanted to retain all the German correspondence in the
meantime. Margaret said she could speak German and would
translate them word for word but the magistrate's view was that
they would get someone from Cambridge to translate them.
Scornfully, Margaret left them to it and took Toshie back to Westwood. It took her days to clear up the mess the soldiers had made.
Toshie wouldn't do a thing. He just sat staring out of the window
at the sea. One had the feeling that if someone had given him a
lamp, he would have signalled the whole German Navy.

Margaret contacted Anna Geddes in London and put her in the
picture. Anna said that Patrick was busy proofing his latest book,
Cities in Evolution (1915) in which, by the way, he made the
rather sweeping statement that:

> 'Mackintosh' was an accepted architectural term from Bel-
> gium to Hungary and his influence was to be seen in city
> after city.[6]

If nothing else, it showed his high regard for the architect, and he
was no less kind towards the man. The Edinburgh-born polymath
was something of a prickly character and presented his good
points to the world much as a hedgehog does when attacked.
There was, however, no denying he had a mind, and was not
afraid to use it. Ostensibly, he was a sociologist but really he was
a bit of everything. Like Mackintosh, he had a gift for making ene-
mies, but his friendships were sound. He now proved it by inviting
the Mackintoshes up to London as soon as they could to stay with
him – as long as Anna saw to everything of course.

And of course she did. But first she had to do something about
these Walberswick magistrates and their military friends. Her

daughter, Norah, was married to influence and, at her mother's request, she used this to get in touch with someone high at the War Office and let them deal directly with the local authorities in Suffolk. Lady Norah Mears, herself, went to Whitehall, backed up by her father's papers and other professional references (but not the German ones) and explained that they were unwittingly holding the most famous architect in Scotland, one whose only German contact was artistic and not political, and that he was totally patriotic. Old as he was, he would have enlisted in the services – except that he had a club foot.

What was said will be on record somewhere in the vaults of the War Office – not that it matters. Whatever she said, she got him off, much as Arthur Balfour saved Robert Louis Stevenson in Samoa when he, too, got entangled in a local war situation. At any rate, someone must have telephoned Walberswick because Mackintosh was summoned to stand before the local magistrates. They ordered him to leave the village at once and not to darken their coastline again. He was also told to stay away from all ports and railway stations for the duration of hostilities. He still did not say a word. It was a totally surreal incident but it was one that further scarred the psyche of this deeply feeling man.

He did go back to Walberswick, many times, after the war was over, often on his own to sketch and paint and stare out to sea. Ginger Winyard was another little boy in Walberswick during this second Mackintosh phase and he had a particularly vivid memory of Toshie urinating into a chamber pot to drown a mouse. Ginger's parents kept one of the pubs in the village, presumably the Anchor, and Mackintosh would often turn up on the doorstep looking for a bed. On the occasions when there was no room at the inn, Mrs Winyard would often ask him to share with their son, Ginger – hence the candle-lit vision of Toshie and the chamber pot.

Ginger remembered that everybody in the village knew the 'little man'. It's hard to think of Mackintosh as a 'little man'. Mary Sturrock thought he was tall as a young man and all through his life he always had presence – he was never a 'little man'. Or had his physique shrunk with his reputation? Mr Winyard goes on:

I knew his name was Mackintosh but everybody called him 'Mac' ... People used to say – 'There go old Mac.' ... Everybody remembered him when he came back to Walberswick. He was so restless, he sort of ran from pub to pub ... But sometimes he'd let a half-pint stand in front of him all night and never finish it. All the customers used to talk about him – 'Old Mac did this and old Mac did that'. In villages people notice things ... My mother said he was never in time for meals, he just wasn't reliable for that sort of thing. He wasn't a smart chap. He wouldn't clean his shoes and he always dressed the same. ... Maybe that was the time of his life when he hadn't got to bother and didn't want to bother. Maybe at nights he had one or two – but in a little village what is there to do between six and ten? Nothing is there?[7]

And nothing comes from nothing. But this was no Lear, he wasn't an old, doddering man, he was fifty-two years of age in 1920 – with an expectation of at least a quarter-century of work ahead of him. Yet he had done so much work already. Perhaps too much. And too soon. But there was more in him yet and it could be brought out again if circumstances were right. He was desperate to resume his real life, his real work, which was creating things on paper to be built for all the world to see – but as the boy said, why bother? After the usual few days, he paid his bill and, with his trilby on his head, his raincoat over his arm, and his shoes still muddy from the beach, he caught the next train back to London and to Margaret. Ginger came to wave him off. Did he have a dead mouse in his hand, I wonder?

In a letter, dated 21 July 1915, Mackintosh announced to William Davidson, 'I am playing around with Geddes here at his summer meeting'. In Mackintosh terms, that meant he was working on something. This was probably plans for 'A Shop, Office-Block and Warehouse in an Arcaded Street' which he prepared for India but it wasn't built. The 'meeting' he referred to was Patrick Geddes's summer seminar on *War – Its Social Effects and Problems* which was being held at King's College. It seems likely that Geddes merely gave his friend something to do while he had the premises, so to speak. As he was due to go out to India next to advise on the rebuilding of Delhi, he no doubt needed something on an Indian theme – hence the 'Arcaded Street' project. Mackintosh also designed a 'War Memorial in a Public Place', which may in fact have been built in India, as Edwin Lutyens was already out there on the same project as Geddes and not getting on at all with the off-putting Scot. 'He seems to talk rot in an insulting way … A crank who don't know his subject.'[8] That was probably because Lutyens didn't know what Geddes's subject was. Mackintosh also designed some lamp standards, no doubt also intended for a New Delhi thoroughfare, but instead something like them later turned up in Skelmorlie, of all places. According to another note to Davidson, Mackintosh might have gone to India himself at one point: 'I have a tentative offer from the Indian Government to go out there for 6 months'. It remained tentative and was never mentioned again, but the mind boggles at the thought of Geddes and Mackintosh together in the Indian heat. Lutyens might then have had genuine cause to be concerned.

Although not quite as close as the Newberys, the Geddes family had been friends with the Mackintoshes since their student days. At a time when the Four were at their height, Patrick Geddes had written a book, *The Evolution of Sex* (1889), in which he posited that the love between a man and a woman, and their acting in that togetherness, represented the fullest ideal of human love. Two beings, uniquely different but equal. They united their genders to become as one. It was the fusion of opposites, thesis and antithesis. This thinking appealed to Margaret and Toshie particularly. They both remembered Professor Max Muller's lectures at Glasgow University on 'Soul and Spirit' and how everything came from one source. Even if it divided itself into opposite and opposing strands it came together in the end, entwined and as one again. This idea can be seen in all their early work together.

One has only to think of the Willow Tea Rooms, and how both their homes illustrated the mutuality which, at the same time, displayed their individuality, particularly at Florentine Terrace (Southpark Avenue). Juliet Kinchin puts this so well in her article, *Mackintosh and the City*. In Southpark Avenue, as she calls it:

> The Mackintoshes created a circuitous journey of the imagination, aestheticising the daily round of activities within their home as a series of visual and tactile experiences representing different facets of spiritual transformation. The inhabitants ... ascend through the house into increasingly intimate spaces, ever more removed from the outer world ...[9]

Ms Kinchin goes on nicely to suggest that we throw off the world with our coats and find, as we go through the day and the house, that we rise gradually to 'the unclothed intimacy of the white bedroom'.

All this is in keeping with Mackintosh's view of the finished architectural project as an artwork in itself, being the sum of all its parts, each part in its place to create the whole. The holistic experience is tangible, a house to him is a living thing, an experience to be felt as much as to be viewed. This attitude was entirely in accord with the Geddes idea about the individual in society being part of a design that links all living things. This in essence was the basis of Theosophy, which was advocated by Helena Blavatsky and upheld by her pupil, Annie Besant, who went to India to spread the need for birth control. Mrs Besant was also a pupil of Geddes and a good friend. She may have initiated, indirectly, the invitation for Geddes to visit to India, where he went soon after the Mackintoshes arrived in London.

Toshie spent that first London summer alone as Margaret had to be away again in Glasgow on other family business. Philip Mairet remembers Mackintosh from this time. Mairet was a draughtsman in the office of CR Ashbee, a very successful London architect, when he was asked to do some work for Patrick Geddes, who by then had left for India. Mairet had known the work of Frank Lloyd Wright in America but he was totally unprepared for the work of Charles Rennie Mackintosh when he turned up out of nowhere. Mairet wrote to Murray Grigor on 2 March 1967:

> Mackintosh and I shared the same room at King's College, London, for a few days in the summer of 1915. I was working at the wall lecture diagrams for Patrick Geddes and Mackintosh was doing some plans ... Were these something Geddes wanted to take back to India with him, I wonder? ... I knew enough to be impressed by the originality of Mackintosh's conception and the skill of his draughtsmanship ... in work that seemed inspired by Japan ... His personality, unfortunately, did not make a very congenial impression ... chiefly because his aura was suffused with the alcoholic potations to which he was addicted. About this I was perhaps rather puritanical ... I attributed his evident intemperance to the trials and tribulations he had just been through ... As you will know, he was arrested on suspicion of espionage ... Geddes took a particular interest in his case; doubtless because he had previous knowledge of his work... He found him a room to work in (which I also used) ... The impression that remained with me was that of a brilliant man ... who was going down-hill. I never fully realised the genius in his work until I saw the exhibition at the Edinburgh Festival of 1954.[10]

Philip Mairet may have seen a small exhibition at the Royal Botanical Gardens in 1954, as he says, but the more important event was the Exhibition of the previous year, which was held at Gladstone's Land in the High Street of Edinburgh during the Festival of 1953. Curated by Tom Howarth in conjunction with Robert Hurd, an Edinburgh architect, in association with the Saltire Society and the Arts Council of Great Britain, it was a great success and threw a much-needed spotlight on Mackintosh. This was the precursor of a much more ambitious Exhibition organised for the 1968 Edinburgh Festival by Professor McLaren Young with William Buchanan and others. This latter event, which later showed in London, really opened the floodgates and led to the later auction-room sensations that made Mackintosh known worldwide.

This, however, was not the case in 1915 when he was ignominiously frogmarched out of Walberswick and forced to head for London and make yet another fresh start. This, coming right on top of his illness and depression and the toll taken by the last few years in Glasgow, made him a changed man. He had just come to life again with his Walberswick flowers and now even they were snatched from his hand. From this time on, he became more self-enclosed. He drew a cloak of self-preservation around himself, as encompassing as the Inverness cape he wore with his deerstalker cap. He retreated not only to London but also into himself. The great talker now left all the talking to Margaret. He had nothing he wanted to say.

CHAPTER TEN

Chelsea Bohemians

1915–1919

The day is happily passing away when Architecture may be
deemed a thing of quantities of diletantism and drains.

CRM

WHILE STAYING WITH the Geddes family, Margaret began to look
for their own base in London. It was George Walton, an old friend
from early Cranston days, who suggested Chelsea. Walton had
been a member of the Chelsea Art Club since he had come to London in 1910 to work on the Kodak building and he told Margaret
there was no better place for artists. Margaret took him at his
word. After first finding lodgings in a bed-and-breakfast establishment in Oakley Street, she took two rooms linked by an interior
common doorway at 2 Hans Studios, 43a Glebe Place, only a little more than a hundred yards away, off Cheyne Walk. Soon they
were settled in with some of their panels and pieces from Glasgow
and Mackintosh was ready to start work as an architect again.
This was not immediately forthcoming.

With a war going on, their well-known Viennese connections
made them slightly suspect. Although their main correspondents
had been Austrian, they were German as far as England was concerned, and that did not help Mackintosh make the new
architectural connections he needed in London. In some circles,
Toshie's work with the Four, although long past, still linked him to
the older world of Art Nouveau, and those tendrils still clung –
undeservedly. Mary Sturrock verifies this:

Mackintosh didn't like Art Nouveau. He liked simplicity and everything handmade. He fought against these things with his straight lines ... things you can see for yourself are like melted margarine or slightly deliquescent lard ... Mackintosh didn't fit in, didn't connect with anyone else artistically ... [he] didn't get much work in Glasgow because it was too provincial. They thought there that the tea-rooms were a joke and the Art School very peculiar ... He had done all that work and it came to nothing.[1]

This testimony suggests that if he had been allowed to continue with either the College of Domestic Science or Jordanhill Training College, he might have stayed in Glasgow and won an established place on his own. Who knows? That's just another 'if' in the conjectures that litter the Mackintosh story. All we know for sure was that by 1915, he had left his great work behind him, most of which had yet to be seen by most of the British architectural world. What few realised was that the whirls and whorls of Art Nouveau were not in keeping with his new rigour and, most significant of all, the stark modernity of his houses and the Art School extension. Appreciation of this had to wait for Marriott's positive reassessment in 1924.

In the meanwhile, the Mackintoshes didn't seem in that much of a hurry to get started again. Margaret's income was fixed enough to deal with the basics and the occasional sales of Toshie's cut flower watercolours – *Anemones*, *Begonias*, *Peonies* and *White Rose* etc. – in addition to book covers for his old patron, Blackie, in Glasgow – *Wireless*, *Our Railways* and so on, were just enough to cover any extras. Blackie still thought the world of Mackintosh, but at this time there were few who had the same high opinion. Some never thought of him as an architect at all, which is not to be wondered at as he didn't seem anxious to practise. Professor Randolph Schwabe, from the Royal College of Art, thought that the London Mackintosh was 'not a great architect but a gifted eccentric and a much-loved friend'.

Margaret's occasional tea parties in their studio attracted a whole new circle of friends – the Schwabes (the Prof and 'Birdie'), Augustus John and Ida, WO Hutchison and his wife (the 'Hutchies'), and Harold Squire. All artists, and not one architect. Why did he never think of knocking on Mr CR Ashbee's door in Cheyne Walk, which was only minutes away from their own studios? Ashbee had built most of the houses in that part of Chelsea and his own house, at No 71 Cheyne Walk, lay between the Magpie and Stump, a pub, and the Blue Cockatoo, a small, unpretentious restaurant, where the waitress, Hettie Swaisland, she of the 'bird's nest hair', made the newcomers very welcome. She took to Toshie at once, although he was by no means the most celebrated of her patrons.

Her clientele was a virtual roll-call of the artistic London of the day and all attended from time to time – the musical Goosens, Eugene, Leon and Sidonie and composers (Sir) Arnold Bax and Clifford Bax, the literary Sitwells, Edith and Osbert, and George Bernard Shaw, the poet Ezra Pound, EO Hoppé, the photographer, and the theatrical director and designer, Edward Gordon Craig, whose mother, Ellen Terry, known to all as 'ET', lived round the corner in Glebe Place. This Chelsea set represented the last Edwardian flourish in a very special metropolitan enclave and one that contained the seeds of the post-war flowering in the arts in Britain that was to come during the Jazz Age. Meantime, it was dressed in khaki, so to speak, and keeping its head below the parapet.

A reminder that bloody happenings were afoot across the Channel came when Mackintosh heard that Captain Eugene Bourdon, formerly of the Glasgow School of Art, had been killed at the Battle of the Somme. He was only two years younger than Mackintosh, and was the same man who had made the patronising remarks about the new School of Art and its architect in 1909. It seemed very unimportant now. Nothing was important now, or everything was. It was a time to live, a time to survive, and Margaret saw that they did.

Their daily routine was very pleasant. Some work after breakfast, a walk after lunch at the Blue Cockatoo and then perhaps letters before returning in the early evening for dinner at the Blue Cockatoo among congenial friends. Then home again by midnight so that, as Toshie said, he wouldn't turn into a cat and start prowling again. He was on his sixth life now, with Dennistoun, studenthood, prodigy days at Honeyman and Keppie, black days at Honeyman and Keppie, and Walberswick now all behind him. The sixth stage, his first Chelsea period was a kind of rebirth or rethinking of his artistic odyssey. Either way it was a testament to his tenacity. His attitude was exactly in keeping with the times – yesterday was irretrievable, tomorrow uncertain to say the least, therefore, today was to be enjoyed.

Not that all the paired and shared experiences were enjoyable. The *künstpaar* had their disappointments. In September 1916 an Arts and Crafts Exhibition was held in London and the Mackintoshes were invited by Robert Anning Bell to contribute. However, the invitation came very late – giving them only two months to prepare something. They worked together on a panel entitled *Voices in the Wood*, which was entered as a mutual work and listed as 'by Margaret Macdonald and Charles R Mackintosh of Glasgow'. It ended up being hung on a staircase and drew only mixed reviews. The *British Architect* thought it was 'meant for execution in needlework'. So much for critics. The couple merely shrugged and returned to their newest interest – textile design.

Over the next decade, they were to produce more than 120 designs for commercial firms like William Foxton, Sefton's and others. It was this work that gradually moved them away from their trademark rose *motif* to more geometric patterns offset by vivid and contrasting colouration. They were unwinding themselves from the sensuous Vienna waltz and getting ready for the Charleston. Short skirts would soon be the order of the day and all the 'isms' were bracing themselves for the new freedoms. This kind of work proved Mackintosh's theory that the true artist can turn his hand to anything and make it workable and beautiful – just as William Morris had advocated. And anyway, there was money in it.

There was an opportunity to design a studio for Augustus John, but that volatile bohemian elected to go for a Dutch architect he met in a pub in the King's Road who produced for the painter a studio which, by all accounts, was quasi-Mackintosh. The next job offer was not from a Cockatoo contact, as one might say, but from a complete stranger. Quite out of the blue, Mackintosh was sought out by Mr WJ Bassett-Lowke to design, or rather re-design, an existing small house at the Derngate in Northampton. Wenham Bassett-Lowke was a successful engineer and builder of model boats, trains and motorcars, who was then living with his parents in Kingwell Street near the family's factory.

However, he was soon to be married and, not being able to build new, he wanted a modern house made out of his very ordinary terraced dwelling which he had bought in the Derngate in centre of Northampton. So who else to make a silk purse out of such a sow's ear than a man who was then designing book jackets and patterns for curtains and cushions. However, Mr Bassett-Lowke knew what he wanted. And Mr Mackintosh knew what he needed – a job.

Nobody is quite certain how the two men came to be in contact. In a typescript written in September 1939, Bassett-Lowke said, writing of that First World War time, 'During a holiday in Cornwall I met a friend from Glasgow who held forth to me on the merits of the architect, Chas. Rennie Mackintosh'.[2] During the Second World War, on 3 July 1944, he wrote to Howarth – 'I cannot remember the friend who introduced me to Mr Mackintosh but he was from Glasgow and in connection with the School of Art, and I met him during a vaction at Ravenglass in Cumberland in 1916.'[3]

The Art School connection would indicate the loyal Newbery, but, as we have seen, Newbery was not in the best of health in 1916, although that also could be why he was on holiday in Cornwall or Cumberland. Then again he was such an obvious Englishman that 'coming from Glasgow' would seem rather to suggest a native Glaswegian. This might better apply to Alexander

Ellis Anderson, a Northampton-based architect who was trained in Glasgow and whose brother was at Art School with Mackintosh. It was he, AE Anderson, in fact, who did the drawings for 78 Derngate and lived only a few doors away at the time. He could conceivably have been a friend of Bassett-Lowke's.

Incidentally, Anderson is famous in motoring circles for having buit 'the first house for a car' – the garage – in 1901. This so offended Frank Lloyd Wright that the American countered with the 'car-port', properly relegating the car to the outside of the house. Alex Anderson paid Mackintosh the ultimate compliment by later re-modelling his own house at 70 Derngate, inside and out, along the lines created by his celebrated fellow-Scot at 78. It is doubtful that a fee was ever discussed, although a bottle of whisky might have changed hands during one of the Mackintosh stay-overs in Northampton.

Dr Sylvia Pinches, the present House Curator at the Derngate, adds another piece to the jigsaw by saying that the first set of inlaid bedroom furniture was done for Bassett-Lowke's parents as early as 1915, but this is entirely anecdotal. Not that it really matters. What is important is that a very great talent was coaxed out from behind his Chelsea curtains and brought to bear on what was really quite a small job with results that showed, nonetheless, that the master had not lost any of his old ingenuity. He 'painted space' in a sense by a resort to extraordinary decorative schemes. The master was still the master after all. He re-used the inverted triangular theme from the Scotland Street scheme for the wallpaper in the lounge/hall, but this time in a brillant yellow Art Deco pattern. The effect was electrifying. No wonder it gave people a shock.

He was still capable of still provoking the same old controversy. Bassett-Lowke described the completed decor in the bedroom as 'distinctly futuristic' and this may have worried him when George Bernard Shaw came to stay on one occasion. Shaw, who was visiting the local repertory theatre with which Bassett-Lowke also had an interest, was being shown to his guest bedroom, and was asked politely by his host if the very modern décor of contrasting stripes might offend him? 'Not at all,' Shaw is said to have replied in that famous falsetto, 'Sure I always sleep with me eyes shut!'

The holism that marked all Mackintosh's work was very evident here with his design of everything from furniture and fitments to soft furnishings and decor. At times this concern with linking all the parts to the total design led to some friction between client and architect – or perhaps it was rather more with the client's newly-married bride, Florence Jones, who was aghast at Mackintosh's more extreme notions, especially in the use of black in the hall. This was in perfect contrast to the white employed in the rear extensions, but Mackintosh had to give in and tone things down – or up – as required. One remembers that this was the same designer who sent a posse of disgruntled Glasgow painters into Sauchiehall Street looking like the Christie Minstrels after he had insisted they paint one of the ceilings in the Willow Tea Rooms with black lead.

Most architects borrow from other architects but Mackintosh was rare in that he frequently borrowed from himself. This can be seen in the way in which he got something out of Queen's Cross Church and inserted it at Windyhill, took something from there and put it into Hill House, saw something from there and realised it again in another way in the Art School. This project turned out to be a veritable cache of effects to be later used as required. As did the tea rooms. One can see the Chinese Room in the hallway of Derngate. Each project was a step up. Until he found that there was nothing at the top of the ladder but a way down. Yet nothing was ever completely wasted. He thought you could never get too much of a good thing. His was always an artistic response to formal problems and this did not always make it easy in dealing with a client's expressed wishes.

For instance, Bassett-Lowke wanted a plain frontage with a 'severe door'. Mackintosh gave the required door but added a bay window to its right which immediately softened its look to the street. However, it was at the rear he made the biggest change and here he so altered and extended the elevation that it immediately suggests the Willow Tea Rooms in its stark contrast to its rather dowdy red-brick neighbours. The open veranda from the first floor bedroom was an innovation and a revelation. This wasn't a matter of keeping up with the Joneses – it was leaving them well behind.

I saw this for myself when I went to Northampton and found that 78, The Derngate was undergoing total restoration at the hands of William Anelay of York, experts in this delicate field of historical rebuilding. They had covered every brick of the place in protective clothing, so to speak, and on the temporary front door was a cardboard notice, on which was scrawled – 'Knock loud and ask for Phil'. I did so – loudly – and the door was opened by Phil Sharp, the foreman on the job, who wasn't impressed by the fact that I had come all the way from New Zealand to see inside the house. However, when I mentioned that my brother Jim had once played centre-half for York City when Sam Bartram was the manager, I was immediately handed a hard hat and invited in. Phil was a keen supporter of York City Football Club as was his father before him.

It was impossible to see anything but ladders and scaffolding inside but I followed Phil through the maze until he came to a spot on the dusty wall where he pointed to a little patch of faded wallpaper circled by a marker. 'See that,' he grinned. I could just see under the dust a series of inverted triangle shapes. 'That's all that left of your Mackintosh now,' Phil added, 'but we thought we'd leave it there while we're doing the job. It reminds us of the bloke that did the original. After all, that's why we're here, isn't it?' I was really quite touched. I hope they find some way of preserving that worker's gesture. I was allowed to peep through the canvas awning on to the veranda but not to go out. 'Anyway, you can see it better from the back garden.' When I had returned my hard hat and wished Phil and York City the best of luck (they had been rescued from bankruptcy by the Supporters' Club only the week before), I went out to find my way through to the back garden.

I did so by climbing over someone's wall further down and was rewarded by a most exciting glimpse of white rear elevation. It must have been quite startling in its time. The *Ideal Home* for August 1920 is before me as I write this, and in this issue and the next one for September, the editor dealt with how an 'old-fashioned and unsightly house was brought right up-to-date'. By means of detailed plans and photographs spread over seven pages we are taken through the whole place and invited to marvel at 'the unique transformation that Mr WJ Bassett-Lowke has effected at 78 Derngate, Northampton ... In some respects, it is almost a house of the future ... Mr and Mrs Bassett-Lowke are to be congratulated.' Nowhere in those entire seven pages is Mackintosh even mentioned. It is possible that Bassett-Lowke himself might have had an editorial say here. He was a self-made man and he saw no reason to suddenly deconstruct himself for the sake of giving credit where credit was due.

Not that he didn't admire Mackintosh immensely. Following on the remaking of his own home, he asked Toshie to do the same to a pair of cottages he had bought a few years before near the village of Roade, which lies south of Northampton. The two cottages been knocked into one and he wanted Mackintosh to design the furniture for the place and add decor – 'to his instruction'. Mrs Bassett-Lowke had obviously put her foot down. Never mind, Mackintosh obliged and the furniture was duly made as designed. You can see it today in the Art Gallery, Brighton.

Much later, in 1924, the model-maker Bassett-Lowke was older and richer – and tried to contact Mackintosh about building a house for him from new. He had found a site in Wellingborough Road, Northampton, and wanted another 'up-to-date' design but when he tried the Chelsea address it was to find that the Mackintoshes had left for 'somewhere in France' and no one could give him a forwarding address. This was a real shame because this opportunity could have kick-started Mackintosh's architectural career in England and who knows what that might have led to. It is another one of the little hiccups that so affected the course of the Mackintosh career. It was always a small brick that brought the wall down.

Bassett-Lowke might have found him had he been more assid-
uous in the search through known contacts like Anderson, or even
Newbery in Dorset, or perhaps he thought he might more easily
get his own way with another architect. He still wanted a modern
'Mackintosh' kind of house so he looked for someone who might
give him just that. He explained in an aide-memoire:

> After the war I purchased a piece of land 300 ft by 600 ft on
> the outskirts of Northampton of which the garden was
> already laid out. Mr Mackintosh was to have designed me a
> house for this site but he went away to live in the Pyrenees
> and I lost touch with him. I could not find any other archi-
> tect with modern ideas in England, and when looking
> through a German publication called 'Werkbund Jahrbuch'
> of 1913 I saw some work by professor Peter Behrens which
> I thought was very simple, straightforward and modern in
> its atmosphere. I obtained Dr Behren's address from the
> German Consul and got in touch with him. This was the
> year 1924.

And that was that. Beherens eventually completed the house,
called New Ways, a very striking house indeed, which the
Northampton neighbours thought was Bassett-Lowke's new factory. Shades of the Art School reaction. In this case, however, the
building was hailed as the first modern house in Britain – and
Behrens took the honours. Honours which so easily might have
been Toshie's.

As it was, much of 78 Derngate was repeated in the new house
so there is a shade of Mackintosh in it, but Bassett-Lowke had the
complete say this time and Behrens did as he was told. Perhaps
that is the Mackintosh difference. 78, Derngate was sold to an
architect, Harold Scrivener who only lived in it for a couple of
years before selling it to a maiden lady who had a draper's shop in
the town and so on until a local doctor bought it for his mother in
1948. In 1964 it and the house next door, number 80, were taken
over by the Northampton School for Girls which was already
established in the Derngate (at number 44). Seventy-eight was

then leased to the Victoria Wine Company for their offices until 1996 when the Borough Council took it into its care and the process of rehabilitation was begun thanks to the efforts of Mackintosh enthusiasts who formed the Derngate Trust in 1998 to secure its future as a Mackintosh site.[4] By March 2004, the house will be exactly as Mackintosh refurbished it for the Bassett-Lowkes in 1917 and, Scotland's most famous architect will have a substantial remembrance, at last, in the middle of England. And somewhere on the walls might there still be that tiny patch of the original wallpaper? Even if it's under glass. Speaking of glass, one of the many neat Mackintosh ideas in the conversion was the mirrored shaving pane in the bathroom window set at exactly the right height to catch the morning light. Once again, it shows his fastidious attention to detail – but how clever too.

Meantime, back in Chelsea, Mackintosh exhibited with the Society of International Society of Sculptors, Painters and Gravers at their 1917 show at the Goupil Gallery, London, with no great benefit, it would seem, to Sculptor, Painter or Graver – or himself. In the same year, the 'Dug-Out' scheme, designed at Walberswick, was installed at the Willow Tea Rooms and the last link with Kate Cranston had been forged. In October, the Major (John Cochrane) died and Kate Cranston, like Queen Victoria and her Prince Albert, spent the rest of her life grieving for him. She gradually gave over the day-to-day running of her tea rooms to her manageresses, and, again like Victoria, the sun had begun to set on her empire. The war changed a lot of social habits and men returning from the trenches wanted something more than a nice cup of tea – no matter how enticing the surroundings.

Miss Cranston sold her beautiful home at Hous'hill with all its Mackintosh effects and contents and, with typical Cranston style, left the new owners a flower-filled house and a warm note of welcome. She took to spending more time in the North British Hotel in George Square where she maintained a suite and soon became a familiar figure in black sombrero and long black skirt taking her constitutional around the square twice a day. She still looked in at her 'shops' as she called them just to make sure they were keeping up her standards. They were, but in the changing times it was becoming harder and harder to do so. They were born of more leisured times and the pace of life was quickening fast as the hectic Twenties approached.

Hous'hill, the house on the hill, was to change hands several times before a disastrous fire in 1933 damaged it irreparably. Most of the furniture was saved and a public auction was held to dispose of what had survived. The response was meagre to say the least. A revolving bookcase was listed as a wireless aerial, which gives an idea of the level of aesthetic awareness by all involved, and in the end many of the pieces couldn't be given away and were destroyed. This was the first of the Mackintosh furniture disasters and, regrettably, it was not to be the last. Miss Cranston died in the following year. Her once-proud mansion was left to moulder into a ruin and was later demolished by Glasgow Corporation to make way for the Nitshill Housing Estate. One by one, the tea-shops closed or were given over to Cooper's, the Grocers, and soon it was as if the colourful Kate Cranston had never been. But she lives on today by virtue of her Mackintosh connection – and deservedly so.

At the eleventh hour of the eleventh day of the eleventh month of 1918, as the immortal phrase has it, the Armistice was signed in a railway carriage in the forest of Compiègne and the Great War was over. It would take almost a year for the politicians to cobble together the iniquitous Peace Treaty at Versailles that would prepare the way for World War Two but in the meantime, ten million young men had died, a whole generation lost – and for what? In no time, the old order would re-assert itself as it always does and things would return to much as they were.

The shattered remains of that confident volunteer army of 1914 came home and only Charlie Chaplin was left to *Shoulder Arms*. The Kaiser abandoned his country and fled in a convoy of twelve cars carrying relatives, followed by a trainload of twenty carriages full of luxuries, to sit out a padded exile in Holland. The Mackintosh exile in London continued with no great change in their fortunes and with money getting perceptibly scarce. Or rather, what they had from Margaret's allowance and the rent from Glasgow didn't stretch as far as it once did. The 'exquisite teas' became a rare event. Mackintosh felt he had to do something.

He entered into a scheme with a new and dear friend, the artist John Duncan Fergusson, to turn the disused army huts in Hyde Park into a colony of painting studios and exhibition area for returning artists, but the War Office refused to sanction their use. The project was really Fergusson's, and it was a good idea, but like most good ideas in the arts, it came to nothing because of the unartistic attitude shown by officialdom.

Fergusson, or Fergus, as he liked to be called, was a tall, good-looking Scot, six years younger than Mackintosh, and now a near-neighbour in Chelsea. Born in Leith, within the smell of Edinburgh as they say, his family was from Pitlochry in Perthshire and Fergus always regarded himself as a Highlander. He was educated at the Royal High in Edinburgh and went on to Edinburgh University to study medicine, but after the first term he knew it was not for him and, inspired by the work of Whistler, he went off to Paris in 1905 to train as a painter.

There he was greatly influenced by Matisse and by Leon Bakst's work for the Ballet Russe and in 1911 met up with the literary world in Middleton Murray and Katherine Mansfield, with whom he worked on the magazine, *Rhythm*. In 1913, he met a beautiful young dancer, Margaret Morris, known as Meg, and together they went to Antibes in the South of France, following Van Gogh and Cezanne in the search for clear light. The outbreak of war in 1914 brought them to London and to their first house at 22 Cheyne Walk in Chelsea with its proximity to the Blue Cockatoo – where of course, they met the Mackintoshes. The new foursome hit it off at once, especially Meg and Toshie, and all four were to grow even closer in the next phase of their London life but that is dealt with more fully in the next chapter.

For the moment, however, an anecdote Fergus himself told Margaret best illustrates their relationship and throws a nice light on Toshie. It seems that Fergusson was sitting one day in the little square at Antibes waiting for Meg to finish her shopping and, like the artist he was, he was sipping his absinthe and admiring, with a painter's eye, the white house opposite with its grey gable, green shutters and the high plantan tree growing alongside. He goes on:

> They're interesting these plantans; the branches are wonderful where the bark is off and they are almost flesh colour ... the way the branches compose is amazing, fascinating; what a wonderful thing a tree is ... It's so old, so full of time ... [yet] it's just a tree and just taking its time; the shade it's making seems to be part of it; it doesn't flash or scintilate this old plantan, it accepts its friend the sun and absorbs it [and] with it makes beautiful patterns on the ground – wonderful. There is form, colour, depth, shade, dignity, friendliness, protection, comfort – yes, all that, but there's something else, a tremendous lot more. Then we just stand still and look and see nothing [but] something is happening slowly ...

Just then Meg returned with the shopping and interrupted his arboreal reverie, but one can see already why this man is a good friend of Toshie's. It might even be Mackintosh speaking. Fergus at this time was into woodcarving. The story goes on:

> When I got back to London I went to the woodyard and bought a batten four inches square and seven feet long. With the idea of the plantan still in my mind I drew two intertwined lines on one side, like the movement of the branches. I put it in the corner of the room where I could see it nearly all the time. It stood there for about two years, I couldn't get a start on it.

> One day the bell rang. I went down, opened the door and found old Toshie – Charles Rennie Mackintosh – with a delightful, happy smile, holding a small flower-pot with two, intertwined twigs, two leaves near the bottom and two more at the top. He laughed and said – 'I saw this on a barrow and had to bring it to you – it's so like you.' What a

charming thing to do and how amazingly sympathetic – real sympathy. I hadn't seen him for some time ... We talked ... Delightful old man, I always had the greatest admiration for him and his work, long before I knew him.

When he left I sat looking at the twined twigs ... I started to make a careful drawing of the movement and the plane relation of the leaves. As I went on I began to feel I had done it before – you know the feeling ... I felt I had fixed it and put it aside. Then one day, long after, I noticed the pencil lines on the batten – they were just like Toshie's plant.[5]

Fergusson did follow through with a carving based on the idea given him by the little pot plant and some years later, the finished work was exibited as *The Dryad* at the Leicester Gallery as part of the Scottish Group with paintings by Peploe, Hunter and the rest. Sickert, in his catalogue notes said of it, 'The Dryad is the best use a four inch batten has been put to in recent times.'

The reason that Fergusson had seen little of Mackintosh before he called at the door was that, in 1919, he and Margaret were as near to being broke as they had ever been. So much so that Mackintosh had to write to their old friend, William Davidson, in Glasgow and ask, if not beg him to buy one of flower paintings so that they could pay the studio rent. On April 1, 1919, he wrote:

I find myself for the moment very hard up and I was wondering if you could see your way to buy one of my flower pictures or lanscapes [sic] for 20 or 30 pounds ... as my rent of 16 pounds is overdue and I must pay or leave.[6]

Mr Davidson replied at once with 30 pounds and got his picture. Mackintosh had to make a similar appeal not long afterwards and one can well imagine the pain it caused this proud man to write such letters. The second appeal was dated August 15 and was occasioned by a sudden demand for income tax, a measure, by the way, which had been brought in by Prime Minister Lloyd George to help pay for the recent war; this 'temporary measure' has lasted to this day. Mackintosh had written:

I fully expected that I would be out of the wood by this time but alas I am still very hard pressed to make ends meet. If you propose taking some of the pictures could you please wire me 7 pounds this week as I have tax to pay that must be settled at once or the law will move.

Needless to say, Mr Davidson was only too happy oblige as requested and when he got the pictures he realised it had not only been a lifesaver for the Mackintoshes but was good business for him. The pictures have remained in the Davidson family till now.

Mackintosh even tried to sell some of the small 'poster stamps' he had made for Bassett-Lowke's business through Davidson but Glasgow businessmen failed to take up the offer. Advertising was a matter of word of mouth to them rather than any hard sell. It was word of mouth that had done the damage as far as Mackintosh was concerned. Rumours about his errant Glasgow behaviour had reached the capital and, as with all rumours, they grew in the telling and Mackintosh's professional reputation was almost in ruins. Had anyone taken the trouble to check out the work he had actually done even during his wayward years, they would have been astounded at its audacity and verve. What he ought to have done was to make a poster stamp of his own output.

Times, of course, had changed and clients were few. They were still waiting for war-time prices to come down. If 'homes were to be built fit for heroes to live in', as the slogan had it, then Mackintosh rightly thought – and so did Margaret – that he should have his slice of the action. Unfortunately, it took a heroic kind of client to fit the Mackintosh bill and it would seem that the Davidsons, the Cranstons and the Blackies were not to be found within commissioning distance of the Blue Cockatoo. In any case, stylistically, architecture's European axis had moved from Vienna to Paris, leaving Mackintosh stranded on the peak he had reached with the Secessionists at the turn of the century. Even in Germany, the Bauhaus had been founded and, together with Dr Behrens, Gropius, van der Rohe and Le Corbusier were now the coming names. Mackintosh was already yesterday's man to many but he had foreseen in his own work the tomorrow that was the evolved Functionalist design of the day, but his first signpost towards the modern was now more than 20 years old and nobody noticed it now in the Twenties.

Allan Ure, a respected figure in the Mackintosh world of recent times, remembered that Hugh Crauford, instructor in painting at Glasgow School of Art after the First World War was, with colleague Somerville Shanks, the only one to uphold the Mackintosh name in Glasgow at the time. Ure said that Crauford once asked a student about Mackintosh. The student looked blank – 'Who?' he asked.

Some small work did trickle his way. He did some interior renovation for Miss Florence Brooks in Burgess Hill and the German connection resumed when EO Hoppé, the celebrated photographer, asked him to do restoration work on his house, Little Hedgecourt at East Grinstead in Sussex. Hoppé could only afford to do half of what Mackintosh advised for the small house, but he was still surprised and pleased with the way Mackintosh could 'paint space' by virtue of design ingenuity and make it look larger without adding an inch to the construction. This was something Mackintosh had learned at the Derngate: how a room looks is how a room is.

Their financial position continued to decline and, this time, Margaret took decisive action. Now it was she who wrote to William Davidson and she came directly to the point – would he like to buy 6 Florentine Terrace, and if so would he remit the market value to her account as soon as was convenient? This approach showed her trust in her own commercial acumen as well as his proved friendship. Her timing could not have been better. William Davidson had been meaning to sell Windyhill in any case as he found the commuting more and more tiring, so he agreed to buy Florentine Terrace, with contents, for a nice round sum and move into it himself. That decided, everyone was happy.

Margaret gave a very special tea for close friends like Fergus and Meg, and the Schwabes and Hoppe. On this occasion, Toshie dressed in his black cape played the butler with all the dignity of a cardinal in a deerstalker hat. Hoppé said he must take a photograph. Hoppe took several portrait photographs of Mackintosh in this garb. This was the first likeness captured by the lens since the famous Annan portrait of the artist as a young man, but it is a very different face we see now. Of course a quarter of a century has passed and the face has filled out and the hair has turned grey but the eyes are in shadow. What was Hoppe trying to show – *la misère de l'artiste?* Or that a great artist/architect had lost his vision – that he could no longer see? Did he know, I wonder, the story of Sinan, the Architect?

> Sinan, the Architect of Agra, built a city for Babar ... When it was completed it was a City for Tomorrow, a city that was everywhere but nowhere. The omnipotent ruler called for the prophetic architect to reward the marvel of his performance. And to ensure that nothing so splendid should happen again, he condemned the architect to the immediate loss of both eyes.[7]

CHAPTER ELEVEN

The Last Fling

1920–1923

The craftsman of the future must be an artist not what they too often are just now, artistic failures.

CRM

THE PRESENT ALICE, Lady Barnes, is the widow of Sir Henry Jefferson Barnes CBE, and the daughter of the late Professor Randolph Schwabe of the Slade School of Art in London. She talked to Alistair Moffat in 1986 of her early Mackintosh memories at the Blue Cockatoo when she was a small child. The following comments are extracted from this conversation:

All the people of that period were there and they all ... went and had lunch. I was looked after by the lot of them and mostly by the Mackintoshes. When they were there I used to sit at their table. In the evening, I recall them very clearly. The little restaurant was lit by candles and the Mackintoshes sat at the back in a nook. Margaret was a very striking person ... she always stood out ... because of her lovely hair. [She] made her own clothes, luminous, lovely, clothes, beautiful colours ... She did most of the talking and Toshie smiled but he didn't say much. They were wonderfully good with me ... We went twice together to Worth Matravers ... I was seven then ... We stayed in a small cottage ... I remember going up and down the hill with Toshie, collecting flowers for him ... I was always worried he would fall because of his bad foot ... I collected the flowers so that he could paint them ...[1]

Mary Newbery Sturrock continues:

> [We] also stayed [with them] at Worth Matravers and
> Mackintosh did beautiful watercolours of that stepped hill
> there – a very pretty place, and of course he was doing flow-
> ers ... he'd a great pile of them ...[2]

Many of these flower studies did not sell in his lifetime and only
came to light at the Memorial Exhibition of 1933 in Glasgow and
two of Worth Matravers' paintings, *The Downs* and *The Village*
went for twenty pounds each, a fair price for watercolours then.
This output was the result of several very happy holidays spent
with the Schwabes at the Newbery home, Corfe Castle, in Dorset.
It can be seen by these works that Mackintosh was improving rap-
idly as a painter but he still thought of himself primarily as an
architect, and back in Chelsea he had at least to make a show of
being willing to work at it. His office diary for this time shows
that he was as busy on speculative architectural schemes as ever he
was in his halcyon Honeyman days. He had written to William
Davidson as early as 1919 telling him that he had 'a lot of schemes
in hand'. This was for a series of three studios in an area within
sight of his own door in Glebe Place. Mackintosh must have
thought that his ship had come in, or at least the tide had turned.
It was only a matter of getting this particular fleet of three little
ships into harbour. The problem was tying them up.

The first client was Harold Squire, an artist friend from the
Cockatoo circle. In January 1920, he came to Mackintosh asking
him to design a studio for him. What wasn't mentioned was
that his sister, Mrs Evelyn Claude, who lived at the Hyde Park
Hotel, was to foot the bill. This made for an uneasy relationship with the architect. Not that this was anything new for the
architect but it caused the client to be tentative and uncertain. He
was certainly no Bassett-Lowke. Mrs Claude's reluctance to pay
for the first scheme suggested led to a rethink, and then another,
and another, until the job slid down the economic chute and hit
basic requirement.

The studio was eventually built in 1921 – the only one to be so – but having costs cut to such an extent, it ended up being a very poor single-story cousin to its original self. Then, because of all the alterations to the first plan, which included a comprehensive heating system, the finished space was difficult to heat, and then to compound its miseries it was said to be haunted. Tom Howarth explains:

> It seems that the site was originally part of a large garden of a curious house owned by a Dr Phene – whom the locals regarded with some suspicion. It was rumoured that he indulged in mystic rites of a most unpleasant kind ... When building work started, the studio site was found to be littered with the remains of an old church and numerous pieces of carved stone, presumably from an altar, were unearthed. And directly under the site for the studio were the remains of a horse ... On making tactful enquiries [of the servants] Mr Squire was told they had seen the spectre of a man on horseback – and they promptly gave notice ... Mr Squire himself saw the apparition in broad daylight and when he had the case investigated by a medium, she too saw the horse – and explained that [it] had once saved Dr Phene's life ...[3]

Professor Schwabe confirmed this story and also that Harold Squire had difficulty in keeping live-in staff. When Dr Howarth checked with Harold Squire in 1946 about the studio, he received the following reply that, ghosts or not, 'The studio had a magnificence which no other in London possessed.' And yet, only three years later, Squire, was writing to Howarth about Mackintosh himself: 'He was an intelligent man but I fancy he drank too much which accounted for his strange manner at times.' This has all the flavour of the gin bottle calling the whisky bottle drunk.

Squire found the studio too expensive to keep up and sold it after only two years. It lay unoccupied for a long time afterwards and its sad interior showed its neglect. On examination after the war, Howarth found that not one trace of the original Mackintosh had survived all the 'improvements', yet its proportions and sense of space hinted that it still was haunted, not by a horse, but by the golden prodigy of a Scottish architect, who was held by some to have had feet of clay – one of them twisted. The premises spent the war years as an emergency ARP store, and by some quirk, escaped the bombs that rained all around it.

In February 1920, Mackintosh did two more studio designs, one for painter, Arthur Cadigan Blunt, who specialised in painting glass and lived at number 48 Glebe Place and the other for sculptor, Francis Derwent Wood, who was at number 50. These men were friends and neighbours in the literal sense but they were also professional artists with specific professional needs in their domestic arrangements and Mackintosh met these with aplomb. Nearly a hundred drawings were found to have emated from this period so he wasn't at all idle. In April, he was approached by Randolph Schwabe who introduced him to a lady from Chile, Anita Berry, who wanted him to design studio premises for her Arts League of Service which she ran from a shop in John Street, Adelphi. The idea was to build a block of low-rental studio flats in Chelsea on a site of the old Cheyne House on Cheyne Row and adjacent to Harold Squire's studio.

The Arts League of Service was a public venture which tried to assist artists of all kinds to obtain working space on a co-operative basis with some degree of funding through subscription. Mackintosh was all for such an enterprise and he obliged Miss Berry with a scheme that fitted in well with the fashionable Ashbee houses on Cheyne Walk. Despite this environmental acknowledgement the scheme hit a snag – planning consent. The ground landlords were the Glebe of Chelsea, with their office at Cheyne House, and they had appointed a surveyor, Mr WE Clifton, to safeguard their interests. Mr Clifton had the final say in whether permission to build would be granted. He had his own views on architecture as he made plain to Mackintosh when he called – on appointment – at Cheyne House to discuss the situation.

Mr Clifton made his reservations clear from the start when he insisted that his superiors looked for 'more architectural considerations'. By that, he meant more ornamentation. Without it, in his view (as a chartered surveyor), it wasn't architecture – or at least, architecture enough. Mackintosh was told bluntly that the whole thing was too flat, too dull. What was needed were a few swags here and there, a pediment or two – something to break up the plain surfaces. Bear in mind this was being told to a master architect by a minor official. And a Londoner at that, who couldn't have been more patronising to someone just down from Scotland, as he believed Mackintosh to be. He probably thought they had snow all the year round up there and, consequently, wouldn't appreciate London requirements. Mackintosh was smugly informed by this nonentity that there were too many problems with his scheme, which he considered too modern for today's taste and, consequently, he could not see his way to recommend the plans to the Board.

Toshie had heard it all before from officials who always found it easier to say 'no' to anything, because a 'yes' would involve commitment – and action. Anyway, what would this little man behind his desk know about spatial organisation, or the congregation of mass, the flow of line, the need for rhythm in the whole and the style that sings through any building when, inside and out, it's RIGHT. All Mackintosh knew was that his job was worth too much time, and effort and worry to waste it on yet another petty mandarin. Of course his scheme was modern – because he (Mackintosh) was modern but it was certainly architecture, and of the highest order. However, he could not make Mr Clifton see this, and the plans were refused. As it happened, the plans were later passed by another assessor in December of that same year but by that time, the money, and the enthusiasm for the League of Arts, had run out, and the whole project was shelved indefinitely. Yet another Mackintosh 'castle' disappeared into the air.

Mackintosh shrugged off the disappointment and found solace in the developing friendship with JD Fergusson and Margaret Morris. The Mackintoshes regularly attended the theatre club which Meg ran for her friends, and their friends, and Toshie and Margaret even assisted in the productions which were mounted there, Toshie with the painting of scenery and Margaret in the making of costumes. They proved very popular as a couple with their new company and Mackintosh was able to put his architectural problems behind him for a time.

Meg and Mackintosh got on famously and when she asked him to design a theatre for her in Flood Street, he complied with a quick design which, frankly, does not bear too close an inspection, but it might have been worked on further had the project taken off. Once again money was the bugbear. What is strange is that one of Meg's greatest friends and admirers was George Davison, a remarkable capitalist with communist sympathies. He had built up the Kodak photography business in England and was worth a fortune, which he now wanted to spend in 'good works'. Why couldn't the Arts League have approached him for their studios or Meg for her theatre? After all, she knew him well. He had come to Meg's summer school in Devon and she and Fergus often stayed with him in his mansion in Holland Park, but she never asked him. Pity. He might have been a patron for Mackintosh. What is odd, in terms of patronage, is that he had his Mr Davidson in Glasgow and might, with Meg's help, have found the same friend, in Mr Davison in London – but it was not to be.

Meg Morris's original theatre club, which she called the Plough, grew out of her dancing classes and from there it developed into a general arts club with discussions, dancing, of course and musical recitals. The premises consisted of one floor of a building, 100 feet long with a stone staircase at either end and a raised performance space in the middle, very like the original Traverse Theatre in St James Court, Edinburgh. The club met on 7th, 14th and 21st of each month and the Mackintoshes were there most evenings. Meg had made them both honorary members. Fergus was delighted to see so much of them again. He had known of them and Jessie King in the very early days and he never lost his deep respect for Toshie's work as an architect and designer. He got Mackintosh to design the sets for a Maeterlinck play which was put on and he did the lighting. With Margaret on wardrobe, it was a formidable backstage crew. Some of the young actresses given their first chance here were the Baddeley Sisters, Angela and Hermione and Elsa Lanchester who was later to go to Hollywood and marry Charles Laughton.

Slowly this professionally disappointing year of 1921 grew to a close, but the Fates weren't finished with the Mackintoshes yet. While preparing for the Christmas festivities at the Plough, they received a letter from Charles Macdonald telling them that Frances had died on December 12 at Gibson Street 'of a cerebral haemorrhage'. Margaret left for Glasgow at once. She found the household devastated. Bertie McNair had been shocked into immediate sobriety and had gone off with his son Sylvan to a sister in Linlithgow. Before going, however, in one towering day of grief and rage, he had burned or destroyed nearly everything that Frances and he had painted or worked on over the years, including material from their only twin exhibition at the Baillie Gallery in London. He had now given up on art in all its shapes and forms. The price it had asked of their lives had been too much. He had lost that part of his life he had treasured most and when the Macdonalds arranged for Sylvan, now of age, to emigrate to South Africa, he made no attempt to stop him. The little Biblical threesome that had fled out of England on a tricycle instead of a donkey was no more and Bertie went to run a garage in Linlithgow. During the Second World War he moved to another sister's in Argyll and after it to an old folks' home in Innellan in the Borders, where he was to die, quite forgotten, in 1945. It was a sad end to a weak but good man – and a fine artist.

For Margaret in 1921, the worst thing to bear was the suspicion held by some in Glasgow that Frances had taken her own life – that she had died after a fall and not through a sudden brainstorm. The family closed ranks around the incident and not a word was said. The only obvious reaction was that Mrs Frances Macdonald, her mother, took to her bed, and seemed to turn her head to the wall. The practical Margaret dealt with everything expected of her, and she and her brother attended to the appropriate matters, but the truth was her heart was broken. Her little sister had been the only daughter she had never had. She had poured all her latent maternal instincts into protecting Frances from McNair, and she couldn't understand the deep love that was between them when it only seemed to bring misery and pain to both.

Friends thought it had been the dreadful time Frances had in delivering Sylvan in Liverpool that had much to do with Margaret's decision to stay childless. She had seen for herself what Frances went through. Now, the delightful, mischievous, impish, laughing talented Frances of Dunure's 'roaring camps' was gone and Mrs Charles Rennie Mackintosh of Chelsea was bereft. It was then that she too made her decision – she would never paint again. She owed that to Frances at least. And she didn't.

She returned to London and dragged herself through 1922. Toshie tried to comfort her but it was now her turn to be withdrawn. Understandingly, he waited for her to come back to him and, together, they went through the motions of living. All their friends tried to help, the Newberys, the Schwabes, Fergus and Meg, and between them all the Mackintoshes got through their days. They went less to the Blue Cockatoo, although they had no real provision for cooking at their linked studios. Nevertheless, they turned them into a kind of flat and pulled their studios and their mutual life around them like a comfort blanket.

Significantly, Mackintosh painted a watercolour at this time, *Palm Grove Shadows*, which may well have typified their mood. They were in their own shadow but there was light outside somewhere. Otherwise, one could not have shadows. They must make their way towards that light. Painting, once his hobby, was to do that – but not yet. The 'straight-forward, frank work' much thought of by Eddie Walton and other artists at Walberswick, had given way to a freer style that promised even better results as reaction to exhibitions at Chicago and Detroit had shown. He was getting better all the time.

For instance, he painted a very rare interior study, *Yellow Tulips*, which had the inside of their Chelsea studio as a backdrop, a backdrop so meticulously painted that is almost half the picture. Another work was the basis of a Christmas card sent to the Bassett-Lowkes. It was another water colour called simply *Ships* and it was perhaps an augury for travel. They had never been out of the country since their heady days in Vienna and Turin but it had been another world then and he had made much of the fact that all expenses for such trips had been paid by their hosts. No such offers came now, but they knew that Eddie Taylor and his wife, Jessie King, friends from student days now lived in Paris. Eddie had given up design in favour of painting full-time. Mackintosh could do the same – but he needed money to get established, and somewhere cheap to live while he converted himself from architect to painter.

Matters were decided for him when, at an architectural exhibition held in December 1922 by the RIBA, Mackintosh submitted a collage of Chelsea studio drawings instead of plans and photographs of his great Glasgow work, particularly the Art School. Considering the modernity of the latter, it is all the more ironic that HR Goodhart-Rendel in the *Architectural Review* called his work, as seen in the studio drawings, 'curiously old-fashioned'. Toshie had missed the bus again, and another wasn't due for a long time yet. It was at this time he told Fergusson, 'I'll never practice architecture again.' And he didn't.

I feel we should pause here – like one does at that moment in Schubert's *Unfinished Symphony* when the conductor puts down the baton. It is a gesture to acknowledge that a master has passed. Life went on of course, as it invariably does, and there were more flower paintings: *The Grey Iris*, *Pinks* etc. He still played about with book covers for the ever-helpful Blackie but his heart wasn't in it and it showed. The novels of GA Henty, however popular, did not bring out the best in him. One of their friends meeting both of them in the street one day, asked politely how things were going. Toshie made some kind of stock reply to the effect that they would have to wait and see – meantime, they would have to trust in Providence. 'And I am Providence,' replied Margaret, taking his arm and wheeling him away.

In January of 1923, at the 48th Exhibition of Decorative Arts, his *Landscape Panel* was not even hung. It was the last straw. London had failed him – or he had failed London. He knew he didn't 'belong' – he belonged to Glasgow but that was too far away now. It was Fergusson, 'dear Fergie' as Mackintosh insisted on calling him, who suggested a solution. Theirs was a mutal admiration society from the beginning and now Fergusson told them bluntly that what they both needed was a good holiday. They needed to get away from London for a bit. But where? It was Meg who suggested France. She and Fergus had been so happy there. She said they could rent out their studios and they could live on that while Toshie painted his heart out in the lovely light. A shilling went as far in Paris as a pound did in London. It was a tempting thought – but how to get to France – and where would they go? Toshie thought they could look up the Taylors in Paris or Patrick Geddes and Anna in Montpelier. Whichever way, it would cost money and her present investments and property rents could only just keep them in Chelsea. Mackintosh had no money at all.

It was then that Providence did intervene – and it was through Margaret, of course. Another letter came from Glasgow telling her that her mother had died. That was sad, of course, but it was expected. She had been failing since Frances died. What was not expected was the next letter from Charles Macdonald enclosing a sizeable cheque which was Margaret's part of her mother's estate. That decided her. She now had the fare to France for both of them and enough funds to let them get started. Arrangements were put in hand at once.

Half the Blue Cockatoo's clientelle had lived in France at some time or other so they took advice from all sides, but mainly from Fergus and Meg. They advised the South of France. The light was better and the rents were cheaper. They could live there on ten pounds a month. Fergus also said that it was better to keep to the Spanish side rather than the Italian as it was so crowded now around Nice since Matisse moved there. However, there were lots of lovely little spots where Fergusson had also worked near Per-pignan – Colioure or Port Vendres for instance; but he suggested it would be best to make up their minds when they got there. They decided that was what they would do.

There was very little packing to do. Such furniture as they had in the studio they would leave in the care of the tenants who would come in. They weren't sure how long they would be away. It was, as Fergus had said, to be a long holiday and they would come back to London refreshed and ready to do battle again. But they had said that when they set out for Walberswick before the war. They had always intended to return to Glasgow when Mackintosh was 'refreshed and ready' but somehow, they never did. Things just kept them going and almost a decade in Chelsea was the result. Would the same happen in France? If it did, would it really matter? Where they lived was really of little consequence, it was *how* they lived, that was the question. And they would not know the answer to that until they got there.

It was at this time that Allan Ure visited them again. He had called on them before, in 1921, when he was living at Kensington Gate, off the Bayswater Road, and working at Sir John James Burnet's London office as a draughtsman. He didn't like the work there. He didn't like Sir John much either, so when he heard that the famous Charles Rennie Mackintosh had set up in Chelsea, he decided to go and see him and find out if there was any chance of working with him. He had always admired his work in Glasgow and remembered that as a wee boy, around 1903, he had been taken by his uncle to see the funny house they were building at the top of the hill in Helensburgh. His uncle, like most of the locals, had been horrified by what they saw rising up before them but little Allan liked it. It was a regular Sunday afternoon walk for everybody just to go up and see it.

After the First War, when he was student in Glasgow, he had kept up his interest in the architect but nobody wanted to know then and the buildings, even the Art School, were beginning to look what he called 'untidy' here and there. He didn't know what had happened to Mackintosh himself until he came to London and heard that he was somewhere in Chelsea – and not doing all that well. That's when Allan decided to go and see him, and just ask him straight out – 'Any chance of a job?'

It was a girl who answered the door, he remembered, a kind of sulky young girl, English, but then Margaret came in and she looked lovely. That hair. What a colour – Titian, he thought. He reminded him immediately of Mrs Patrick Campbell. (Mr Ure had two nieces who were famous actresses in their time, Gudrun Ure and Mary Ure, so he knew his theatre.) Margaret brought him through to the other room where Mackintosh was sitting. She was talking all the time, he couldn't remember what about, and Mackintosh just sat there saying nothing, but nodding and smiling now and again. He wasn't rude or anything, just silent. Allan said he had known that Mackintosh could be withdrawn. He heard that from the young draughtsman in the Glasgow office. 'He had his days,' they had told him. All the same, sitting in that Chelsea studio nearly ten years later, young Ure couldn't keep his eyes off him – just sitting there. He knew he was looking at somebody *important*. That was the word he used.

The greatest architect Scotland had ever produced – just sitting there. The girl brought in tea on a tray and some biscuits but Mackintosh didn't take anything. Margaret told him that Mr Mackintosh wasn't taking anybody on just now and he was doing his own drawings. Allan noticed some of the drawings lying on a table – these were probably the studios. They looked good, even though it was only a squinty glance he had at them. The Mackintosh penmanship was always superb. 'That's what used to annoy Henderson in the Keppie office', Allan told me, laughing. 'The presentation was always first-class even though he might take a drink in the forenoon. John Keppie could take a good drink too – but never in the forenoon. That was maybe the difference.'

It was two years before Allan Ure saw the Mackintoshes again. Now he had come to tell them he was still with Burnet but had thoughts about going back to Glasgow. They didn't seem very interested and he had the feeling he was in the way, although Margaret was much too polite to tell him so. This time, there was no girl – and no tea. Mackintosh was still quiet – but this time, no nodding smiles. He sat at the window smoking a pipe while Margaret went back and forward between what looked like a wardrobe trunk and some boxes. She was putting things in one box and taking them out of another. One box was for rubbish, so Allan said he would take it down to the area for her when he left. He went as soon as he could. Mackintosh turned and gave him a nod and a wee wave. Then he smiled – and it changed his whole face.

Mr Ure told me all this during one of our chats at Windyhill in 1975. He still looked wistful when he talked about that last visit. There wasn't a mawkish muscle in Allan Ure, he wasn't at all sentimental, but something must have touched him on that day if he remembered it so clearly more than fifty years later. He then showed me one of his treasures – it was a piece of headed paper he had saved from the rubbish bin that day. It was small and neat and simple, announcing:

C. R. MACKINTOSH

F. R. I. B. A. –   -

2 HANS STUDIOS -

43A GLEBE PLACE

CHELSEA   S.W. 3

I found it very moving just to look at it. Allan promised to send me a photocopy 'as soon as he could get to the shops', and it is this I'm looking at now on my computer desk in front of me. A single sheet of paper. All that was left of a glittering career in architecture. I remember saying to Allan that leaving Glasgow must have broken Toshie's heart. His reply was trenchant to say the least. 'There was nothing wrong with his heart,' he snapped. 'The Glasgow establishment sucked away his soul, that's what happened. You can't blame London for ignoring him. He never went halfway to meet them, so they just turned their backs. Look at Sir John and the success he had. That's because he knew what they wanted and who to talk to away from the drawing board. Mackintosh was always a loner. That's where he made his mistake. I've never met anyone in the architectural line', he went on, 'who was so much talked about and so little used.' Allan had the strong impression that Mackintosh was glad to be shot of the whole thing although he maintained his FRIBA to the end and his name appeared as usual in the 1926 Edition of *Who's Who in Architecture*.

Allan Ure did go back to Glasgow after the Second World War, staying near the Botanic Gardens until he was able, eventually, to buy Windyhill. He was the third owner, and in taking it over he felt he was paying Mackintosh back for stealing that sheet of headed paper in 1923. I had one little regret myself. I was preparing to play Mackintosh on the stage in the dramatised lecture at that time and was desperate to know how Mackintosh sounded – did he have a Glasgow accent, for instance, but, on both occasions he had called, CRM never said anything.

'Not a bloody word,' said Allan.

There were many in Chelsea who were sad to see the Mackintosh couple leave. Not least was Mrs Hettie Swaisland from the Blue Cockatoo. She had seen so many coming and going in the artistic world – yet she vividly remembered the Mackintoshes and their regular table in the nook:

> He was a customer at the <u>Blue Cockatoo</u> for nine years. He and his wife always had the same table and they would be very annoyed if they were unable to have it. Mr Mackintosh was a very distinguished-looking gentleman in spite of his club foot and defective eye. He was the soul of Chelsea. He and Mrs Mackintosh gave quite an air to the shop and they were greatly missed when they left.[5]

CHAPTER TWELVE

Painting a Paradise

1923–1927

I am struggling to paint in watercolours – soon I shall start
in oils – but I find I have a great lot to learn, or unlearn. I
seem to know far too much and this knowledge obscures
the really significant facts – but I am getting on.

CRM

THEIR FIRST STOP in France was Collioure, as recommended by
Fergusson. It is a town which seems totally given over to artists as
any casual walk around it would show. Throughout the tight little
cobbled streets winding up from the harbour, one can see at every
second doorway a print fixed to the wall or tied to the railings,
which is as likely to be a Corot or a Derain or a Matisse, set
directly against the very house or view represented in the painting.
It is a nice idea, but the effect was to make one wonder which was
the more real – the subject or the subject painted? It appeared to
be in direct ratio to the skill of the painter. This is obviously a
painter's world where texture, light, colour and weather all con-
spire to make it ideal for the artist – except that, in the week I
visited, it snowed.

Which was why I was sitting in the bar of the Hotel de Templiers admiring the walls that were thick with canvases. Apparently,
the old-time painters used to exchange their paintings for drink
here, but I saw nothing by Mackintosh. Yet we know from the
account given by M Rene Pous, the patron, to Alistair Moffat in
1986, that he did visit from time to time, sometimes with Margaret – 'She had red hair I remember,' said M Pous. He had

opened the Hotel des Templiers in 1922, just before the Mackintoshes arrived, and it was he who 'discovered Mackintosh was an
architect'. He was *l'architecte devient peintre*, as the locals put it.
There was a rumour that Toshie had designed a house in Collioure
but there was no trace of his style anywhere. It certainly would
have stood out in that old, walled town. Monsieur Pous went on –
'I thought his paintings were very good – he knew his craft very
well. All architects, nearly all of them, know how to draw which is
a great help to them when they turn to painting ... I remember
[his] friend, M Ihlee. He was a painter who stayed a long time at
Collioure ...'[1]

Rudolph Ihlee, or Ely as Toshie called him, had known the
Mackintoshes at Chelsea and was the owner of one of the few
motorcars then in Collioure. He used to pick up Toshie from his
hotel and drive him around the countryside. It is odd to think of
Mackintosh, that essential Victorian, in a car, but that was often
how he was taken to the Templiers, which was then little more
than a small café, for coffee and cognac and talk of painting. Pous
mentions conversations with Mackintosh but they must have
been in English for Toshie had little or no French. Ihlee had,
because he had painted in the area since 1923 and he was to marry
a French wife.

After Collioure, the Mackintoshes went up to Amelie-les-
Bains, a mountain spa, for the summer, and then, quite
unexpectedly, they returned to London – very briefly. Margaret
why explained why in a letter to Jessie Newbery:

> We went back to London in September – intending to stay
> perhaps till January, but, strange to say, the studios this year
> let almost at once – and each tenant wanted to get in at once
> – so we had a very short stay in Chelsea ... So here we are
> back in our beloved Pyrenees ... We got here on November
> 22 ... back to this lovely, rose-coloured land, back again to
> its warmth and sun ...[2]

This time, they came back to Port Vendres – which was to serve as
their base camp throughout their time in France. Port Vendres is

in the Pyrenees-Orientales, right on the Spanish border, and it is known that the Mackintoshes were in Spain, and also in Italy, at some brief points during this Southern phase as their letters show. They moved around a lot, principally by train. No wonder Bassett-Lowke couldn't find him. They would generally winter in Port Vendres and travel about by train, following the weather, as it were, through the rest of the year. Their habit was to go high to Mont Louis for the 'fine air' in the summer and come down to the coast again in the winter. It is Port Vendres, however, and its Hotel du Commerce on the Quai de la Ville (now called Quai Pierre Forgas) that was the nearest thing they had to a home in the next four years. This was despite the foul smell that pervaded the frontage. Barrels of anchovies were stacked on the quay at most times and they could get very high, but Port Vendres was a working port and it did not mind who knew it. That would not worry a Clydesider like Mackintosh and he revelled in its colourful, commercial activity.

The most one can say of the Hotel du Commerce is that the Ritz it is not. Homely would be the word that comes to mind and the best description would be 'accommodating', and that is exactly what the Mackintoshes needed in 1923. The lady-caretaker showed me round. I had the feeling that not much had changed in 80 years. It was eerie to think that Toshie and Margaret had mounted these same wooden stairs and walked along the same narrow corridor to Room 19 on the first floor, the room that was his. Hers was directly opposite. Margaret liked her own space. After a look at the dining room, and their corner table, with its two chairs, where he had sat so often alone, the lady, who had no English, handed me a one-page *Petite Biographie* of 'Monsieur Rene' as she kept calling Mackintosh. She told me about the American film crew that had taken over Room 19 to make a film about it. She told me, too, about all the people who come who are writing about Mackintosh. I had to admit that I was in that category, and having exhausted my little store of French, I left to continue my search for 'Monsieur Rene'.

Walking round by the harbour, taking the Route de la Jetée, and going through two tunnels, I arrived by way of the Chemin du Mole at Fort Mailly. It was blowing hard, and climbing up through the gorse, it was hard to believe that he ever held a paint brush to canvas in such a wind. But he had done, and to stunning effect, as the 44 pictures he painted in his four French years, more than half of them here in Port Vendres, well testify. Seeing the actual sites of many of these works, I marvelled all the more at the strides Mackintosh had made as a painter since Walberswick – where, incidentally, his output was only slightly less. The only difference was it took him four times as long to paint almost the same number of pictures, but he was now into 'lanscapes', as he called them, and it became clearer as time went by that he was no so much renouncing architecture as embracing painting.

It may only have been the reaction to the disappointing Chelsea period, but the time spent in the South of France was to prove the happiest of his life and almost the most fulfilling artistically. The whole French move was less a retreat than an advance on a new front. If he were now a painter then he would paint his landscapes in an architectonic style. These were pictures, as Mary Sturrock said, that you could build. He could never entirely forget his training or totally redefine his architectural technique. This is what he meant by 'knowing too much'. He was still the perspectivist of his peak years, with the same delight in line, but in deserting the drawing board for the canvas, he had come back to himself, to his beginnings. If he had made himself in Scotland, and lost himself in England, then he found himself again in France.

His exile may have denied him full recognition as an architect, but it gave him a whole new perspective as a painter. This was a born-again Mackintosh. He was ecstatic in his new body of work – and it showed. As Margaret wrote to Jessie Newbery:

Toshie is as happy as a sandboy – tremendously interested in his painting, and, of course, doing some remarkable work. I hope he will have a show sometime – but that remains to be seen about – when he has got enough work

together. In the meantime, he is absorbed in this landscape
... from 9.30 till 3 in brilliant sunshine...We live, the two of
us, for 8 shillings a day, wine included ...[3]

His last work shown in London had been the Walberswick painting – *Venetian Palace, Blackshore-on-the-Blyth*, dating from
1914, which was exhibited at the Royal Academy in 1923. Now,
from this time on, under a new light, en France, he created works
like *Palalda* and *Boultenere* where one can see that the brush is
still held in the architect's hand. Before long, however, he was
capable of masterpieces like *La Rue du Soliel, Port Vendres* (1926)
and *The Rocks* (1927). And all done with a few brushes and a
watercolour set that any child would own. What a pity he never
did get on to oils.

If he had appeared to have forgotten architecture, it had not
forgotten him. Charles Marriott, architectural critic of *The Times*,
wrote an article, later reproduced in a book, *Modern English
Architecture*, in which he stated, under the first published photograph of the completed Glasgow School of Art, 'It is important
because of the great influence of Mr Mackintosh's work on the
Continent – in Germany, Holland and Sweden. It is hardly too
much to say that the whole modernist movement in European architecture derives from him.' It was *nearly* too much to say, but
Marriott's comments were sweeping enough to make their effect felt
in British architectural circles and ensure that an exiled, Glasgow
artist-designer, still had a place in the brick-and-mortar world.

He, for his part, wanted nothing to do with architecture. When
Christian Barman, editor of the *Architect's Journal,* was later to
ask him to write about contemporary English architecture, Mackintosh replied:

I cannot write about present-day architecture in England,
because it does not exist – nor will there be any daylight
until it is made impossible for pompous bounders, like a
well-known (at least well-advertised) professor at Liverpool
to have any say in architectural education. He is teaching

efficiency – but even then he is a 23rd rater because they already do it better in America.[4]

This was a rare good comment on America. He liked nothing about America. He also disliked HG Wells, and most journalists, but the only real enemy he ever made in his life, and the one person he actively despised, was Professor Charles Herbert Reilly, who had been Roscoe Professor of Architecture at Liverpool since 1904, which was around the time of Bertie McNair's difficulties there and not long after the disappointment of his own Liverpool Cathedral:

> I have waited twenty years to get one back at Reilly – and during twenty years I have not said a word about him to any outsider. Now I can get a few more nails in his nasty, stinking, cheap coffin – I am not vindictive – far from it – you know how much I want to paint well – but I think I have one stronger passion and that is to make Reilly a discredited outsider before I am finished with him. When I get him on the run I will drive him like a fiend until he is a raving lunatic. Sweet idea? But true. I know where to get the nails and by God if I drive, I will drive them home.[5]

One must remember that, even if the Mackintosh fires were banked, the flame was not quite out. The unexpected rages of his boyhood were still latent in the man as witness his anger at Keppie, the fight with the soldiers at Walberswick and the row with the unfortunate Mr Clifton in Chelsea – and now this letter. It is not known how Reilly reacted to this kind of attack, if he did know about it, but he lived until 1948, long enough to see Mackintosh seemingly discredited. However, much more hurtful to Toshie, in that same year of 1924, was the news that the 'Wee Troot' had died. After Bertie McNair, James Salmon Jr, was the closest friend Mackintosh had in Glasgow. While he may not have touched the heights that Toshie did, Salmon nevertheless did good work in a proto-Mackintosh, Art Nouveau style that acknowledged their common aims in design and symbolised their friendship. Now another architectural thread had been broken.

In February 1925, the pair were again at Ille-sur-la-Tet, as Toshie called it, and he was writing to Fergusson following the latter's successful show at the Leicester Galleries. He writes here about Fergusson's 'beautiful Scottish pictures' and Walter Sickert's review of them in the *Observer* of 11 January, which had been sent to them in France:

> It is quite understandable that Sickert should appreciate them so much and I do hope that at last the buying public have come to realise their true artistic value. I have not forgotten the impression they had on me when we saw them at Chelsea. I still have such a vivid, mental picture of them that I can pass them in review one by one making a sort of subconscious 'peep-show' and see them quite clearly just as you showed them to us. This is a most valuable gift I possess as I can see your pictures whenever I like and for as long as I like ...

This is a letter more typical of the man, warm, generous and, quite unselfishly, one artist to another. He always responded well to good work wherever he saw it. He goes on:

> There is nobody here but ourselves and we are as happy as sandboys.
> I wish you and Meg could come here for 3 or 4 months either to work or rest... The food is good and plentiful, and the people are simple and kind... The eating room is a delightful feature. At the end is a long table the full length of the room at which the workmen sit – usually 8, 10 or 12 splendid fellows sitting here and having a gorgeous feast and discussing the affairs of the world. It always somehow reminds me of 'The Last Supper' only there is no frugality here and the wine flows in a way that would have given life and gaiety to Leonardo's 'popular masterpiece ... We shall be here until the end of May then we go to Mont Louis for 2 months and then back here or perhaps we may go to Montpelier to stay with Professor Pat Geddes for a month or so ...[6]

This letter exemplifies their good spirits and also illustrates their gypsy, whimsical lifestyle. It was little wonder that neither wanted to go back to London. Margaret added a small note with Toshie's letter and enclosed a poem for Meg, who at that time was daringly living with Fergus in Paris – in sin, in some people's eyes, but not in theirs, nor in Margaret's. The poem was by the Jacobean, Thomas Carew:

> Then shall thy circling armes embrace and clip
> My willing body, and thy balmie lip
> Bathe me in juyce of kisses, whose perfume
> Like a religious incense shall consume,
> And send up holy vapours to those powres
> That blesse our loves, and crowne our sportfull houres.
>
> No wedlock bonds unwreathe our twisted loves;
> We seek no midnight Arbor, no darke groves
> To hide our kisses; there, the hated name
> Of husband, wife, lust, modest, chaste, or shame
> Are vaine and empty words, whose very sound
> Was never heard in the Elizean ground.
>
> All things are lawfull there, that may delight
> Nature, or unrestrained appetite;
> Like, and enjoy, to will, to act, is one,
> We only sinne when Love's rites are not done.[7]

Margaret at this time was sixty years of age and her husband only four years younger and although both were obviously still enjoying the 'heat of the sun', they had rented two rooms at the Hotel du Commerce. Was all passion naturally spent? Not according to his letters to her – 'I am tired and lonely and I want *you*'. They are the letters of a lover.

They did go to Montpelier and they did stay with Patrick and Anna Geddes and saw the Scots College Geddes had founded there the year before. Not even the hottest of suns could deter that man's energies. By the same token, the architect-builder in Mackintosh just would not die, whatever he said. Wherever he went, he made a bee-line for the nearest church. He loved pottering around the old graveyards, looking at the stones just as he did when he was a boy around the Glasgow Necropolis, but here he had the extra pleasure in having 'so many interesting little churches lying all around them'. As he wrote to Newbery on 28th December 1925:

> Personally, I have been, what they say, 'struck-dumb' – Elne, Arles-sur-Tech, Prats de Mollo, and many others are surprising stone structures and of course built to hear the spoken word and not to follow the service by the reading of the printed word. The artistic problem of lighting the interior of the church for these two conditions seems to be one of faith or visability. Of course we have the advantage over you of having stayed in the country longer and thus having the chance of seeing some of the more inaccessible and the most delicious small churches such as Montalba, Montbolo, Marian, Jujols, Canavels, Palalda etc, etc. These are all simple stone structures with the most georgeous altarpieces in carved and gilded wood – wood that is not carved but cut showing every mark of the tool and gilded but clothed in gold leaf ... Very Rococco but very beautiful ...[8]

This is surely the voice of a master-craftsman still very much in love with his craft and excited by the material under his hand and the way in which it can be turned into something beautiful. He never lost this excitement nor the eye that could see the truth in honest workmanship. Similarly, he could quickly detect the spurious and the phoney. He added a postscript to this letter, 'P.S. I found Florence just as artificial in a stupid way as I found it 25 years ago when I went as a small lad.' Actually, it was 34 years ago and he was 23. Not that it matters. What is important is that, essentially, he still had all his boyish enthusiasm for the basic aspects of his trade.

And a considerable learning by now. Mary Sturrock remembers how he pointed out to the same Newbery while on holiday with them at Corfe Castle some years before, that the lower stones of a chapel near Scoles were Saxon because of the way they were set, herring-bone fashion, in the lower wall. Newbery was slightly put out for not having noticed this himself. This was the sort of thing that Mackintosh stored away against further use. Not that there was to be any 'further use' unfortunately. Still, the days were warm, bright and filled with painting possibilities. What else could he want? A little more money, perhaps.

Margaret performed wonders on their finances but prices were going up every year – and he still hadn't sold a painting. Although he was to show his landscape of *Collioure* at the 6th International Water Color Exhibition in Chicago, and receive several invitations to come to America, he refused to even think about it. Mackintosh consistently maintained a strong prejudice against America and Americans. This transatlantic antipathy wasn't helped by their meddling with his pipe tobacco:

> I begin to dislike this French tobacco since the Americans undertook its manufacture – formerly it was light and fragrant, now it is sordid and sickening.

He did not know how apt this last word was in this context. Was he already reacting to tobacco – any tobacco? The pipe was rarely out of his mouth, often remaining there, unlit, as he painted. The letter continues:

> I think I dislike everything the American touches commercially – his idea is to work for the millions and dam the individual – our idea is to work for the best kind of individual and the crowd will follow – Dam them – I have to keep the lid of my tin open now to dry the tobacco before I can smoke it ... Dam them – Moving pictures – Architecture – Theatres.[9]

Architecture always gets in there, whatever the topic, and if there is an American connection, it is not linked to any of the known American architects, such as Sullivan or Frank Lloyd Wright. However, the architect engaged to oversee the building of Devonshire House in Piccadilly was an American, Thomas Hastings, from the New York firm of Carriere and Hastings. He was appointed on the advice of Mackintosh's *bête noire*, CH Reilly, who was consultant on the project. That may well be at the nub of the matter.

Other than these petty quibbles, their life at this time was almost serene. They were in a lovely country, among friends, and, he at least, was doing good work. Margaret had no wish to work, but there was no question that they were both healthy, happy and in love – but how long could the idyll last?

During 1926, Sir John Burnet was building Adelaide House in London and Mackintosh was painting Port Vendres green – or rather, trying not to. As he said, it was almost the first tube of paint he opened each day, whatever he was painting, but even with this handicap, he was turning out good work in what may be called his *annus mirabilis ars picturae*. They rolled off his self-determined production line, even if it were with an ever-increasing anxiety as his technique improved. He was trying for something new as much as he ever did with his building. One can only described the paintings as a kind of heightened reality, an abstract naturalism. Rocks were rocks and water was water but seen with his eye they were patterns of light and colour and often his brush could not keep up with what he wanted to achieve. But with each canvas or cardboard attempt he was getting nearer.

If there were indeed 44 completed in the four years from 1923–7, then that works out about one every three weeks as he took time to get going, but each one is not only his postcard from a place, it is a testimony to his will to work. He could not have found it easy, in the final year especially, but he had grit and a good Scottish doggedness, and he just got on with it. To borrow from Mary Sturrock's remark about wishing to have seen his 50th house, I wish I could have seen his hundredth painting. I am convinced it would have put him up there among the big boys in the fine arts class. Certainly, no architect since Leonardo himself has painted better.

But being Mackintosh, there had to be snags. 1927 did not start off well with news of the death of Hermann Muthesius in

Germany. Another link to their golden past snapped. Things could not go long in any direction without some kind of problem arriving, and the next was Margaret's teeth. Whatever the cause, her condition was beyond local care, which meant London attention. She also required electrical treatment for an unspecified ailment, which may have been her heart. And while she was in London, she could deal with their other business affairs. There was the matter of her property in Liverpool, her rents in London and the business of pushing for a showing of her husband's work at the Leicester Galleries. She had also been asked to help in the design of a doll's house for Queen Mary, so there were right royal reasons for her going back, other than the dentist, and only one for Toshie's not – he had no wish to. He hated the thought of London now. All he wanted was his time in the sun with as few interruptions as possible.

As a good husband, however, he also wanted his wife well and happy. It could not have been easy for her latterly, with no real work to do, and relying on Mudie's library books and long walks and letters to pass the hours while he worked. She had still not got over the loss of Frances completely, and now that the honeymoon period with France was over, she was becoming increasingly listless, and not like her old dynamic self at all. While Toshie went from strength to strength, she appeared to stand still.

She needed to get herself going again, so, on a May morning, she left for Paris, *en route* for London and the start of another phase in their life together. He was left at the Hotel du Commerce with the pipe in his mouth and a paintbrush in his hand – which he promptly laid down and took up the pencil to write the first of the 23 letters he was to write to his wife between Thursday 12 May and Saturday 25 June 1927.

For a proper consideration of this correspondence I can only refer the reader to Pamela Robertson's excellent edition produced by the Hunterian Art Gallery at Glasgow University in 2001 under the title *The Chronycle*, being only one of Mackintosh's several misspellings of the word. I was given the chance in 1974 to see the same letters as part of my research into a possible Mackintosh film, which became instead the dramatised theatrical lecture and also a television script. I quote from my own notes made at the time with reference to the Robertson volume for confirmation and additional information. The letters, as now edited in a slim volume, constitute a compact research instrument as well providing fascinating sources but even from my own notes I got a glimpse of Mackintosh as he was in his own time, with all warts visible, and none the worse for it. He begins on 12 May:

My Dear Margaret,

This is a sort of chronacle. I hope you arrived safely in Paris and had a good journey to London ... I dined quite alone and they have the happy idea to give me a full bottle of wine and I have the good and happy idea to drink only about half of it ... I had a good morning's work and the picture of <u>The Rock</u> goes well. Nothing could be more perfect than sitting where I was this morning – only you did not come to meet me at the end of the tunnell – that was a great sadness ... It seems queer to have your room opposite empty – very queer and very lonely ...

13 May

Half-past-four Friday afternoon and no letter no PC from you – I wish I could get some word from you to say you are all right ... My crow is still faithful and comes to see me each day wherever I am – he told me a lot this morning but being ignorant I did not know a word he said ...

You see how I spend my afternoon, as I can't come to tea with you. I sit down and cover sheet after sheet with a lot of rambling notes that may not interest you in the least. My only excuse is that I have painted my little town so nicely that I feel I deserve some relexation and my idea of relexation at the moment is to write to you ...

14 May

Do you like such long screeds or would you prefer a few facts baldly told?

I have just put your tea in the tin box it nearly fills it but not quite – it seems good and has a nice smell

The French working men are amazing. They will argue for ten minutes in the most excited way – instead of giving the fellow one on the jaw. That is a kind of kindly progress

15 May (Sunday)

It has been a perfectly glorious morning – no wind the sea the same as I painted for Fort Mouresque – absolutely flat and bright blue – I only got as far as the Tamaris Trees where I sat on my three-legged stool and tried to do three things – to read – to look about me – and to think. I know I did not read – I may have looked about me – and I know I thought and partcularly about you ...

16 May

Just had my lunch alone with Catherine.

My tongue is swollen – burnt and blistered with this infernal tobacco ... I never found it warm and burning before. What to do I don't know ...

All the house folks and all the staff are much concerned about your ... present well-being in Londown ...

I have to commence my big <u>Rock</u> – perhaps it will come out all right but I seem to work very slowly ...

17 May

The only reason for writing ... is that I miss you and I want you and I look forward to the time when I dont need to write because you'll be here.

18 May

I shall have to sharpen my pencil and write a little closer ... so if I put too much lead pencil on each sheet it may be overweight – but if I keep to light observations and light remarks I and avoid all heavy and deep arguments I may get through all-right ... This paper is all wright but I don't think I could write on both sides ...

19 May

Thursday – One week since you went away and one less till you return ...

20 May

Middle-aged painter and his wife arrived today...She is a nice bright girl but he is rather an acid drop ...

21 May

Ely [Rudolph Ihlee] wishes you could have taken a colour photograph of me to London to let them see how I look.

22 May (Sunday)

I am feeling tired and lonely. I shall go to bed soon hoping for a good morning ...

23 May

Beautiful day but the wind seems to be shrieking – blowing from every direction – I met Ely when I was coming home. He said that they [he and Edgar Hereford] would come and have dinner with me tonight – so that's that – you can't get out of it.

24 May

This morning has been superb – sun and no wind... I have now broken the back of the <u>Rock</u> and it will now do what I want it to do ...

I have been smoking 'Piccaduros' – My tongue is gradually recovering its normal shape & size

25 May

Brilliant sun and no wind so here's for the <u>Rock</u> – not yet finished but getting on ...

I hope you are remembering to keep quiet and dont worry no matter what occurs ... and dont get excited – everything either blows straight or blows away eventually... nothing matters but your health – You must come back at least as well as you went away ...

PS There has been nobody in your room – Rosa keeps the door open so that I always see a bed – a table and a chair that is all?

I have discovered how to spell 'CHRONYCLES' that looks better???

And so it went on for another month of days – with trivia, wise saws, good sense and nonsense, good humour and some wit. There is also evidence of reading but most of all there was concern and warmth for 'My Margaret' from 'Your Toshie'. As shown, for instance, when he comments on the cobwebs gathering on 'her' chair at their table. Which doesn't say much for Rosa, the house-keeper. No trace of her letters to him remains and we know that she did write for at one point he wrote, 'My chronycle beats yours hollow'. I'm sure it did, for here the man Mackintosh is revealed in all his endearing contradictions as he went steadily on, five mis-spelled, unpunctuated pages a day, until the last one on 24 June – or what he thought would be the last.

Their plan was that they should meet up in Perpignan Station and go from there via Villefranche to Mont Louis where she could rest and recuperate. He had written on June 22:

I arrive according to time-table a few minutes before you and I shall meet you on the platform... so if you are first just sit tight, till you see me like a glorious rising sun

> appearing I shall be quite visable among all the pale faces. I must take a day off work tomorrow and settle down to answer all the questions you have put in the last 3 or 4 letters – I have really only two interests You first and my work next and when I get working I get thinking about it and letter writing unless I am doing nothing else seems to me a heavy task ...

All the more creditable then his feat of writing daily throughout her absence, although as he did tell her, all he was trying to say could be summed up in three little words.

On 23 May, he wrote – 'I'm sorry you did not see *The Great God Brown* – but as Schwabe and Birdie enjoyed it that is some compensation.' This was a play by Eugene O'Neil about an architect who would rather have been a painter. A case of *dramatic* art imitating life, perhaps? In the same letter he promised to bring her big sun-hat, carrying it in his hand and he ended: 'Let me know in good time at what hour you reach Perpignon and I shall be there waiting – eagerly.' Then on the 24th – the final epistle:

> Well Margaret good night I am writing at 10 o'clock at night – this will be my last letter to London – I shall add a little more in the morning just to emphasise the three words ... MMYT

Next morning he received a bit of a shock. There was a letter from Margaret asking him to meet her at the Lord Warden Hotel at Dover. He had no idea what had happened to make her change her plans but there was no time to dither. Apparently, a registered letter from Harrods explaining everything had not reached him in Port Vendres. Despite a slight panic about his passport, and last-minute decisions about their luggage (which he sent on to Mont Louis) he made arrangements to arrive in England on the Tuesday. Did he mean to carry her sun hat all the way to Dover?

Margaret was indeed brought back to share 'the fine air of Mont Louis with her life-long lover' – but not for long. Within weeks it would seem, it was not she who was the cause for health concern, but Toshie. The lump in his tongue had hardened and he returned to Port Vendres to see his old friend, the doctor, there. That gentleman immediately saw the need for surgery and advised a quick return to London. So, where Mackintosh had fussed so recently about getting to an invalid wife in Dover, it was now he who was hurried to England, a very sick man indeed.

Whether Margaret had gone ahead to London before him, or was in Paris arranging for the showing of his *Le Fort Mauresque* at the British Artists Exhibition there, is not known, but she did not seem to figure in the immediate arrangements. Madame Isabelle Ihlee, widow of Toshie's other great friend, Ely, remembers that time well. It was in the autumn, and she told Alistair Moffat in 1986:

> When M Mackintosh became ill, my husband told me that he was leaving Collioure to take him to England. I can't remember if it was London or Glasgow he took him too. Mackintosh had something wrong with his throat. I myself think it was a cancer. He could not even speak. My husband said that M Mackintosh was very overcome and that it was a very difficult journey.[10]

It must have been – a sick man, on those trains, in that heat and probably, crowded. It might have been worse. They might have gone in Ely's car. What makes it all the more ironic is that these two travellers had been the merry companions of many a night in Port Vendres and Collioure and together with the third member of the trio, Edgar Hereford, another young English painter in the district, Ely had seen that Toshie was never short of society while Margaret was in London. Dinners, car drives, what Mackintosh called 'Gramaphone Nights', had all helped to pass the leisure hours and a good time was had by all. Toshie remembered especially a time when Ely called at the Hotel du Commerce. It was Wednesday 25 May. He writes:

> I was sitting at 5.30 eating my heart out with depression when Ely arrived down in the dumps – he looked at my <u>Rock</u> and said that's going to be a very fine thing ... I

assured him I was trying to make it a fine thing. After a while he said, by jove Mackintosh you are a marvel you never seem depressed. You're always so cheerful and happy – I told him it was health – but I didn't tell him that I was much more depressed than he was when he arrived – nor that his deepest depression was something equivelant to my not being very well – I keep my deepest depressions to myself he shows them all the time like a young child – and that in a way makes him an object of sympathy and attraction – he came in his car, we had a drink and he departed – But he thinks he will come again because I am a cheerful soul …"

Now, such a short time later, he was not so cheerful while young Ihlee escorted him north on that purgatorial journey to the English Channel, the pain, I am sure, increasing with every kilometre. It can only be hoped that one of them had laudanum or at least a bottle of Scotch. Mackintosh had long beaten his old drinking problem, thanks to painting and the good life in France, but there would have been times during those tortured days and nights on the journey when he needed to block everything out – even painting – even Margaret. In any deep crisis, the individual is finally alone with their God – or their Devil. What else is there? There is a wife. And she was waiting for him – eagerly.

When I left Port Vendres myself, after three full and wonderful days, I couldn't help feel a little guilty somehow about Mackintosh. The first thing I did on the plane to London was to order a large whisky and drink to Charles 'Rene' Mackintosh – a hero in exile – may he never be forgotten.

They want to remember him in Port Vendres. They want to start a summer Mackintosh Festival. They want to stick his paintings on the railings or fix them to a wall at all the various sites just as the Town Council has done with all the old masters up the road at Collioure. This would be fitting because, as he was dying, as we know, Mackintosh had asked Margaret to come back to France and scatter his ashes – 'on the waters of Port Vendres'. She did. So it might very well be that some spirit of 'Monsieur Rene' is still there yet. I hope so, because, for him, it was a place of rare peace and real happiness.

CHAPTER THIRTEEN

A London Epilogue

1927–1928

If I were God, I would design like Mackintosh.

Robert Mallet-Stevens

IF MARGARET WERE GOD, or, on her own assertion, Providence, in all Mackintosh affairs, than her Divine interventions were few and far between in the last months of 1927. Indeed, her movements were rather more ghostly than Godly as she remained uncharacteristically uninvolved in the arrangements that finally saw Mackintosh accepted as a patient at the Westminster Hospital. She may also have been ill herself. She had returned to France half the woman she once was, and Mackintosh's sudden cancer could not have improved her heart condition.

From being co-star in the partnership she virtually left the stage for a time. Once more, it was the Good Samaritan Newbery family who came to the rescue. Margaret may very well have been with them when she wrote the first letter asking Toshie to meet her at Dover, as Corfe Castle is within striking distance of the seaport, but we know that it was Jessie Newbery who met the travellers from the train, and it was she arranged the hospitalisation after a fashionable clinic had confirmed cancer of the tongue.

Since they had rented out both their studios, Mackintosh must have gone first to the room Margaret had rented in Glebe Place or else the Schwabes offered a bed. Once again, it was shown that while the Mackintosh circle may have been small it had an enduring loyalty. Not to mention, a high practicality when required, as these last years were to show. Indeed, so valuable were their friendships to them that the Mackintoshes ought to have included them among their capital assets. When the question of money for hospitalisation and the necessary radium treatment came up, the Mackintoshes were embarrassed by the prospect of this sudden outlay. It was only Jessie Newbery's intervention with the surgeon-in-charge that allowed Mackintosh to be treated. She explained that Mr Mackintosh was one of Scotland's, no, Europe's most distinguished architects, but her trump card was that she had found out that the surgeon's wife came from Paisley. Caledonian pressure was brought to bear and Toshie was admitted as a 'special' patient. 'Why didn't he tell me hadn't any money?' asked the surgeon. 'He's a very proud man – and besides, it wouldn't occur to him,' Jesse told him. One wonders if Mackintosh ever mentioned that his grandfather, Hugh McIntosh, also came from Paisley.

Mary Newbery Sturrock, to whom so much is owed for information about Mackintosh, also recalls that when he was in the ward, Mackintosh helped the students with their case drawings and anatomical illustrations of various conditions. He even drew his own tongue for them – complete with cancerous growth. The students were very grateful and probably had never had better illustrations on their notes. The drawings would have brightened up the surgeon's daily rounds.[1]

All we can be sure of is that Toshie wouldn't have signed them. He hated signing anything, but had lately neglected to sign his paintings being unsure in some cases that they were actually finished. In any case, the signing of any work mattered little. To him, the real signature was in the work itself. That's why Margaret always had to remind him to sign his pictures, if only on the back. Later, she even signed them for him herself – on his specific instructions: 'You can do it in pencil, then wet with cold, clean water.' She did so many times. The only one we know he did sign was *The Rock* – because he told her so in a letter. He had also written, telling her to sell his top hat and tails as he was likely to have little need for them. He was unfortunately right. Pyjamas and dressing gown were to be the order of the day for most of the days he had left.

In early December of 1927, the kindly surgeon removed the lump from Toshie's tongue and ordered complete rest in hospital. Mackintosh had no option but to comply but as he slowly recovered he found time hanging heavily around his bedside. He did write the occasional letter and one survives to Jessie Newbery, whom he still referred to by her maiden name of Rowat. He writes:

Dear Jessie R,

As Margaret is coming to see you I am taking the opportunity to write a short note and tell you that as far as I can gather from the small scraps of news that the doctors grudgingly let fall, I am making quite good progress. I had a good sleep last night and that is an event so unusual that it stands out as ... something quite out of the ordinary. I don't know when they will be finished with me here but I must be getting better because I am now longing to be out – the days are passing very tediously. Thank you very much for the little garden posy – it lasted quite a time and looked nice and cheerie on my locker. Love to you both – Yours always, Toshie.[2]

As his 'Chronycles' of the year before showed, Mackintosh couldn't face being long away from Margaret, even if it were only from the pale shadow of herself that she was. The problem was that she couldn't take him home because they didn't have one. Once more friends served as the cavalry and came to the rescue. On this occasion it was Randolph and Birdie Schwabe. They found a place near them in Hampstead – well, more Swiss Cottage. The rent was a bit stiff for Margaret but at least the place had a garden and Toshie needed a garden. It was a corner house on Willow Road. There was a huge willow tree in the mandatory garden. He said it reminded him of Sauchiehall Street.

Lady Alice Barnes remembers seeing him when he came out of hospital in the summer of 1928. She explained to Alistair Moffat in the 1986 conversation:

When I came home from school on holiday he came out of hospital for the first time. He had cancer of the tongue and in those days they made him wear a radium collar which was apparently very painful. When he was allowed out, Margaret took these lodgings in Willow Road, Hampstead so as to be near us in New End Square They had taken the ground floor and the people above looked after them. There was a willow tree in the garden and Mackintosh used to sit by it ...[3]

At that time, he could still speak, but only just. One can only imagine how he felt. All the new spirit, all his old verve which he had rediscovered in France, had by now drained out of him. He was 'collared' in Hampstead. The outsider had been roped in at last and tethered like an animal to a tree. He was back in a garden under a tree, but this time there were no cabbages.

Now he could sit, like his father in Dennistoun, and watch the grass grow. Like William McIntosh, he knew that there was always something to see in a garden – if one has the eyes to see it. As he said in his Manchester lecture, 'Life is the green tree. Art is its flower.' Not cut and dried and pressed between the pages, but quick and alive and real upon the branch. He had time to dwell on such things now. To notice that the smallest petal on the smallest flower has its distinctiveness. No two leaves on the tree are the same. Every blade of grass has character. There is nothing in Nature that doesn't have a purpose. The most minute detail of decoration has its point. Nothing is wasted. It's the job it does that gives the thing its special face, and it is this that gives it its form. We must go with it. Follow its line. Straight to its source. Everything has its source in Nature. Or with God if you like, which might well be the same thing. He sat for hours in his chair, alone with his thoughts, just looking at green things.

Mackintosh was not an overtly religious man, but he had God-fearing parents and he might have inherited Presbyterian genes. His early experience of Italian churches didn't endear him to the externals of religion, yet he loved churches – but as buildings not for their liturgical purpose. Nevertheless, as Margaret came to sit with him now in these garden hours in London, did his Biblical familiarity extend to the Psalmist's response – 'Let my tongue be silenced, if I ever forget you'. The truth was, his tongue was killing him.

However, he had not been totally silenced. He still managed a husky croak to young Alice, when she came in to run errands for them. Margaret did most of his talking for him now. How he must have wished that he could have sent Alice out for some good tobacco, but the life-long pipe was no longer part of him. The young schoolgirl would have been appalled at the sad change in her childhood hero from Chelsea, but Mackintosh didn't consider himself as an imminent cadaver. Meg Morris found this out when she came back to London from Paris and sought him out in his garden. She tried to give him voice production exercises, but it was all too painful for both of them. She resorted to sign language, taking his hands in hers and introducing him to the gestures of Commedia del Arte as a means of basic communication but then they could not get on with this for laughing.

Margaret herself told me this when I talked with her in her flat in Clouston Street, near the Botanic Gardens in Glagow. She had just come back from shopping for groceries as I arrived to have lunch, and asked me if I 'would be a darling' and go down and bring up the box of tinned cat food she had left on the bottom steps. Of course I did, and after carrying the box up three flights of stairs to her top-storey flat I was glad to sit down. It must have been a big cat, as it was a large box. Like Margaret Macdonald, Margaret Morris loved cats.

We had met first when she and Mary Sturrock gave a talk about their Mackintosh links at the Art School in March 1976 – and a lively exchange it was.[4] It was then she had asked me to call and have lunch with her. I had not long before presented my dramatised lecture on Mackintosh and was now preparing a possible film script on the subject so I was anxious to hear from anyone who had known him personally – and Margaret Morris – even as an old lady – wasn't anybody. She was a tall, striking lady, looking every inch the dancer that she once was. She was lively, alert, vivacious and a very merry widow, still very much in love with her tall, handsome Fergus. She said he had regarded Mackintosh as 'one of the greatest and most independent artists Scotland has ever produced' but they had never really got to know him or Margaret until Chelsea sometime during the First War – 'about 1915, I think'.

At that time, Meg had her first-floor flat in Callow Street, Chelsea and Fergus 'kept his painting things there', which was her way of saying that, while in London, he officially lived elsewhere. 'Not that anybody minded, even then,' she laughed. 'It was Chelsea, but buyers could be put off by the slightest thing. And Fergus had a reputation. The chatelaine at his studio in Paris was told that he was at home to no one – except attractive females.' And she laughed again. 'When we came to Glasgow, he wouldn't join the Art Club. James Bridie said it was because they didn't allow women. Fergus said the sight of all those men in dark suits all in one room depressed him.'

We were now having lunch among the stacks of Fergusson canvasses of all shapes and sizes which leaned against the walls or were perched on the furniture. I particularly admired a glorious, seated nude holding an apple. 'That's me.' she exclaimed, unabashedly. 'More tea?' Typically she had said 'is' and not 'was'. I tried to steer the conversation back to Mackintosh and she was immediately away on another exuberant flow. 'He was a lovely, lovely man, old Toshie,' she remembered. I wanted to know how he sounded – his voice, did he have an accent, for instance? 'He had soft voice,' she told me. 'Quite Glasgow, but not ugly Glasgow, if you know what I mean. Some Glasgow voices are terrible, aren't they?' I could only nod, as she went on. 'But it was his eyes you noticed first under those lovely shaggy eyebrows – his eyes were always alive, you know – even if he had the teeniest squint in one – I can't remember which. And that pipe. I think it was the cause of all the trouble, if you ask my opinion. It was always stuck in the same corner of his mouth. He'd never take it out. I don't know how Margaret bore it, but she was very patient with him.

And he just adored her. He had lovely hands, you know. You felt he should have played the piano – but he said they were peasant's hands. I told him that they hadn't any peasants in Dennistoun. "Don't you believe it," he would say, then chuckle like a boy. I think there was a lot of the boy in him all his life. A bit of a spoiled boy, may be, but a lovely boy. He could have been anything, Toshie, had he wanted – but he was set on being an architect and that was that.'

Her whole manner changed when she later talked of the final Mackintosh days. Then she spoke quietly and with an engaging reserve. She had obviously liked him very much.

'When I went up to Hampstead to see him, Fergus was in New York. I used to take Toshie's hands and help him make the speech gestures. And he croaked once that I should put two flags in his hand and he would just semaphore. He would always try to make his little joke even when speech must have been very hard for him. Sometimes, I stood behind him, so that I could show him better how to do a particular gesture and he would shake with laughter – but as he got tired I had to stop. One day, as we were working, he wiped his eye with the back of his hand and I thought he was wiping away tears of laughter. They were tears all right – but he wasn't laughing. So I just sat and held his hands until Margaret came out and he stopped. He would never cry in front of her. It would upset her, you see. I didn't go back much after that. I felt so sad for him.'

There was a silence then – the first since I arrived. I tried to break it by asking her about the theatre he had designed for her in Flood Street. Theatre was our business, after all, but she just threw up her hands, and rose from her chair saying, 'Oh that's enough about about old Toshie. Let's talk about my Fergus.' And we did – for the rest of the afternoon.

It was strange that this lovely woman had attended Mackintosh at that time in his life, and in such a manner, for it was she who had invented the Margaret Morris System of Remedial Aesthetics, a movement she developed worldwide and which led to her annual summer schools in France. Suzanne Lenglen, the tennis player, was one celebrity who adopted her methods in her tennis training. One wonders if this idea of healing through dance came partly to her out of the sessions with Mackintosh in the Hampstead garden? Should she have danced with him perhaps? No, she did what she could do best; she offered, literally, a loving and helping hand.

Margaret and Fergus came back to Glasgow for good at the start of the Second World War in 1939, when he became the grand old man of Scottish painting, the last of the Scottish Colourists and leader of the new Scottish Group. Meanwhile, she founded the Celtic Ballet. 'As long as they don't call you Morris dancers', he had said. Meg also helped him to institute the New Art Club for the poorer Scottish artist. Thirty or so years later she was one of the mainsprings of the New Glasgow Society, which in turn, spawned the Charles Rennie Mackintosh Society. When Fergusson died in 1961, she created the Fergusson Art Foundation to preserve his name and work. It still does so from its centre in Perth. Margaret herself died on 29 February 1980. Trust her to take a leap into the next world. But then she had always been a dancer.

In the late summer of 1928, the Mackintoshes had to move his chair abruptly from under the tree and find other lodgings because of some trouble with the 'carers' in the upstairs part of the house. One can be sure at least it was nothing that Toshie had said. This time, Margaret turned to yet another friend-in-need, one who was as much her admirer as her husband's, Major Desmond Chapman-Huston. This gentleman, a determined bachelor, turned out to be a friend indeed, and a ready shoulder for Margaret to lean on. It was he who had visited Mackintosh all those years before at Florentine Terrace when Chapman-Huston was an actor with the Benson company. He had, after that, stayed with the Mackintoshes whenever he visited Glasgow – 'in the best digs in the world' – as he called the attic spare room. And now, here he was, about to return their hospitality.

The Hustons had Scottish roots, as being from Houston in Renfrewshire. The Chapman was added to indicate the Anglo-Irish branch to which he belonged. His background was High

Church and there was money enough to sustain a mansion in Ireland with servants to match, but for little else and young Desmond had to earn his living. The church was not for him so he tried the next best thing for a well-spoken youth of reasonable appearance, the stage. He was, in a sense, saved by the First World War and found some kind of status and identity in the Officers' Mess. He began his writing career as a Boswell to one of his generals and he never laid down his pen after that. He was, by 1928, a successful biographer of other military and minor royal figures and travelled Europe from palace to schloss, assisting in the memoirs of the richly forgettable. He now had to go off on another of these well-paid trips and he told Margaret they could have the upper floors of his bachelor home at 12 Porchester Square for as long as he was away.

He also paid the outstanding rent due at Willow Road. This was most generous of him, but he was a kind and thoughtful man. Unfortunately, the stairs at Porchester Square proved too much for Mackintosh and a sick-room had to be improvised out of the dining-room. This, however, gave Mackintosh a French-windows view of the garden – he still needed to see green. It was life to him and he would hold on to it as long as he could, but his tongue was not responding to the radium treatment and he was finding it difficult, not only to talk, even in a whisper, but to eat. And without eating he had neither the strength nor energy to fight the cancer.

Nor had Margaret the strength or energy to cope with the demands of this kind of nursing. She was near to cracking herself, and craved tranquility. She was cruelly saved by the fact that Toshie had a relapse and was hurried to the nursing home nearby at 26 Porchester Square where his condition was sufficiently restored to have him returned to the Westminster Hospital – so that he could die in good hands.

It was now another autumn and the anniversary of his leaving his beloved France. There was a lump on his tongue then and now there were signs that the cancer had not been completely cut out of his body. They took the whole tongue out. He could not speak at all. He could do nothing but lie there and be – patient. And think.

A lot of people think they are thinking when really they're doing nothing but letting the film run behind their eyes. They're just seeing pictures. So do we all, but the thing is to try and catch the thought behind the picture – to hold it in its frame, as it were, and find the latent image within what is seen. It might be called the artist's view of things. As an artist, Mackintosh never drew people. In his view, they were never natural, never themselves. People rarely are. We are always annoyed with ourselves because we are not what we want to be, what we would rather be. It is not always easy to accept what we are. Consequently, we are rarely happy with ourselves. Perhaps, subconsciously, we are afraid of ourselves. So we try not to dwell on ourselves and are happy to accept the externals.

For Mackintosh, the externals were diminishing all around him. He had to go into himself and give himself to his own silence. As far as he was concerned this was a fact of life and not even a wish of lines upon the page could change that fact. Artist or architect, the man was dying. He was weakening just as gradually and inevitably as the days were getting shorter and the nights drawing in. There is no final perfection. In the end, we come back to our beginnings. But with the special knowledge that at last, we know where we are in the overall design and are at peace.

Margaret, for her part, knew little peace. She worried about how all this medical care was going to be paid for. As it happened, no account was ever received from Westminster Hospital. She was now back in the Chapman-Huston house in Porchester Square. So was the Major. Between them they finally got dates out of the Leicester Gallery people who agreed to take a selection of Mackintosh canvases as part of a forthcoming mixed show. This was better than nothing so between them all, a selection was made, but several were still unsigned. Chapman-Huston undertook to take them up to the hospital one afternoon in a taxi and have Toshie sign them. He did so and, on a Wednesday afternoon, while signing one of them that the pencil fell from his hand. Charles Rennie Mackintosh was dead.

'May God rest his large soul', was Desmond's involuntary reaction, but he later, remembered the lines he had read from Bishop King's *Exequy* of more than 200 years before, which said of dying:

> Once off, our bodies shall aspire
> To our soul's bliss; then we shall rise
> And view ourselves with clearer eyes
> In that calm region where no night
> Can hide us from each other's sight.[5]

Walter Blackie wrote to Margaret:

> His death was a loss to the world. Not many men of his calibre are born and the pity is that when they are gone such men are irreplaceable. In my last talk with Mackintosh, I grouped him with Leonardo da Vinci ... and in looking back I feel I may not have been far wrong. Like Leonardo, Mackintosh it seemed to me, was capable of doing anything he had a mind to.[6]

Around the same time, a group of architects from Vienna tried to contact Mackintosh through the offices Major Alfred Longden of the British Council. The Austrians wanted him to be their guest of honour at a dinner to mark – 'his influence upon the art and architecture of his time'. But they were too late. By the time he was traced from Glasgow to London to France and back to London again, he was dead.

The date was December 10, just one day later than his much-loved mother who had died on December 9 in 1885, when he had been seventeen and just beginning on the career that had promised so much. Now all that was over, and he was safe at last in his own undeniable posterity. The funeral was immediate – the next day – and brief. It was small affair at Golders Green Crematorium. There was little time for anything else and Margaret was escorted to Golders Green by Lady Alice Egerton and a Miss Todd, representing Major Chapman-Huston, who hated funerals and, like Oscar Wilde, hoped he would be spared his own.

On his instruction, Miss Todd paid for everything, including the nursing home bill. Margaret was then handed a plain box containing what was left of her husband – 'Margaret, will you scatter my ashes on the waters of Port Vendres?' How that croaked request from Toshie under the willow tree must have thundered now in her head as she carried him back to Porchester Square. For the first time in her memory, she was alone – no Frances, no Toshie – and no matter the warmth of close friends, there was no substitute for either. For so many years, she had lived entirely for him – he was her *raison d'être* – now he was gone. What did she feel, sitting in her borrowed room with that box in front of her? He had said of her:

> Margaret Macdonald is my spirit key. My other half. She is more than half – she is three quarters – of all that I've done. We chose each other and each gave to the other what the other lacked. Her hand was always in mine. If I had the heart, she had the head. Oh, I had talent but she had genius. We made a pair.[5]

Their life together was their best production. A blend of the melancholy and the enigmatic, suggesting at once, secrets shared, thoughts unspoken, and a deep love articulated in a silence. They were voices from a mysterious past blended in a subtle harmony with the promise of tomorrow, and sounding in it with that force which impelled their mutual fate and was part of their condition. A lifetime of work between the two of them and now at the end, hardly a penny to show for it. Still, they had made their choice. Everything in life is a matter of choice. But it must be one's own choice. Now all the choices would be hers alone. A lawyer came to see her – 'to wind things up' he said.

Mackintosh had left no money at all. His total estate comprised 26 water colour paintings, mainly landscapes, and five flower paintings. There was a clock, and some cutlery, and a lovely cabinet. There was also an armchair and four chairs – all his own design. The four chairs were sold at a pound each –'as being of no value'. Thus was summarised the life of a genius, but then he was a Scottish genius. As he said himself, it's a hard thing to be an artist in Scotland.

The Scottish press made polite noises in their obituaries, although *The Times* of London did acknowledge that 'the whole modern movement in European architecture looks to him as one of its chief originators.' In no sense was his passing looked on as the 'national calamity' Fra Newbery had feared in 1914. In 1928, Mackintosh was as hurriedly tidied away to his posterity as he was to his cremation, and ought, but for the action of a few, to have been completely forgotten by the start of the new decade. Some critics, like Sir John Summerson, thought him 'remembered in Glasgow, if at all, as something outmoded, not worth a thought or a glance'.[6] Who today remembers Sir John Summerson?

His story catalogued the apathy of an era. Had his London schemes been built he would have predated Gropius and Corbusier by a decade. Had he been given Liverpool Cathedral, as he deserved to be, they would have canonised him. At the end there was little anyone could do. Or say. Toshie was, for better or worse, his own man. He looked back as much as he looked forward, but couldn't quite see his way to be straightforward – to conform completely. He followed his own star and in the end it led him on to the rocks of Port Vendres. It was a pity, though, that he ever left Glasgow because he was so very – Scottish. That's the only word for it.

Perhaps the last word, however, should be left to Muirhead Bone, a notable Scottish artist, who, writing of the 1902 Turin Exhibition of Decorative Art, said:

I felt keenly that there ought to have been a central monument to Mackintosh, for he anticipated almost everything there. To this great artist some day surely justice will be done.

CHAPTER FOURTEEN

Surviving Toshie

1929–1933

O, ye, all ye that walk in willowood,
That walk with hollow faces burning white;
What fathom depths of soul-struck widowhood ...

THESE LINES FROM their zenith year of 25 years before must have
echoed painfully for Margaret Mackintosh as she walked very ten-
tatively into widowhood. She remained at Chapman-Huston's
house until May when she left for Port Vendres – presumably with
a certain box of ashes. She met with the Ihlees while there, as we
know from Madame Ihlee's account to Alistair Moffat:

> After her husband's death, Madame Mackintosh came back
> each year for three months in the summer and she stayed at
> the Hotel du Commerce ... We dined three times together
> one summer ... She had a beautiful face [and] seemed quite
> content to me ... I really came to know her after her hus-
> band's death and I remember thinking, all those years ago,
> that she never talked about him.[1]

What could she say? How could she define the sudden, enormous
gap in her life? In that first year of loss, her only defence was to
keep moving. Who is to know how often she read and re-read his
'Chronycle', which she kept with her at all times. When she went
back to the Hotel du Commerce did she try to find some of her letters to him? Perhaps in some hidden cupboard or corner is a box
containing all her replies to him, put there by Rosa the maid per-

haps, for safe keeping? It's odd that all of them should have disappeared. That would be a find and would give us the full picture of a distinct episode.

Meantime. as long as her passport, visa and travelling expenses were in order she drifted around Europe like a leaf in the wind. She went first to Bagnole de l'Orne for a 'heart cure', then spent the winter of 1930 in St Paul, before leaving for Monaco in May 1931. There was no work done in these trips – or no trace of it remains – although she wrote charming letters to friends which indicated that she had not entirely lost her spirit. She went to various spas seeking treatment for her heart, saying that she was 'lugging it about from place to place' as if it were a different part of her. Yet perhaps all that was wrong with it now was that it had been broken; and it is a fact that loving and loved wives are known not to last long after their husband's demise. Like her dear friend, Jessie Newbery, Margaret was to be no exception.

For a lady who was worried about hospital bills she seemed to have regularised funds to an extent that she could 'bloweth where she listeth'. However, we know that the summer of 1931 was spent with her brother, Archie Macdonald, and the Schwabes in England at Charing in Kent. She then continued her valetudinarian tour of England, and January of 1932 found her at Falmouth, in Cornwall. By the summer she was north again at the Hotel Alexander in Harrogate, Yorkshire, from where she wrote to her sister-in law, Elsie Macdonald, saying, 'I am longing to be settled for a while. If I am well enough it is my intention to see about something when I get back'.[2]

She did, in September 1932, renting a studio for a year at 10 Chelsea Manor Studios, Flood Street, her own place still being let out to tenants. As soon as she was settled, she was besieged by a certain P Morton Shand, an architectural writer of no great standing, in her eyes at least. He wanted to know all about Mackintosh in Glasgow for an article he wanted to write on him, but he wasn't in the least interested in Margaret's own art or her work in partnership with Mackintosh. Nor was she interested in his researches either, so she refused to talk to him. She had similarly kept him from Mackintosh while he was alive, so she saw no reason why she should co-operate now that he was dead.

Morton Shand took his revenge in the essay published as *Glasgow Interlude* in the 1935 *Architectural Review*, making denigrating comments on her own painting – 'rather thin, Aubrey Beardsley mannerism of the art-crafty type' and going on to dismiss her as an artist entirely, and as a negative influence on Mackintosh:

> Only when he had to build, and so work in single harness, does he seem to have seen beyond that narrower orbit of his own vision which was his wife's … Her wholly inferior decorative talent … too often led him into uxorious ornamental vulgarity.[3]

Shand saw Mackintosh as a constructor rather than a mere decorator. He saw nothing in Margaret at all. This inflamed her supporters like Chapman-Huston, but it mattered little to her at this stage, as by now she was beginning to fail. Her cousin, Joseph Tilly Hardeman came down from the north of England to persuade her to come back with him to the family home but she refused to leave Chelsea. She was content to live quietly and wait for the end.

It came on Saturday 7 January 1933 when she collapsed in her studio with an attack of cardiac asthma. She was taken to a nursing home where she died aged 69. One has the feeling she was glad to go. It was a release from what had latterly been a wasteful aimlessness. For a talented, clever woman this must have been sore to bear, even if her physical state had deteriorated. And so it was that the Mackintosh story comes to its end – or rather, sort of peters out. It was all very sad, in a shoddy kind of way. Which is astonishing when one remembers the verve, colour, excitement and sheer creative joy that once had been there between them.

Her funeral had a little more dignity than his, although not much. Her cousin seems to have made the all arrangements and he put a notice in *The Times*, referring to her only as the wife of Mr Charles Mackintosh and not as the artist Margaret Macdonald.

Her cremation, also at Golders Green, was an intimate affair. Mr Hardeman accepted the ashes for the family. The Schwabes were there, of course, and Mrs Talwin Morris. And Miss Todd again represented Chapman-Huston. Token obituaries appeared in *The Times* and the *Glasgow Herald* and Robins Millar wrote something about her for the Glasgow *Evening Citizen,* but one has to say it was an untrumpeted end. Desmond Chapman-Huston wrote an article for *The Times* on the Mackintosh pair but it wasn't accepted. It was the final demeaning touch.

Their wound-up estate was adjudged to have a sterling monetary value in pounds, shillings and pence variously as 88 pounds, 16 shillings and 2d or 88 pounds 12 shillings and 6d. Three and eightpence isn't worth arguing about, is it?

Post Mortem

Mackintosh left no disciples, but today Mackintoshism, in its many forms, flourishes as much as does his native city. His survival is due mostly to one man, William Davidson, and to a lesser extent, Professor Randolph Schwabe, who wrote to the estate at once asking that the pictures and furniture be kept together as much as possible so as to form a basis of a collection which would stand as a memorial to both Mackintoshes. This was done sufficiently to suggest to William Davidson in Glasgow that a public exhibition devoted to the two should be held, and to this end he approached the RIBA. Since no help was forthcoming from them, he went ahead with the project himself.

With the help of architect, Jeffrey Waddell, assisted by Somerville Shanks and James Meldrum, he created a three-week Mackintosh Memorial Exhibition at the McLellan Galleries in Sauchiehall Street from the 4th to the 27th of May 1933. This was an astonishing proof of one man's fervour and determination against all odds to justify his confidence in Mackintosh as an artist, and one with staying power over several disciplines. It can be said, without exaggeration, that had it not been for Davidson's strong intervention, the Mackintosh *oeuvre* would have been dispersed and long forgotten by now. Davidson dived fearlessly into the still waters of indifference and brought Mackintosh up from the depths. This public showing of his work gave him what amounted to the kiss of life. Everything that we know about Mackintosh today started from this time.

The first thing that took people by surprise was the quantity and quality of the paintings. As the *Glasgow Citizen* said on opening day, after noting the usual municipal speeches, 'It is not often that an architect is also master of the art of landscape painting.' Many others were of the same opinion. This was the one-man show he had painstakingly worked for. It was a shame it had to be posthumous. Jessie Newbery wrote the Foreword for the programme which ended with the comment of a Belgian artist about a previous International Decorative Exhibition in Paris during 1928, who said: 'There's only one thing lacking in this Exhibition – 'A Statue to Mackintosh'. The 1905 article by BE Kalas from *De la Tamise à la Spree* was reproduced in full, and its gushing prose re-echoed the comment of the Belgian quoted above – 'Why does Paris, City of Light, fail to discern the glory of Mackintosh?'

Professor Allan D Mainds wrote a critique of Mackintosh, which appeared in the *Listener,* the broadcasting magazine, at the time of the 1933 Glasgow Exhibition:

> The new School of Art stands as a monument to [Mackintosh's] vision and genius on Garnethill, Glasgow. To those of us who had the privilege of watching this building grow from its foundations and who have since seen the development on the continent and I these islands – of the new order of architecture, the Glasgow School of Art is recognised as a landmark in the history of architecture and Mackintosh is recognised as a pioneer. That his work has been misunderstood by many and derided by not a few is not to be wondered at; had it been universally understood and accepted at its inception it would not have been worthy to take its place in the new world order that it foreshadowed …

In order to grasp at the significance of Mackintosh and the Glasgow artists who worked with him … it must suffice to show today that it is towards Glasgow and the Continent rather than to England that one must look for the new order of architecture which is sweeping over the world and changing the character of our homes and cities.[4]

What price glory in Glasgow? This was proved by the fact that every picture for sale was sold and those on loan from his friends were much admired. The Davidson treasure trove was much in evidence as well as a portrait of Margaret by Olive Carlton-Smyth, sister to Dorothy, who died before she could take up her post as the first female director of the School of Art. Margaret's own work was well displayed and fetched top prices. A textile design was bought by Allan F Ure but the highest price paid was £35 for a watercolour hung at Chicago in 1923, *White Roses*, which was bought by Miss Jessie Keppie. And thereby hangs a tale.

I must preface it by explaining that I had met Benno Schotz, the sculptor, during one Edinburgh Festival in the Sixties when he came to see my Robert Burns solo performance, and decided he wanted to do my head as the poet. This was done over a series of arranged sittings during which I got to know him almost as well as he got to know me. When the bronze was eventually completed and sold to the Dick Institute in Kilmarnock, we continued to keep in touch with occasional lunches at his studio or at the Glasgow Art Club. It was during one of the Art Club lunches that he told me the following story. The television version of my Mackintosh script had just gone out and Benno was one of the few who liked it.

I asked him if had ever known Toshie, but apparently Benno had come to Glasgow just after Mackintosh had left in 1914. Ironically, he had got to know John Keppie well, as Keppie helped him find his first studio in the city. 'Mr Keppie was very nice. Always the gentleman.' And he added, in that lovely Estonian/Scottish accent: 'And his sister too, Miss Jessie, who looked after him – charming, charming.'

'She loved Mackintosh, I gather.' I said

'Adored him, adored him. Everybody knew that.'

'Except Mackintosh perhaps.'

'He knew too. That's what made it so terrible for her. She never forgot him. I know this because I was at the Exhibition in the McLellan Galleries when she had a fight with her brother because of Mackintosh.'

'A fight?'

'Well, not a fight – but an argument. A very loud argument.'

'Really?'

It appears that the Keppies were walking round the McLellan Galleries looking at the Exhibition, and, naturally, they were talking about Mackintosh. Benno, who was just behind them at the time, couldn't hear exactly what was being said, but he became aware that their voices were rising as they talked, then he couldn't help overhearing. John suddenly said to his sister, 'That's nonsense.' And she said 'No, it isn't. You could have kept him on had you wanted to.' 'You know nothing about it, woman.' 'Don't call me "woman"!' 'Her voice was quite shrill – like an angry bird,' remembered Benno. As the squabble went on, other people began to hear them. Benno tried to hide behind a piece of the furniture nearby. He noticed that she was carrying a picture she had bought and he thought any moment she was going to smash it over her brother's head – but he kept very calm and then they left, with Jessie walking out very fast in front of him. Everybody tried to pretend that nothing had happened – 'The way they do,' he said, and went on, 'I saw John in the tram car some days afterwards. We never mentioned it. That was his way of dealing with things. I never saw Miss Keppie much at all after that. Yet I want to tell you something. She would have kept Mackintosh in Glasgow, that's for sure.'

'How do you work that out?

'They would have married and she would have given him what Margaret Macdonald never gave him.'

'What's that?

'Children. That's what. That would have made him stay. I know it. Keppie would have carried him – for his sister's sake. Mackintosh would never have hit the bottle the way he did, because he would not have been so unhappy with himself, if he had had children round about him.'

Benno was so vehement about this, I wanted to ask him more but then Emilio Coia joined us and the Keppies were forgotten, but I went home that afternoon still thinking about Jessie. There was more to her than I had thought. In 1949, when Tom Howarth was in Glasgow researching Mackintosh for his book, he received a letter from Jessie Keppie. He had written a letter on the subject to the *Glasgow Herald,* and she wrote:

> I have read with great interest your letter on Charles Rennie Mackintosh in yesterday's *Herald.* I knew him so well in his early days and always felt that architecture was to – him the most important thing in his life. I could never understand how Glasgow got the name of not appreciating his work as I think no young architect ever got so many of his ideas carried out – or was so much admired – by so many clients: with the war intervening while he was still at the zenith of his work he had to be content with the lighter phase of his capabilities, otherwise we might have had many more of his beautiful buildings. I think your letter was most enlightening and very fair. And I am sure his work will live long and be appreciated by many.[3]

This is an authoritative voice, whatever the personal tensions, and it deserves to be listened to. Miss Keppie had class, and showed it to the end. She deserves to be remembered in the Mackintosh Story.

At the time of writing, Craigie Hall in Glasgow is up for sale, and among the Mackintosh effects in this house is a carved chair which features a woman's face on the side panels. It is Jessie Keppie, as seen by Mackintosh in 1893. Underneath is a heart. If indeed it is Jessie's, than perhaps she also deserves the last word.

Envoi

ABOVE THE IMPOSING portals of the Musee d'Orsay in Paris is the legend reading – 'CHICAGO – GLASGOW – VIENNA' and beyond the doors the interior is entirely given over to the nineteenth century, with one room devoted to the beginnings of the Modern Movement in Architecture. 'Chicago', of course, takes in Frank Lloyd Wright and 'Vienna' acknowledges Hoffmann, Olbricht and the other Austrians, but the 'Glasgow' element is mostly Mackintosh. This is a compliment in any language, but from the chauvinistic French it is a high honour indeed to accord such a place to a foreign artist, especially one who came from Glasgow. It is certainly more than he ever got from London in his own time, and that complacent capital has never thought of Glasgow as anything more than a conurbation that consists mainly of the Gorbals.

As we have seen, he made his first impact abroad before being recognised belatedly in his home town but not before he had made his colleagues and fellow architects uncomfortable, his friends angry and convinced the Glasgow man in the street that he was quite mad. They only knew him as the eccentric showman of the tea rooms, and never guessed there were cathedrals in him. In a world of antimacassars, draped piano legs and cluttered mantle pieces, he offered the awful prospect of the straight line, and the white wall. And even worse, he jilted a Glasgow girl to marry an Englishwoman.

However, with his pen, he gave Glasgow its own castle on a hill above Sauchiehall Street. Its outline horrified many at the time as it towered above the cake-mix of the Victorian skyline, just as it does today above the empty envelopes that is much of Scottish architecture today. Would that we could lay waste to that unconsidered huddle of commercial outlets that lie below the Art School's uncompromising south facade today, So that in some enlightened tomorrow we might create a Mackintosh place in the centre of the city which might include his circular concert hall and beneath, on Sauchiehall's pavements, his Chelsea art studios, and at each corner, his town and country houses for an artist. In this way, we might have a Mackintosh square mile to rival Edinburgh's High Street, and set up Scotland's greatest artist-architect with a Glasgow flourish that both it and he have for so long deserved. At one stroke it would cancel out the waves of Mockingtosh that have recently buried him under tea trays, scent bottles, key rings, glassware and ashtrays which trivialised a true talent by recreating it as a commercial icon.

To some Charlie Mackintosh, as he liked to be called by the workmen, was merely a designer, a play actor with light, a conjurer with domestic effect and detail. To others, he was supreme architect in the traditional Scotch Baronial manner, cut off at his prime, and prevented from creating the further masterpieces that were undoubtedly in him. Nowadays, he is seen as a considerable painter, and as a most ingenious innovator of unique furniture style ever seen in Europe to this day. He is each and all of these.

In short, he is an artist of world status, and it was his contribution to the 'new art' that gives him his place in the records as the artist of genius that he undoubtedly was. What he has left us, whether on paper, in wood or stone, is the best testimonial to the life of a man who may have been hounded by his own demons but was attended by angels.

The Mackintosh Posterity

1934   Professor Nikolaus Pevsner writes a monograph, *Charles R Mackintosh,* but cannot find a publisher. It was finally published in Italian in 1950 and translated back to English in 1997.
        Kate Cranston dies.
1935   P Morton Shand writes first essay on Mackintosh.
1939   Thomas Howarth comes from Manchester to teach at the Glasgow School of Architecture – 'discovers' Mackintosh via Professor T Harold Hughes. Meets William Davidson and is introduced to the Mackintosh material at the Davidson warehouse.
1945   Howarth registered for a doctoral thesis on Mackintosh at Glasgow University. In the same year, William Davidson dies and Glasgow University inherits Mackintosh property and letters via Davidson family. Howarth returns to Manchester University.
        John Keppie dies.
1946   Fra Newbery dies at Corfe Castle.
1948   Jessie Newbery dies.
1949   Howarth gains PhD at Glasgow.
1951   Jessie Keppie dies.
1953   Thomas Howarth writes *Charles Rennie Mackintosh and the Modern Movement.* Arranges Mackintosh Exhibition in Edinburgh for the Saltire Society in arrangement with the Arts Council of Great Britain.
        Wenman Joseph Bassett-Lowke dies.
        Walter Blackie dies.
1954   T Campbell Lawson buys Hill House from Blackie family.
1955   James Herbert McNair dies.
1960   *Art Nouveau* exhibitions in New York and Paris – Mackintosh a main item in each.

1963   Glasgow University demolishes 6 Florentine Terrace/78 Southpark Avenue.

1964   'Friends of Toshie' formed by Murray Grigor and journalist Bill Williams.

1967   Murray Grigor writes and directs the first documentary film on Mackintosh. A Films of Scotland film for International Film Associates (Scotland) Ltd. with assistance of the BBC, the Scottish Arts Council, the Glasgow Institute of Architects and the Glasgow School of Art. Producer: Forsyth Hardy. Photography: Edward McConnell and Oscar Marzaroli. Music: Frank Spedding. Editor: Bill Forsyth. Graphics: Avril McIlwraith. Narration: Maurice Roeves.

1968   Henry Hellier, Head of Graphics at Glasgow School of Art, designs a set of letters for the Mackintosh Centennial Exhibition created by Andrew McLaren Young and others and presented by the Scottish Arts Council at the Edinburgh Festival.

1970   New Glasgow Society founded. President, Sir Robert Grieve.

1971   Glasgow Corporation buys Ingram Street tea rooms to save them from demolition.

1973   Charles Rennie Mackintosh Society founded in Glasgow, October 4.
Replica Mackintosh furniture produced by Cassina of Milan.

1974   *Furniture by Charles Rennie Mackintosh* – Museum of Modern Art, New York.
August – Glasgow Corporation appoints team of consultants under Sir Leslie Martin to survey existing Mackintosh buildings in the city to see which would serve best as a cultural centre. Princess Margaret tours sites with Lord Provost William Gray, Honorary Vice-President of the Charles Rennie Mackintosh Society. RIBA buy Hill House from T Campbell Lawson for £25,000.

Restored flats offered for rental at £1,000 pa.
Hill House Society formed.

1975 European Architectural Year.
December 5 – Mackintosh Symposium, Kirkcaldy
featuring Murray Grigor's film on Mackintosh, A
Critical Forum chaired by Dr Maurice Lindsay with
speakers including Emilio Coia, Robin Haddow and
Henry Hillier.
Mackintosh the Man – A Dramatic Lecture by John
Cairney with Rose Mcbain and John Shedden and Triple
Screen Illustrations by Murray Grigor, Graham Metcalfe
and Roand Kennedy. Script advisor: Roger Billcliffe.
Sponsors: AH McIntosh & Co Ltd, makers of original
designs – 'After Mackintosh'.
Andrew McLaren Young dies.

1976 March 2 – *I Remember Mackintosh* with Mary Sturrock
and Margaret Morris chaired by H Jefferson Barnes.
June 17 – *A Mackintosh Experience* with John Cairney
with Jan Equi and Robert Docherty for Shanter
Productions at the Martyrs' School, Glasgow in
conjunction with the AGM of the Charles Rennie
Mackintosh Society.
Allan F Ure made Honorary Member of the Charles
Rennie Mackintosh Society.

1977 July – *Mackintosh* – with John Cairney and full cast,
Scottish Television, Glasgow.

1978 August – *A Mackintosh Experience* with John Cairney,
Leonard Maguire and Alannah O'Sullivan for Shanter
Productions at the Netherbow Theatre for the Edinburgh
Festival and repeated at the Lyceum Little Theatre on
December 6 for a week with Russell Hunter replacing
Mr Maguire and Jan Equi added.

1980 February – Mackintosh furniture illustrated in *House
and Garden*.
Margaret Morris dies.

1981   Mackintosh House opened at Hunterian Museum, University Glasgow.

1982   Hill House transferred to the National Trust via endow-ment from National Heritage Memorial Fund. Moira Shearer and Ludovic Kennedy unveil the *Charles Rennie Mackintosh*, a Class 47 railway engine, with Anthony Jones, the Director of the Glasgow School of Art, dressed as Francis Newbery.

1983   Burrell Collection opened in the Pollok Park, Glasgow. June – *A Mackintosh Experience* with John Cairney and Alannah O'Sullivan for Shanter Productions at the Walter Kasa Theatre, Edmonton, Alberta. Sponsor: The Northern Chapter of the Alberta Association of Architectects.
Repeated in Columbus, Ohio as part of US tour.

1985   November 2 – A dramatised play-reading of the Mackintosh-Macdonald Letters adapted by Dr Lorn Macintyre was given at the Tron Theatre, Glasgow, with John Shedden and Anne Lannan.

1986   October 2 – RIBA Awards. John Cairney and Alannah O'Sullivan in *Mackintosh*. With Russell Hunter and Jan Equi. Presented by RIAS.
Wendy Maruyama creates her *Mickey Mackintosh* chair in California.

1987   August – *Dreams and Recollections* by Alistair Moffat, with Tom Conti and Kara Wilson. Channel Four Television, London.
Charles Rennie Mackintosh – Art, Architecture and Design – A CD multi-media documentary on the life and work directed by Jo James and issued by Wigwam Digital, Bellshill, Strathclyde.

1988   The Glasgow Garden Festival features the Charles Rennie Mackintosh Rose.

1990   Glasgow as European City of Culture. The Post Office features the Art School on a stamp. Architectural Symposium at the Glasgow School of Art.

John Cairney and Alannah O'Sullivan read *A Mackintosh Experience* at the Burrell Gallery, Glasgow. *Glasgow Girls – Women in Art in Design 1880–1920 –* curated by Jude Burkhauser at the Glasgow Art Gallery. Sir Denys Lasdun designs Milton Gate office building in London as – 'a homage to one of the great masters of the Modern Movement, Charles Rennie Mackintosh'.

1991 February – *A Mackintosh Experience* with John Cairney and Alannah O'Sullivan for Shanter Productions at the McLellan Galleries, Glasgow.

1993 *Geniuses without Glory* – a Japanese comic strip by Morita Singo for Young Jump illustrating 'CR Mackintosh, The Architect ahead of this Time'. A Mackintosh font made available for computers.

1995 Mackintosh Exhibition at the McLellan Galleries, Glasgow, presented by the Glasgow Museums, University of Glasgow and the Glasgow School of Art. Sponsors: Whyte and Mackay Group. Project led by Stefan van Raay. Project co-ordinator Daniel Robbins. Curators: Pamela Robertson and J Stewart Johnson.

1996 October – The House for an Art Lover, visualised by Mackintosh in 1901, is realised as a building project by Graham Roxburgh in Bellahouston Park, Glasgow, from the original Mackintosh design drawings.

1999 British Council designates Glasgow as City of Architecture and Design. The *Glasgow Herald* building is refurbished as *The Lighthouse* – a Mackintosh Interpretation and Display Centre.

2000 Thomas Howarth dies.

Notes

PREFACE

1 Testo, *Charles R Mackintosh*, Turin, 1997 and Canal Books, 1998, p22.

INTRODUCTION

1 See Defoe's *Tour Thro' the Whole Island of Great Britain*, London, August 1726 and quoted in David Daiches, *Glasgow*, London 1997, pp46–4.
2 See James Pagan, *Sketches of the History of Glasgow*, Stuart, Glasgow, 1847 quoted by Juliet Kinchin in (Ed) Wendy Kaplan, *Charles Rennie Mackintosh*, for Glasgow Museums 1996, pp31–51.
3 Quoted in *Glasgow Herald* interview with Dr Lorn MacIntyre.
4 John McKean & Colin Baxter, *Charles Rennie Mackintosh – Architect-Artist-Icon*, Lanark, 2000.

CHAPTER ONE

1 Essay, with drawing, by Mackintosh in the Art School *Magazine*, 1902.
2 William Forrest Salmon and George Salmon Junior were both Glasgow architects.
3 See John McKean, *Charles Rennie Mackintosh – Architect, Artist, Icon*, Lomond: Edinburgh 2000.
4 See Tony Attwood, *A Guide to Asperger's Syndrome for Parents.*
and Professionals, London, 1997.
5 See Jen Birch, *Congratulations, it's Asperger's Syndrome*, Jessica.
Kingsley, Auckland, New Zealand 2003.
6 See Filipo Alison, *Charles Rennie Mackintosh as a Designer of Chairs*, London 1978.

CHAPTER TWO

1 Thomas Howarth, *Charles Rennie Mackintosh and the Modern Movement*, Routledge and Kegan Paul, London 1952, pp3–4.

² Pamela Robertson, *Flowers – Charles Rennie Mackintosh,* 'Architectural Draughtsman', p9.
³ See CRM Newsletter 68, Winter 1995.
⁴ Op cit, Howarth, p1.
⁵ See CRM Newsletter No 30, Autumn 1981.
⁶ Janice Heland, *The Studios of Frances and Margaret Macdonald,* Manchester University Press, 1996, p23.
⁷ See CRM Newsletter, No 30, Autumn 1981.
⁸ See CRM Newsletter No 22, Summer 1979.
⁹ Elizabeth Wilhide, *The Mackintosh Style,* Pavilion, London 1995, p16.
¹⁰ Op cit, Robertson, p9.
¹¹ See CRM Newsletter No 32, Mid-Summer 1982.

CHAPTER THREE

¹ See William Buchanan, 'The Mackintosh Circle Part Three – The Keppies', CRMSN No 32 Mid-Summer 1982.
² Op cit, Howarth, p20–1.
³ (Ed) Pamela Robertson, *Charles Rennie Mackintosh – The Architectural Papers.*
⁴ Ibid.
⁵ Ibid. 'Diary of the Italian Tour', pp89–107.
⁶ Cited by R Eddington Smith, in letter to *Glasgow Evening Times,* 17 February 1933.
⁷ Programme of 1933 Mackintosh Exhibtion, Foreword, p1.

CHAPTER FOUR

¹ Op cit, Howarth, p58.
² See George Rawson, 'Mackintosh, Jessie Keppie and the Immortals', CRMNS No 62, Summer 1993, pp4–6.
³ See Iain Patterson, 'William McIntosh's Wives', CRMNS No 68, Winter 1995, p5.
⁴ Op cit, (Ed) Pamela Robertson, *Charles Rennie Mackintosh – The Architectural Papers,* pp68, 70 and 115.
⁵ See CRMNS No32, Summer 1982 – Article on John Keppie by William Buchanan.
⁶ Quoted in Alistair Moffat, *Remembering Charles Rennie Mackintosh,* p30.
⁷ Quoted in Anthony Jones, *Charles Rennie Mackintosh,* p15.
⁸ Quoted in Elizabeth Wilhide, *The Mackintosh Style.*

CHAPTER FIVE

[1] GSA *Magazine* 1893.
[2] Quoted in Janice Helland, *The Studios of Margaret and Frances Macdonald,* 1996, p66.
[3] Gleeson White, 'Some Glasgow Designers and their Work', *The Studio,* No 2 1897, p89.
[4] Ailsa Tanner, *Bessie McNicol,* 1998, pp15–17.
[5] Ibid p53.
[6] Ibid.
[7] Letter to Hermann Muthesius, May 11, 1898.
[8] Op cit, Howarth, pp170–3.
[9] Ibid.
[10] Hermann Muthesius, *Das Englische Haus,* 1904 quoted by Anthony Jones, p125.

CHAPTER SIX

[1] Conversation quoted in Alistair Moffat, *Remembering Mackintosh* 1989, p40.
[2] Alan Crawford, *Charles Rennie Mackintosh,* 1995 and 2002, pp57–8.
[3] Letter to the author from Lesley Johnson, May 9, 2003. See also RF Bisson, *The Sandon Studios Society of the Arts,* Parry Books, Liverpool 1965.
[4] Op cit, Moffat, p23.
[5] EB Kalas, *De la Tamise à la Spree: L'essor des industries d'art,* 1905. Quoted in Robert Macleod, *Charles Rennie Mackintosh,* 1968, p116.
[6] Moffat, p39.
[7] Quoted in John McKean, *Charles Rennie Mackintosh – Architect, Artist, Icon,* 2000, p41.
[8] Quoted in Anthony Jones, *Charles Rennie Mackintosh,* 1990, p61.
[9] Howarth, p156.
[10] Ibid.
[11] Ibid, p154.
[12] Ibid, p153.
[13] Op cit, Moffat, p39.
[14] Ibid, p41.
[15] Johnson letter.
[16] Ibid.

[17] Moffat, p45.
[18] Ibid.
[19] Ibid.
[20] Op cit, Moffat, p46.
[21] KE Sullivan, *The Life, Times and Work of Charles Rennie Mackintosh*, 1997, p92.
[22] Op cit, Moffat, p46.

CHAPTER SEVEN

[1] Nikolaus Pevsner, *Charles R. Mackintosh*, (1997), p1823.
[2] Anthony Jones, *Charles Rennie Mackintosh*, (1990), p35.
[3] Ibid, p37.
[4] David Daiches, *Glasgow*, London, (1977), p206.
[5] See Peter Wylie Davidson, 'Memories of Mackintosh', in CRMS Newsletter No 22, Summer 1979.
[6] Ibid.
[7] Ibid.
[8] Moffat, p53.
[9] Ibid, p24.
[10] Desmond Chapman Taylor, *The Lamp of Memory*, London, (1949), pp124–6.
[11] Ibid, p1281.
[12] (Ed) William Buchanan, *Mackintosh's Masterwork*, (1989), p42.
[13] An anecdote by Murray Grigor as recounted to the author.
[14] Op cit, Buchanan, p44.
[15] Records from the Glasgow School of Art by courtesy of Mr Peter Trowles.

CHAPTER EIGHT

[1] John McKean & Colin Baxter, *Charles Rennie Mackintosh*, (2000), p106.
[2] Jocelyn Grigg, *Charles Rennie Mackintosh*, (1987), p25.
[3] Anthony Jones, *Charles Rennie Mackintosh*, (1990), p77.
[4] Murray Grigor, *The Architects' Architect*, (1970), p13.
[5] CRMS Newsletter No 32, Mid-summer 1982.
[6] Letter to Howarth, 30 July 1947, quoted in Neat & McDermott, *Closing the Circle*, p101.
[7] From the Bisson account of the Sandon Society quoted in Janice Helland, *Studios of Margaret and Frances Macdonald* (1996) p169.
[8] Op cit, Neat & McDermott, p147.

[9] Op cit, Howarth, p169.
[10] Op cit, Howarth, p195.
[11] Moffat, p74.

CHAPTER NINE

[1] Janice Heland, *The Studios of Margaret and Frances Macdonald,* (1996), p160.
[2] Moffat, p79.
[3] Janice Heland, Notes, p185.
[4] Alan Crawford, *Charles Rennie Mackintosh,* (1995), p51.
[5] Moffat, p80.
[6] Article in (Ed) Wendy Kaplan, Catalogue for Glasgow Museums Mackintosh Exhibition, (1996), p35.
[7] Moffat, p83.
[8] Gavin Stamp, *The London Years,* Kaplan Catatlogue, p207.
[9] Juliet Kinchin, Kaplan Catalogue, p60–1.
[10] Letter quoted in Moffat, p93.

CHAPTER TEN

[1] Op cit, Moffat, pp72–3.
[2] Letter from Dr Sylvia Pinches, The Derngate Trust Northampton, May 9, 2003.
[3] Howarth, p199.
[4] Lecture by Dr Sylvia Pinches to the Friends of 78 Derngate, 26 November 2002.
[5] Margaret Morris, *The Art of JD Fergusson,* Glasgow (1974), p206–7.
[6] Alan Crawford, pp178–9.
[7] Frank Lloyd Wright, *An Autobiography,* FLW Foundation, (1932), p589.

CHAPTER ELEVEN

[1] Op cit, Moffat, p103.
[2] Ibid, p102.
[3] Op cit, Howarth, p209.
[4] Letter of 14 November 1949, quoted in Neat, *Closing the Circle,* p108.
[5] Letter to Howarth quoted in ibid, p107.

CHAPTER TWELVE

[1] Op cit, Moffat, p131.

2 Op cit, Neat & McDermott, p132.
3 Letter from the Hotel du Midi, Ille-sur-Têt in December 1924, in op cit, Neat & McDermott, p133.
4 Letter from Port Vendres, 29 May 1927. See (Ed) Pamela Robertson, *The Chronycle*, Hunterian Art Gallery, Glasgow University, (2001). Letter 9.4, p74.
5 Letter from Port Vendres, 11 June 1927. Ibid, Letter 15.2, p20.
6 Op cit, Moffat, p109–10.
7 Op cit, Margaret Morris, Glasgow, (1974), pp154–5.
8 Op cit, Moffat, p113.
9 Op cit, (Ed) Robertson, *The Chronycle*, Letter 2,5a, p52.
10 Op cit, Moffat, p149.
11 Op cit, (Ed) Robertson, *The Chronycle, Letter* 7.4–5, p66.

CHAPTER THIRTEEN
1 Op cit, Moffat, p149.
2 Timothy Neat, *Part Seen, Part Imagined*, (Edinburgh 1994) p132.
3 Op cit, Moffat, p152.
4 See CRMS Newsletter No 11, Spring 1976.
5 Desmond Chapman-Huston, *Lamp of Memory,* (London 1948) p18.
6 Anthony Jones, *Charles Rennie Mackintosh*, (London 1990) p70.
7 Op cit, Crawford, p192.
8 Op cit, Jones, p82.

CHAPTER FOURTEEN
1 Op cit, Moffat, p156.
2 Op cit, (Ed) Robertson, *The Chronycle*, p22.
3 Op cit, Neat & McDermott, p107.
4 Ibid, p88.

End Note

WITH THE PASSING of Howarth in Toronto the circle had been completed and it was time to let Mackintosh go, to let him find his real level in the market place, which is the surest test of any artist's durability. He has met the challenge superbly as the following table shows. It is by no means a complete list of sales to date but it gives a fair indication of his continuing saleability. If he was discovered in the showrooms by the new Moderns then it is in the showroom he will surely continue to thrive.

29 August 1974 – at J&R Edmistons, Glasgow
Wag at the wa' clock sold for £960.
Low-backed waitress's chair for £495.

13 March 1975 – at Sotheby's of Belgravia, London
Mackintosh armchair from Music Room at Hous'hill sold for £9,200.
Two silver spoons and a fork – £3,500.
Cabinet with bowed recess – £2,700.
2 July – Small, straight-backed chair – £1,400.
Square oak armchair from Hill House – £2,100.
27 November – Fire Irons (Derngate), Hearth Rug (Hill House), Oval Tea Table and four straight back chairs for total of £2,060.
New York – One writing-desk, the property of the artist – £90,000.

1984 – Sold at Edinburgh, one cabinet by CR Mackintosh and Margaret Macdonald dated 'Glasgow 1899' £115,000.

5 February 1991 – at Sotheby's
A water colour painting of Anemones by CR Mackintosh purchased by the Fine Arts Society, – £198,000.

6 November 2002 – at Christie's

For *Port Vendres*, a painting by CR Mackintosh –
£200,000.
To one high-backed chair by CR Mackintosh – £340,000.
Ebonised mahogany writing cabinet designed for Walter
Blackie by CR Mackintosh – £1,000,000 (including VAT).

The total sales figure to date amounts to almost £5,000,000 in all
from works he could hardly give away in his life time. And with
that last irony, common to so many greats in art, we salute his
name as he takes his rightful place on Parnassus – and fades into
the fabric of history...

GOING – GOING – GONE.

A Mackintosh Chronology

1837   William McIntosh born Belturbet, County Cavan,
        Northern Ireland, fifth son of Hugh McIntosh of Paisley
        and Marjory Morris of Methil in Fife.

1841   Margaret Rennie born Ayr, Ayrshire.

1845   McIntosh family returns to Scotland.

1851   Move to 94 Glebe Street, Townhead, Glasgow

1858   March 17 – William McIntosh joins Glasgow Police.

1862   August 4 – Marriage of William McIntosh and Margaret
        Rennie at 54 McIntosh Street, Dennistoun, Glasgow.

1865   William McIntosh becomes Chief Clerk to the Chief
        Constable of Glasgow.

1868   Charles Rennie McIntosh born on 7 June at 70 Parson
        Street, Townhead, Glasgow.

1874   William McIntosh now a Police Inspector. The McIntosh
        family moves to a tenement flat at 2 Firpark Terrace,
        Dennistoun.

1875   Mackintosh attends Reid's Public School.

1877   Attends Allan Glen's High School.

1883   September – Enrols as Chas. R McIntosh, part-time
        student (evenings/Saturday afternoons) for a course in
        drawing and ornamentation at the Glasgow School
        of Art.

1884   Formally articled as an apprentice with John Hutchison,
        architect. Sketching on the Isle of Bute.

1885   Charles Mackintosh wins prize for 'Painting and
        Ornament in Monochrome from the Flat'.
        Sketches Old College, Glasgow.
        December 9 – Margaret Rennie McIntosh dies aged 48.

1886   Begins formal course in Elementary
        Architecture at the Art School under Thomas Smith.
        Sketches Glasgow Cathedral.

1887   Passes in Building Construction.

Wins Book Prize awarded by Glasgow Institute of
Architects. Wins Bronze Medal at Kensington.
1888　Completes Modelling Course. Awarded National
Queen's prize for design of Presbyterian Church.
John Keppie joins John Honeyman from Campbell,
Douglas and Sellars to form partnership in Glasgow at
140 Bath Street. Herbert McNair, from Skelmorlie, joins
as draughtsman. Mackintosh designs Celtic headstone
for Chief Constable McCall at Glasgow Necropolis.
Wins £1 prize from Glasgow Institute for 'A Town
House in Terrace'.
1889　Mackintosh completes apprenticeship and joins
Honeyman and Keppie as a junior draughtsman. Works
with Bertie McNair on measuring trips to Achamore
House, Gigha and the Abbey, Iona. Visits father's family
in Moray. Sketches in Elgin. Wins prize in Architectural
Design and a free studentship (First Class Honours).
Wins Design Prize at Glasgow Institute plus 15/- for
sketching ornament from the cast and 30/- for the best
set of three drawings. Meets Alexander McGibbon.
July – Receives first payment of £5 from
Honeyman and Keppie.
Works with Bertie McNair on interiors for Keppie home
in Prestwick. A relationship is begun with Jessie, one of
the five Keppie sisters.
Chief Inspector William McIntosh leads Glasgow Police
team to World Tug-o'-War Championship.
1890　September 26 – wins Alexander Thomson Travelling
Studentship of £60 with design for public hall.
Receives half to finance tour in Italy. Wins National
Silver Medal with design for Museum of Science and Art
but fails to win the British Institution Scholarship.
Mackintosh designs Redclyffe House as a pair of semi-
detached houses at 140/2 Balgrayhill Road for his uncle
on his father's side – Gavin Hamilton, a haulage
contractor from Dennistoun. The first Mackintosh

building design to be completed.
October – Receives second £5 from Honeyman
and Keppie.
Honeyman and Keppie enter three schemes: Classical,
English Renaissance and Scottish Renaissance for the
new Art Galleries in Glasgow but none is premiated.
Promoted to designer. Sketches at Largs with McNair.
Paints frieze of cats in room at Dennistoun.

1891   February 10 – Reads paper on Scotch Baronial
Architecture to Glasgow Architectural Association.
March 21 – Leaves Glasgow for London and Paris en
route to Italy.
Arrives Naples April 5. Visits Rome, Orvieto, Siena,
Florence, Pisa, Ravenna, Ferrara, Venice, Padua, Verona,
Cremona, Brescia, Bergamo, Como and Pavia until July.
Wins first prize in Glasgow School of Art Student
Exhibition with Italian watercolours. Wins National
Silver Medal at Kensington for Public Hall scheme.
July – fails for Soane Prize with 'A Chapter House'
under the name of 'Griffen' but won a Gold Medal when
it was submitted to South Kensington later in the year.
Designs writing desk for Michael Diack.

1892   Goes on to regular salary and becomes engaged to Jessie
Keppie, now an assistant lecturer at the School of Art.
July 8 – Superintendant William McIntosh marries
Christina Forrest, a widow from Dennistoun. Changes
surname to Mackintosh. Weekends at 'roaring camps'
with 'The Immortals' at Dunure, Ayrshire. Works on
interiors for Glasgow Art Club, 185 Bath Street, Glasgow
with Keppie.
September 6 – reads paper 'A Tour in Italy' to the
Glasgow Architects.
October – the extended McIntosh family moves from the
East End to the South Side of Glasgow, to 2 Regent Park
Square (now No 6). Decorates his cellar room with
Japanese prints and a frieze of cats. Exhibits sketches

and watercolours at the annual show at the Glasgow Institute of Fine Arts. These were unsuccessfully submitted for the Pugin Scholarship in the following year but received acclaim in the *British Architect and Builder*.

November 19 – first graphic work on invitation to first meeting of the Glasgow School of Art Club founded by Francis Newbery. Here he introduces evening-students, Mackintosh and McNair to the day-student Macdonald sisters and suggests that all four might work together on future projects related to the decorative arts.

A railway terminus scheme (longitudinal section) for Manchester Technical School fails for the Soane Medallion despite receiving better reaction than winner. First symbolic watercolour – *Harvest Moon*. Gives it as gift to John Keppie. Gives Jessie brass casket with two rosebuds inside. Reads paper on 'Elizabethan Architecture' to Glasgow Architects.

1893   February – Lecture on 'Architecture' with reference to the progressive elements in contemporary British architecture given to audience of 'picture painters. Sketchbook of Scottish and Italian drawings. Works on designs for *The Glasgow Herald* building in Mitchell Street.

May – Completes ten years at Art School and leaves. Increasingly involved with the Macdonalds and McNair in design schemes. The Four exhibit at the School of Art autumn show. Macdonald sisters design Invitation Card for the School of Art Club 'At Home' on 25 November. It is the beginning of the Glasgow Style. Sketches at Lamlash on Arran.

Canal Boatsman's Institute, Port Dundas, Glasgow. Photographed by Annan.

October – Mackintosh family moves to Holmwood at 82 Langside Avenue.

First furniture for fellow-student, David Gauld and rents

his first studio to work on furniture for Guthrie and Wells of Glasgow.

November 1 – Jessie Keppie writes *A Faerie Storie,* an allegory about her situation with Mackintosh, for the first issue of *The Magazine.*

1894   April 4 – In the next issue of *The Magazine,* Jessie's big sister, Jane, writes a similar allegory contrasting the contented life of Portia with the sad end of Ophelia. Jessie added a drawing and short piece entitled *Silly Ophelia.* Meantime, Mackintosh completes three watercolours for the same magazine including *Cabbages in an Orchard* with his own satirical commentary. Works on Conservative Club house for Kidson family at 40 Sinclair Street, Helensburgh. Designs *Converzatione* programme for the Glasgow Architectural Association. Works with John Keppie on Queen Margaret College design, a warehouse for Pettigrew and Stephens and on designs for the Fairfied Shipyard Offices. Also for schemes for the Royal Insurance building and Paisley Technical School, neither of which was completed. Works on *Glasgow Herald* scheme in Mitchell Street. Hyndland Tennis Club incident. Jilts Jessie in favour of Margaret. Quarrel with John Keppie. Jessie declines to pursue for breach of promise. Sketches in Langside, Stirling, Ascog on Bute and southern England.

September – sketching in Worcester and the northern Cotswolds.

Watercolours published in the *Glasgow Architectural Sketchbook.*

November – exhibits with Macdonalds and McNair at the Glasgow School of Art Club.

1895   January – paints pair of symbolic watercolours. Both featured in the student *Magazine.*

February – Poster in the style of Aubrey Beardsley for Glasgow Institute of Fine Arts.

Designs furniture for William Davidson at Gladsmuir, Kilmacolm and recreates cats' stencil for the nursery. Works on design for Martyrs' School sited on the very street where he was born.

June – Sketches on Arran, Maybole (The Castle), Lennoxtown, Oxford, Lyme Regis, and in Hampshire, Dorset and Somerset.

October – McIntosh family return to Regent Park Square, this time to No 27.

Re-does cat frieze in cellar. Works with George Walton on stencil decorations for Kate Cranston's enlarged tea room at 91–93 Buchanan Street, a four-storey building designed by George Washington Browne. Fancy Dress Fair held at the Glasgow Institute Galleries to raise funds for the Ladies Arts Club. Mackintosh on 'stage management'.

1896   March 7 – Sir James Fleming. Chairman of the Governors of the Glasgow School of Art, proposes the building of a new Art School. A competition is suggested. April – Gives Margaret present of *Part Seen – Imagined Part,* original watercolour in special frame.

May – Newbery draws up conditions of competition for Art School design and prepares block plan. Assessors appointed (Sir James King and Sir Renny Watson) and a Building Committee formed.

June – The competition is announced, limited to eight, then twelve, architectural firms. Honeyman and Keppie enter and give the brief to Mackintosh as his sole responsibility. The deadline is set for 1st October.

The Four exhibit with the Arts and Crafts in London to mixed reaction. Sketches in Orkney, Prestwick, Maybole Castle and Langside.

1897   January – Mackintosh design wins Art School contract. Salary raised to £12. John Keppie is made responsible for the erection of Art School to first stage.

February – All competition designs for new Art School

on view at Corporation Galleries.

CRM designs St Matthew's Church, Maryhill for the Springburn Mission. This was to become Queen's Cross Church and the offices of the Charles Rennie Mackintosh Society from 1973.

Organ case and stool for Craigie Hall, Glasgow.

Works on furniture designs for Argyle Street tea rooms Gleeson White pubishes an article on the Four in *The Studio,* making them known on the Continent for the first time.

August – Sketches in Walberswick, Suffolk during first visit with Newberys.

Visits Worstead and other places in England.

October – First stage plans for the Art School approved by the Dean of Guild Court.

November – construction begins.

1898   Designs a Grand Hall and Concert Hall, and also designs an Industrial Hall for the Glasgow International Exhibition of 1901.

Works on offices for the National Bank on the St Vincent Street/Buchanan Street corner, Glasgow. Designs furniture for Alexander Seggie of Edinburgh. Hall for Free Church, Ruchill Street.

May 25 – Foundation stone laid for Glasgow School of Art in Renfrew Street by the Lord Provost of Glasgow.

Works on gravesones for James Reid at Kilmacolm August – Sketches in Tavistock, Ashburton, Stoke Gabriel and Exeter, Devon.

Bedroom for publisher, Robert McLehose at Westdel, 2 Queen's Place, Glasgow.

September 16 – Results of International Exhibition Competition – he is unplaced.

September 30 – William McIntosh retires from Police with rank of Superintendent.

Article on Mackintosh by Beresford Pite in the *Architectural Review.*

November – first article by Hermann Muthesius in *Dekorative Künst*, Munich.
Designs dining room at Nymphenburgerstrasse 86, in Munich for Hugo Brukmann of *Dekorative Künst*.

1899   Year given over to design of Art School interiors. Salary increased to £16 monthly. First sod cut at Windyhill by William Davidson Junior. Assists Keppie in design for Redlands at Bridge of Weir.
April – completes interiors and designs furniture for Miss Cranston at 114 Argyle Street.
May – The Four exhibit with Society of Sculptors, Painters and Gravers in London. Queen's Cross Church completed.
December 20 – Formal opening of first stage of new Glasgow School of Art by Sir James King with long key designed by Mackintosh on a cushion designed by Margaret Macdonald.

1900   Works on own flat at 120 Mains Street, Glasgow. Designs Luncheon Room for Miss Cranston's Ingram Street tea room.
May – Design for the *Daily Record* building go before the Dean of Guild Court.
Sketches at Falkland Palace. Design for St Serf's Church, Dysart. Redesigns Walton's interiors at Ingram Street for Kate Cranston.
August – completes designs for Windyhill at Kilmacolm for William Davidson. On 22nd, marries Margaret Macdonald at St Dunstane's Episcopal Church, Dumbarton. Honeymoon spent on the Holy Island, Northumberland.
Moves into Mains Street flat. Visited in Glasgow by Fritz Wärndorfer.
November – in Vienna to install exhibits for the Vienna Secession with the McNairs, George Walton and Talwin Morris who are also showing – Strong critical reaction. Remained in Vienna for six weeks. Feted by students.

1901   Mackintosh becomes junior partner in Honeyman,
Keppie and Mackintosh. Salary increased to £20
monthly. Practice moves to 4 Blythswood Square. Works
on House for an Art Lover for German competition
promoted by Alexander Koch at Darmstadt. Entry under
the pen name 'Der Vogel'. Wins a 'Special Purchase
Prize' of 600 marks.
June – sketches on Holy Island, Northumberland,
with Margaret.
Second Glasgow International Exhibition – opening of
Kelvingrove Art Gallery. Designs Gate Lode at
Auchenbothie, Kilmacolm. Works on *Daily Record*
building and on interiors for the Rowat family at 14
Kingsborough Gardens, Glasgow. Also a bedroom
interior at Queen's Place which was featured in
Dekorative Künst in 1902. Designs An Artist's Town
House – not executed. Designs An Artist's Country
House. Designs menu for RIBA annual dinner in Glasgow.
December 20 – first stage of Glasgow School of Art
opens.

1902   William McIntosh family moves to Tynemouth, near
South Sheilds. Toshie's salary now £240 p.a.
March – first drawings for Hill House, Helensburgh, for
Walter Blackie. Work of both Mackintoshes published in
Dekorative Künst. Music Room at Carl-Ludwigstrasse
45, Vienna for Fritz Wärndorfer of the Weiner Werkstätte.
Frieze of gesso panels by Margaret Macdonald. Article
on the two Mackintoshes by Hermann Muthesius in
Dekorative Künst.
April – In Turin for the International Exhibition of
Modern Decorative Art. Dines with Grand Duke
of Hesse.
Designs Scottish section, including the Rose Boudoir
with Margaret. Fritz Wärndorfer buys furniture,
including the writing cabinet, from Rose Boudoir.
June 23 – Meets Glasgow School Board to discuss design

for Scotland Street School.

July – sketching on Holy Island with Margaret, the McNairs and Charles Macdonald.

September – Whole issue of *Dekorative Künst* devoted to Scots at Turin.

November – designs submitted for Scotland Street School.

December – Gives paper on *Seemliness* to Glasgow architects. Moscow Exhibition at the Petrovka, *Architecture and Design of the New Style* includes Mackintosh

1903   February – plans for Willow Tea Rooms at 217 Sauchiehall Street for Miss Kate Cranston, approved by Dean of Guild Court.

Designs steel frame for George Frampton's portrait of Sir James Fleming to be built into the half-landing above the museum gallery in the Art School.

March – Design for Liverpool Cathedral published in *The British Architect* – 'highly commended'.

May – suffers from eyestrain and overwork. Takes trip to Orkney Islands.

June – appointed by Glasgow School Board to design Scotland Street School, his last public commission.

September – enters competition for Anglican Cathedral in Liverpool. Fails at first stage. Norman Shaw and GF Bodley, the Assessors, but Professor Reilly of Liverpool School of Art has influence. The competition won by Giles Gilbert Scott, an architectural apprentice.

Designs interiors and furniture at Hous'hill for Mrs John Cochrane (Kate Cranston). Shop and apartment above for Mr Macpherson at Dunira Street, Comrie.

December – exhibits bedroom for the Dresdener Werkstätten fur Handwerkskünst at Dresden. Josef Hoffmann vists Glasgow to persuade Toshie to join the Werkstätte in Vienna. Declines offer of a studio and workshop in Vienna.

1904   John Honeyman retires due to increasing eye failure
March – Hill House is completed *under* budget.
October 29 – Willow Tea Rooms opened and acclaimed
by Glasgow.
Mackintosh and Newbery godfathers to Muthesius's son,
Eckart. Toshie evolves ladder-backed chair for Miss
Cranston. Furnishings for Holy Trinity Church, Bridge
of Allan. Sketches in Scilly Isles.

1905   March – Fernando Agnoletti eulogises Mackintosh and
the Hill House bedroom in Alexander Koch's *Dekorative
Künst*.
Shows rectilinear dining room in exhibition sponsored
by AS Ball, Berlin.
April – article on Willow Tea Rooms in *Dekorative Künst*.
August – sketches in Saxlingham, Norfolk.
Fireplace for Miss Rowat in Paisley.
Works on Auchenibert, a neo-Tudor house at Killearn,
Stirlingshire for Francis J Shand. Gravestone for Rev
Alexander Orrock Johnston at East Wemyss, Fife.
November – sketches in Sussex.

1906   Mackintosh completes interior of boardroom at Glasgow
School of Art.
March 30 – buys 6 Florentine Terrace, Glasgow, (the
later 78 Southpark Avenue) for £950.
August – sketches on Holy Island and at Bowling.
September 27 – Art School governers appoint a Building
Committe to oversee extensions to School.
November – Approval given to designs for Balgray
Cottage (later Mossyde) at Cloak, Kilmacolm.
Dutch Kitchen for Miss Cranston at Argyle Street tea
rooms. Pulpit for Abbey Close Church, Paisley. Scotland
Street School completed at cost of £15,000.
December 3 – elected Fellow of RIBA.

1907   February 1 – Honeyman, Keppie and Mackintosh
appointed architects for Art School extension.

April 22 – Plans approved by Building Committee.
Works on Oak Room at Ingram Street tea rooms.
June 26 – *Glasgow Herald* names Mackintosh as the
architect for the Art School extension.
Return visit to Walberswick with Margaret.
November 14 – Plans passed by Dean of Guild.

1908   Became FRIAS on John Keppie's recommendation. Keppie
become President of the Glasgow Institute of Architects.
Supervising Art School extensions. Designs black door
and Entrance to Lady Artists' Club, 5 Blythswood
Square.
February 5 – Building Committe protests about
'unauthorised and extravagant work' on the entrance
porch. Five days later, William McIntosh dies aged 70
and is buried in Sighthill Cemetery, Glasgow.
June – sketches at Cintra, Portugal.
Cottage extension at Cloak (renamed Mossyde)
Kilmacolm for HB Collins.
October – Dresses up as Morgan le Fay for fund-raising
pageant at the University.

1909   January – Building Committe objects to the Gallery in
the Art School Library.
Oval Room interiors at Ingram Street tea rooms.
June – sketches at Blairgowrie and in Sussex.
Interiors at Hous'hill for the Cochranes.
Sketching in Withyham and Groomsbridge, Sussex.
September – Mackintosh reports completion of Art
School extensions.
December 15 – Wednesday at 2.30, the formal opening
of Art School wing by Sir John Stirling-Maxwell.
Mackintosh makes a speech and presents a casket which
he had designed to Sir James Fleming.

1910   Revises plans for Art School extensions. Designs furniture
for Art School. No further architectural work.
April – Flower studies at Bowling.
May – sketches in Kent.

December – Governors of Art School report that the building has been paid for and that they are 'completely satisfied with what they have got for the money'.

1911   Interiors for White Cockade tea rooms at Scottish National Exhibition in Glasgow. Chinese Room and Cloister Room in Ingram Street tea room show effects of latest work on Art School. Art Nouveau abandoned in favour of repetitive squares and straight lines. Designs hairdressing salon at 80 Union Street, Glasgow. Talwin Morris dies. Mackintosh designs Rosicrucian gravestone.

1912   March 11 – transfers ownership of 6 Florentine Terrace to Margaret.
Sketches at Bowling.

1913   Exhibited in Moscow. Sponsored by Elizabeth of Hesse. February 13 – Newbery presents his painting of Building Committee in Session (1906–09) to the Governors of the School of Art. Mackintosh seen at left with plans in his hand. Meantime, working through the night, Toshie fails to complete designs for College of Domestic Science in Woodlands Road and a competition for the building of a Teachers' Training College at Jordanhill. Keppie and assistants finish the drawing and win the competition. Mackintosh loses partnership. Sets up on his own at the old Keppie office at 140 Bath Street but does not attract one client. Drinking increases and a deep depression sets in.
July – sketches on Holy Island.
Extremely ill with pneumonia. Depression now very severe. The Mackintoshes leave Glasgow for Walberswick. Extended stay at Walberswick to paint flowers for book to be published in Germany. Paints 40 watercolours of flowers.
October – Designs book covers for Blackie's – *Rambles Among Our Industries*.

1914   John Honeyman dies. Partnership of Honeyman, Keppie and Mackintosh formally dissolved. John Keppie promotes Henderson, the chief draughtsman to form

Keppie, Henderson and Partners with offices at 257 West George Street.

May 18 – Building Committee Group portrait formally unveiled by Sir John Struthers.

July – Mackintoshes decide to remain in Walberswick and rent out Florentine Terrace for a year to William Davidson.

August 14 – War declared with Germany. German links broken. Paris visit cancelled.

1915   Arrested as German spy. Acquitted, after intercession by Lady Norah Mears (daughter of Patrick Geddes) at the War Office in London.

July – Attends Summer school run by Patrick Geddes at King's College on *War – its Social Effects and Problems*. Shares room with Philip Mairet. Plans for 'Shop, Office Block and Warehouse in an Arcaded Street' prepared for Geddes in India, but not built. Designs lamp standards for Patrick Geddes and also supplies a drawing of 'A War Memorial in a Public Place'.

August 5 – Tentative offer from the Indian Government to go out there for some six months.

Margaret returns to London and they settle in Oakley Street, Chelsea. Rent studios at 2 Hans Studios, 443A Glebe Place and at Cedar Studios, 45 Glebe Place but two studios linked by interior common doorway. Mackintosh paints flowers. Mackintosh is sought out asked by Wenman Joseph Bassett-Lowke, an engineer and member of the Design and Industries Association, and asked to design interiors for his house at 78 Derngate, a Georgian terrace in Northampton.

1916   Exhibits at International Society of Sculptors, Painters and Gravers at Goupil Gallery, London.

October – Mackintoshes exhibit *The Voices of the Wood* for the Arts and Crafts Exhibition Society in London.

December – Designs approved for The Dug-Out, a basement tea room under the Willow Tea Rooms at 217

Sauchiehall Street.

1917   March – completes interior and exterior alterations at Derngate in time for Bassett-Lowke's wedding to Florence Jones. Dug-Out completed at Willow Tea Rooms. Buchanan Street tea rooms sold to become a bank. Miss Cranston later gives Ingram Street premises to her manageress there, a maiden lady, Miss Drummond who ran it until her own retirement in 1930. She sold to Coopers Ltd, who leased until 1950 when the premises were acquired by Glasgow Corporation. Exhibits for Society of Sculptors, Painters and Gravers in London. Works on textile designs with Margaret. These show Viennese influence. Clients include Templeton's in Glasgow, Sefton's in Belfast and Liberty and Foxton in London.

1918   Interiors at Candida Cottage, Roade, near Northampton for FM Jones (Bassett-Lowke's brother-in-law). Also a 'German room' for Harold Bassett-Lowke as a wedding present for his brother. Designs 'Peace Panels' for Miss Cranston. With Fergusson, re-organises the London Salon of the Independents but plans to use disused army huts in Hyde Park fall through because permission refused by War Office. WR Davidson buys 78 Southpark Avenue from Margaret.

1919   Bedroom at 78 Derngate, Northampton and re-designs of interior for Bassett-Lowke's wife, Florence Jones. Alterations at Little Hedgecourt, East Grinstead, Surrey for photographer, EO Hoppé. Sketches at Buxted.

1920   January 8 – Designs studio/house for painter, Harold Squire, at 49 Glebe Place, to be paid for by his sister, Mrs Evelyn Claude.
February 13 – Designs house for painter, Arthur Cadigan Blunt, at 48 Glebe Place.
March – Designs studios and workshop for sculptor, Francis Derwent Wood, at 50 Glebe Place, but neither of these schemes were carried through.

April – On suggestion of Professor Schwabe and JD
Fergusson and at the request of Anita Berry of the Arts
League of Service, works on block of studios and 27
studio flats. The first site chosen was on the site of the
old Cheyne House on Cheyne Row. The ground land
lord, the Glebe of Chelsea, appoints as their planning
consultant, a surveyor, WE Clifton.

May – Clifton insisted on 'more architectural
considerations' on the final Mackintosh elevation and
building plans were halted. When they were finally
passed, the Arts League of Service had effectively ceased
to function and the project came to nothing.

June – asked to design small theatre in Flood Street,
Chelsea for dancer, Margaret Morris and the Plough
Theatre, but this project was also not carried through
due to lack of funds.

July – The Mackintoshes holiday at Worth Matravers,
Dorset with the Schwabe family.

August – Derngate extensions illustrated in *Ideal Home*
but Mackintosh not mentioned. Bassett-Lowke given
total credit.

December – Another plan for studios and flats for the
Arts League of Service, this time at 48 Glebe Place, also
aborts. Resolves to give up architecture.

Portrait photographs taken by EO Hoppé.

1921 Designs bindings for GA Henty novels.

1922 Exhibits studio designs at RIBA, London, in December
and is dismissed by HS Goodhart-Rendel as
'old-fashioned'. Mrs Macdonald dies and leaves legacy
to Margaret. JD Fergusson and Margaret Morris suggest
the Mackintoshes take a long holiday in South of France.

1923 January – 48th Royal Academy Exhibition of Decorative
Arts. His exhibit, *A Landscape Panel*, was not hung.
Allan Ure visits on the day they were packing to leave
for France. Mackintoshes arrive first at Coullioure in the
Pyrenees-Orientales.

Toshie becomes a regular at the Hotel des Templiers – patron René Pous.

1924 Move to Hotel du Commerce (patron, M Dejean) on the harbourfront on Quai Pierre Forgas, Port Vendres, and in the hot summer go up into the mountains at Mont Louis. Mackintosh paints outdoors at Amelie-les-Bains. Margaret in London to prepare designs for the Queen's Doll's House and try to place Toshie's flower paintings. She returns to walk, sew and read English newspapers and library books from Mudie's which are sent out. Meantime, Bassett-Lowke is trying to find Mackintosh, He wants the Scot to design a new house for him. Failing to find Mackintosh in the Pyrenees, he hires the German architect, Peter Behrens, born the same year as Mackintosh, who designs New Ways, based on the interiors and furniture at Derngate.
Charles Marriott, architecture critic of the London *Times* writes piece under the title of 'Modern English Architecture' in which he argues that the whole Modernist Movement in European Architecture stems from Mackintosh.

1925 Mackintoshes travel by train around the region to let Mackintosh paint – Amelie-les-Bains – Ille-sur-Têt – La Lagonne Boultenere – Mount Alba – Palalda and Mount Louis. Stay with Geddes at Montpelier. Watercolours exhibited in Chicago.

1926 Brief ventures into Spain (Fetges) and Italy (Florence) but return to Port Vendres.

1927 Hermann Muthesius dies.
May – Margaret in London for dental treatment and to tidy up their affairs in Glasgow and London.
Mackintosh alone at Hotel du Commerce till July.
Continues to paint landscapes.
May 10 – starts on *The Rock* and it is finished by 27th. Writes his daily 'Chronacles' to Margaret. Margaret returns. Exhibits his watercolours at British Artists

Exhibition in Paris. Finally beats his drinking problem. Soreness of the tongue is diagnosed as cancer. Rudolph Ihlee takes him back to London for radium treatment. Met by Jessie Newbery who arranges admittance to Westminster Hospital.

1928   Toshie enters Westminster Hospital as private patient of the surgeon. Draws tongue as an aid for medical students. Improves enough to be released to convalesce in furnished rooms in Willow Road, near Hampstead Heath. Visited regularly by Margaret Morris who teaches him sign language. Trouble with the other tenants causes them to leave hurriedly. Desmond Chapman-Huston offers them the upper floors of his house at 72 Porchester Square. Suffers sudden relapse and is moved into nursing home at 26 Porchester Square, where he dies. He is sitting up in bed, signing the pictures that Chapman-Huston has brought to the bedside from the exhibition of watercolours at the Leicester Galleries when he dies. The date is December 10, one day later than his beloved mother's death-date in 1885.
December 11 – Cremated at Golders Green.

Bibliography

Attwood, Anthony	*Asperger's Syndrome,* London 1997.
Barnes, Henry Jefferson	*Charles Rennie Mackintosh – Furniture* and *Charles Rennie Mackintosh – Ironwork and Metalwork,* Glasgow School of Art, 1968.
Billcliffe, Roger	*Flower Drawings by Charles Rennie Mackintosh,* London 1977; *Mackintosh Watercolours,* London 1978; *Charles Rennie Mackintosh – Complete Furniture and Interior Designs* (2nd edition) Lutterworth 1980; *Mackintosh Furniture,* Lutterworth 1983; *Mackintosh Textiles,* Lutterworth 1993.
Bisson, RF	*The Sandon Studios Society of the Arts,* Liverpool 1965.
Blake, Fanny	*Essential Charles Rennie Mackintosh,* Bath 2001.
Bliss, Douglas Percy	*Charles Rennie Mackintosh and the Glasgow School of Art,* Glasgow School of Art, 1961.
Brett, David	*Charles Rennie Mackintosh – The Poetics of Workmanship,* London 1992.
Buchanan, William M	(Ed) *Mackintosh's Masterwork,* Glasgow 1989; *Charles Rennie Mackintosh – CD Rom,* Wigwam, 1997.
Burkhauser, Jude	*Glasgow Girls,* Edinburgh 1990.
Cairney, John	*A Mackintosh Experience –* A Reading for Four Actors Shanter Productions, Edinburgh, 1975; *Mackintosh –* Scottish Television 1977; *Toshie –* A play manuscript, November 1989.
Chapman-Huston, D	*The Lamp of Memory,* London 1949.
Connolly, Sean	*Charles Rennie Mackintosh,* London 2000
Crawford, Allan	*Charles Rennie Mackintosh,* London 1995.
Daiches, David	*Glasgow,* London 1977.
Davidson, Fiona	*Charles Rennie Mackintosh,* The Pitkin Guide, 1998.
Fiell, Charlotte and Peter	*Charles Rennie Mackintosh,* London 1995.
Grigg, Jocelyn	*Charles Rennie Mackintosh,* Glasgow 1987.

Grigor, Murray (with Richard Murphy)	*The Architect's Architect, CR Mackintosh.* Glasgow 1995.
Grogan, Elaine	*Charles Rennie Mackintosh's Early Sketches,* London 2002.
Hackney, Fiona and Isla	*Charles Rennie Mackintosh,* Sandstone 1996.
Harris, Nathaniel	*Life and Works of C. Rennie Mackintosh,* Glasgow 1996.
Helland, Janice	*The Studios of Frances and Margaret Macdonald,* Manchester 1996.
Herman, Arthur	*The Scottish Enlightenment,* Fourth Estate, London 2001.
Howarth, Thomas	*Charles Rennie Mackintosh and the Modern Movement,* London 1952; *Queen's Cross Church – An Appraisal,* Scottish
Ecclesiological	Society 1945; *Poems,* Gillemot, Toronto 1996.
Jones, Anthony	*Charles Rennie Mackintosh,* London 1990 and 1995.
Kaplan, Wendy	(Ed) *Scotland Creates,* National Galleries of Scotland, 1990; (Ed) *Charles Rennie Mackintosh,* Glasgow Museums, 1996.
Kinchin, Perilla	*Miss Cranston,* NMS Publishing 1999.
Larner, Gerald and Celia	*The Glasgow Style,* Edinburgh 1979.
Lethaby, WR	*Architecture, Mysticism and Myth,* London 1892.
Macauley, James	(Ed) *Glasgow School of Art – Charles Rennie Mackintosh,* London 2002.
MacLeod, Robert	*Charles Rennie Mackintosh,* Country Life 1968; *Charles Rennie Mackintosh, Architect and Artist,* London 1983.
MacInnes, Ranald	*Building a Nation,* Edinburgh 1999.
Masini, Lara-Vinca	*Art Nouveau,* Secausus, New Jersey 1984.
McKean, John (with Colin Baxter)	*Charles Rennie Mackintosh,* Moray 1998
McLaren Young, Andrew	*Architectural Jottings by Charles Rennie Mackintosh,* Glasgow Institute of Architects, 1968.
Moffat, Alistair (with Colin Baxter)	*Remembering Charles Rennie Mackintosh,* Colin Baxter Photography, Lanark 1989.
Morris, Margaret	*The Art of JD Fergusson,* Glasgow 1974

Moss, Michael (with John Hume)	*Glasgow as it Was,* Vol 2, Hendon Publishing Nelson, Lancs, 1975
Murphy, Richard	*Architect's Architect – A Celebration of Charles Rennie Mackintosh,* London 1993.
Neat, Timothy	*Part Seen, Part Imagined,* Edinburgh 1994; *Closing the Circle: Thomas Howarth, Mackintosh and the Modern Movement,* London 2002.
Nuttgens, Patrick	(Ed) *Mackintosh and his Contemporaries,* CRM Society and Cameron Books 1988.
Pevsner, Sir Nikolaus	*Pioneers of the Modern Movement,* London 1936; *Charles R. Mackintosh,* London 1950 (re-published Turin 1997).
Robertson, Pamela	Charles Rennie Mackintosh – The Architectural Papers MIT (USA) 1991; *Art is the Flower – Charles Rennie Mackintosh,* Hunterian Art Gallery, University of Glasgow 1995; *Chronycle,* The Mackintosh Letters to Margaret Macdonald Mackintosh – Port Vendres 1927, Hunterian Art Gallery at Glasgow University 2001.
Ruskin, John	The Seven Lamps of Architecture, London 1848.
Scott, Richard	Artists at Walberswick (East Anglian Interludes), Bristol 2001.
Steele, James	*Synthesis in Form,* London 1994.
Stuart, Andrew	*Old Dennistoun*, Richard Shenlake, Ochiltree, Ayrshire (ND)
Sullivan, KE	*The Life, Times and Work of Charles Rennie Mackintosh,* Caxton Editions, London 1997.
Swinglehurst, Edmund	*Charles Rennie Mackintosh,* Thunder Bay 2001.
Tanner, Ailsa	*Bessie MacNicol,* Privately published 1998.
Walker, Frank Arneil	*Glasgow.* Phaedon, London.
Wilhide, Elizabeth	*The Mackintosh Style,* London 1995.

also
Scottish Arts Review, Special Number, Vol XI, No 4, 1968
and

Catalogue	Memorial Exhibition – McLellan Galleries, Glasgow 1933.
Catalogue	Mackintosh Exhibition – Saltire Society and Arts Council of Great Britain 1953.
Catalogue	Centennial Exhibition – Scottish Arts Council, Edinburgh Festival 1968.
Catalogue	Margaret Macdonald Mackintosh – Hunterian Museum Glagow 1984.
Catalogue	*The Mackintosh House* – Hunterian Museum, Glasgow 1987.
Catalogue	'CR Mackintosh – The Chelsea Years' – Hunterian Gallery, Glasgow and RIBA, London 1994.

with
Back Numbers of the Charles Rennie Mackintosh Society's *Newsletters* on demand from Queen's Cross Church, 870 Garscube Road, Glasgow, G20 7EL.

CRMSN 11 (Spring 1976) 'I Remember Mackintosh', Sturrock & Morris.
CRMSN 22 (Summer 1979) 'Memories of Mackintosh', Peter Wylie Davidson, pp4–6.
CRMSN 30 (Autumn1981) 'The Newberys', H Jefferson Barnes.
CRMSN 31 (Winter/Spring 1981/2) 'MMM', Pamela Reekie (Robertson).
CRMSN 32.(Summer 1982) 'Mackintosh, John and Jessie Keppie', William Buchanan.
CRMSN 33 (Autumn 1982) 5–9 'James Herbert MacNair', R Billcliffe.
CRMSN 53 (Spring 1990) 'Geddes and Mackintosh'.
CRMSN 62 (Summer 1993) 'Mackintosh, Jessie Keppie and the Immortals; Some New Material', G Rawson.
CRMSN 64 (Spring 1994) 5–8 'The Honeymans', David Walker.
CRMSN 67 (Summer 1995) 5–8 'William McIntosh' Iain Paterson.
12 'Review of the Architects Architect' Patrrick Nuttgens.
CRMSN 68 (Winter 1995) 'Note on Current Popularity of CRM', R Billcliffe.

Charles Rennie Mackintosh
The Glasgow Legacy

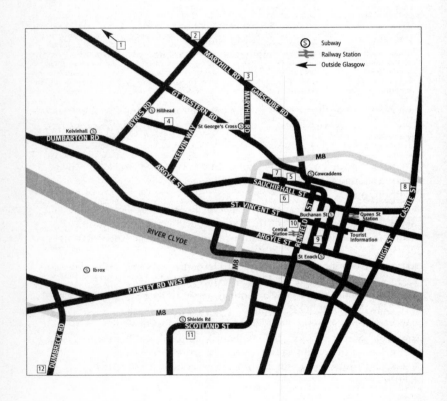

1 **The Hill House**
Upper Colquhoun Street,
Helensburgh G84 9AJ.
T:+44 (0)1436 673900.
F:+44 (0)1436 674685.
E: thehillhouse@nts.org.uk
www.nts.org.uk
The Hill House, originally
designed for the publisher
Walter Blackie, is now in the
care of The National Trust for
Scotland. The original furni-
ture, fittings and interior
designs have been reinstated
or restored.

2 **Ruchill Church Hall**
15/17 Shakespeare Street,
Glasgow G20 9PT.
Built as a mission before the
adjacent church which was
not designed by CRM. It consists principally of two halls
and two committee rooms, all
currently used by an active
congregation and is considered to be a well-planned
minor work.

3 **The Mackintosh Church**
Queen's Cross
870 Garscube Road,
Glasgow G20 7EL.
T: +44 (0)141 946 6600.
F: +44 (0)141 945 2321.
E: info@crmsociety.com
www.crmsociety.com
The only church designed by
Mackintosh to be built and
now the Society's
international headquarters.
Magnificent stained glass and
exceptional relief carving on
wood and stonework are
highlights of the interior
where light and space are
used to dramatic effect.

4 **Hunterian Art Gallery**
The Mackintosh House,
University of Glasgow
Hillhead Street, Glasgow
G12 8QQ.
T: +44 (0)141 330 5431.
F: +44 (0)141 330 3618.
E: hunter@museum.gla.ac.uk
www.hunterian.gla.ac.uk
The interiors of 6 Florentine
Terrace, Glasgow home of
Mackintosh and

Margaret Macdonald from
1906 to 1914, meticulously
reassembled within the
University's Art Gallery.
Changing displays of items
from the Mackintosh
Collection in the upstairs
Gallery.

5 **McLellan Galleries**
Glasgow Museums,
270 Sauchiehall Street,
Glasgow G2 3EH.
T: +44 (0)141 565 4137.
F: +44 (0)141 565 4111.
www.glasgowmuseums.com
The Glasgow 1900 gallery dis-
plays furniture, decorative
objects and paintings which
set CRM's work in its local
context and contrasting it
with that of his contempo-
raries including the
Macdonald sisters, Talwin
Morris, E.A. Taylor,
George Walton, John Ednie,
George Logan and the
'Glasgow Girls'.

6 **The Willow Tea Rooms**
217 Sauchiehall Street,
Glasgow, G2 3EX.
T: +44 (0)141 332 0521.
E: sauchiehallstreet@wil-
lowtearooms.co.uk
www.willowtearooms.co.uk
Behind the remarkable façade
which Mackintosh created for
Kate Cranston, tea and light
meals are still served in the
Room de Luxe and on The
Gallery. Many of the original
features survive. The ground
floor houses Henderson The
Jewellers. The Tea Rooms also
have a branch at 97
Buchanan Street.

7 **The Glasgow**
School of Art
167 Renfrew Street,
Glasgow G3 6RQ.
T: +44 (0)141 353 4526.
F: +44 (0)141 353 4746.
E: shop@gsa.ac.uk
www.gsa.ac.uk
Justifiably the best-known
architectural work, occupying
a whole city centre block with
the design skilfully balanced

around the central entrance.
Tours, lasting approximately
one hour, visit rooms containing many of the well-known
pieces of furniture and
include the breathtaking
Mackintosh Library.

8 **Martyrs' Public School**
Glasgow Museums,
Parson Street,
Glasgow G4 0PX.
T:+44 (0)141 553 2557.
www.glasgowmuseums.com
Uniquely built on the street
where CRM was born and
clearly visible from the top of
High Street. The solid red
sandstone construction is
topped by three ventilators
with highly decorative finials.
Inside there are lime-wash
plaster walls and spectacular
roof trusses.

9 **The Lighthouse**
11 Mitchell Lane,
Glasgow G1 3NU.
T: +44 (0)141 221 6362.
F: +44(0)141 221 6395
E: enquiries@thelight-
house.co.uk
www.thelighthouse.co.uk
The former Glasgow Herald
Building is now home to
Scotland's award winning
Centre for Architecture and
Design. The Mackintosh
Centre incorporates technology, original objects and a
fascinating illuminated wall to
plot Mackintosh's contribution to architecture and
design. The Mackintosh tower
with its helical staircase provides magnificent views
across the city. The Lighthouse
offers world class exhibitions,
displays, events, a rooftop
café/bar and viewing platform.

10 **Daily Record Building**
20 – 26 Renfield Lane,
Glasgow G2 5AT.
A large building which lies
between two city centre
lanes, west of Drury Street.
Mackintosh surprises us with
his striking use of colour on

the façade and skilfully
combines sculpted sandstone
and white glazed bricks to
maximise light.

11 **Scotland Street School**
Museum
Glasgow Museums,
225 Scotland Street,
Glasgow G5 8QB.
T: +44 (0)141 287 0500.
F: +44 (0)141 287 0515.
www.glasgowmuseums.com
Mackintosh's last major commission in Glasgow showing
evidence of the genius
of the mature architect.
Impressive leaded glass towers, magnificent tiled entrance
hall, unique stonework and
mastery of the interplay of
light and space. Period class-
rooms, exhibitions and activity
programmes throughout the
year. New displays on the history of the school and local
area, including interactive displays and our schools
photographic database.

12 **House for an Art Lover**
Bellahouston Park,
10 Dumbreck Road,
Glasgow G41 5BW.
T: +44 (0)141 353 4770.
F: +44 (0)141 353 4771.
E: info@houseforanart-
lover.co.uk
www.houseforanartlover.co.uk
The House was completed in
1996 inspired by CRM's port-
folio of drawings of 1901
which were submitted as a
competition entry to a
German design
magazine. A permanent exhibition of decorative furnished
rooms have been
realised by contemporary
artists and craftspeople.

Map and accompanying text
© CRM Society from their
leaflet The Glasgow Legacy.

Index

Grez 30
Grieve, Sir Robert 256
Grigor, Murray 3, 6, 7, 8, 144, 145, 150, 178, 256, 257
Groomsbridge 279
Gropius, Walter 195, 244
Guthrie, James 30, 64

H

Haddington Park 53
Haghill 21
The Hague 31
Haldane Academy 39, 94
Hamilton, David 134-135
Hampshire 273
Hancox, John 8
Hans Studios 180, 210, 281
Hardeman, Frances Grove 28
Hardeman, Joseph Tilly 247, 248
Hardy, Forsyth 256
Harrison, William 11, 106
Harrogate 246
Hastings, Thomas 221
Haudebert 29
Hawthorne, Nathaniel 14
Hedderwick, Ruth 127
Heggie, Alex 8
Helensburgh 7, 123, 125, 208, 272, 276
Hellier, Henry 7, 256
Henderson, A Graham 153, 158, 167, 168, 209
Henderson, John 94, 146
Henry, George 30, 145
Henty, GA 206, 283
Hereford, Edgar 226, 229
Hesse, Elizabeth of 280
Hesse, Grand Duke of 276
Hill House 7, 124, 125, 127, 144, 157, 160, 186, 255, 256, 257, 258, 266, 276, 278
Hillier, Henry 257
Hoffmann, Josef 31, 114, 122, 172, 253, 277
Hogarth 15
Holland 191, 216
Holland Park 203
Holmwood 82, 85, 271

Holy Island 110, 125, 164, 275, 276, 277, 278, 280
Holy Trinity Church 278
Honeyman, John 29, 34, 36, 46, 48, 50, 56, 57, 58, 65, 73, 82, 84, 92, 100, 101, 102, 110, 116, 126, 135, 142, 143, 146, 148, 150, 153, 157, 158, 160, 183, 199, 269, 270, 273, 276, 278, 280
Hope Street 35, 84, 89, 92, 140
Hoppé, EO 182, 196, 197, 282, 283
Hornel, Edward 29, 30, 51, 79, 80, 98
Hous'hill 135, 144, 190, 191, 266, 277, 279
Hous'll 135
House for an Art Lover 259, 276; see also Art Lover's House
Houston Street 106
Howarth 3, 5, 6, 7, 8, 9, 17, 37, 41, 55, 67, 68, 103, 115, 158, 178, 184, 200, 252, 255, 259, 266, 287, 288
Hughes, Professor T Harold 255
Hunter 194
Hunter, Russell 257, 258
Hurd, Robert 178
Hutchison, James 36, 37
Hutchison, John 16, 36, 37, 38, 42, 45, 46, 49, 268
Hutchison, WO 182
Hyndland Tennis Club 86, 89, 272

I

Ihlee, Rudolph 213, 226, 229, 230, 245, 285
Ille-sur-Têt 265, 284
The Immortals 56, 68, 289
Ingram Street 38, 43, 93, 116, 132, 142, 151, 256, 275, 279, 280, 282
Iona 49, 269
Italy 45, 55, 60, 62, 63, 71, 82, 124, 214, 269, 270, 284

J

Jackson, Enid 109
James, Henry 14
James, Jo 258
John, Augustus 118, 119, 182, 184

The Luath Burns Companion

John Cairney
ISBN 1 84282 000 1 PBK £10.00

'Robert Burns was born in a thunderstorm and lived his brief life by flashes of lightning.'
So says John Cairney in his introduction. In those flashes his genius revealed itself.

This collection is not another 'complete works' but a personal selection from 'The Man Who Played Robert Burns'. This is very much John's book. His favourites are reproduced here and he talks about them with an obvious love of the man and his work. His depth of knowledge and understanding has been garnered over forty years of study, writing and performance.

The collection includes sixty poems, songs and other works; and an essay that explores Burns's life and influences, his triumphs and tragedies. This informed introduction provides the reader with an insight into Burns's world.

Burns's work has drama, passion, pathos and humour. His careful workmanship is concealed by the spontaneity of his verse. He was always a forward thinking man and remains a writer for the future.

Immortal Memories: A Compilation of Toasts to the Memory of Burns as delivered at Burns Suppers, 1801-2001

John Cairney
ISBN 1 84282 009 5 HB £20.00

The annual Burns Supper, held on or around his birthday, January 25, has become something of a cult in virtually every country in the world where 'Scottish' is spoken - and even where it is not. This is an occasion when people gather around a dinner table to give tribute to a Scottish poet who died more than two hundred years ago. It really is an extraordinary phenomenon.

Thus begins John Cairney's latest work

focusing on Scotland's national bard, Robert Burns. To be asked to deliver the 'Immortal Memory', the chief toast and centrepiece of the traditional Burns Supper, is recognised as a privilege cherished by Burns enthusiasts the world over. Immortal Memories is an extensive collection of these toasts, spanning two hundred years from the first Burns Supper in Alloway in 1801 to the Millennium Burns Suppers of 2001.

For over thirty years Cairney has been recognised as the embodiment of Burns thanks to his portrayal of the poet in the 1968 Scottish TV production Burns. He has delivered toasts 'To the Immortal Memory of Robert Burns' or performed his Burns one-man-show in almost every country in the world.

THE QUEST FOR

The Quest for Robert Louis Stevenson

John Cairney
ISBN 0 946487 87 1 HB £16.99

In this book John Cairney examines the intimate relationships in the life of Robert Louis Stevenson, and their often destructive effects on his personality and work.

By introducing the boy Stevenson to the terrors of Hell did Alison Cunningham, his Calvinist nanny, irrevocably affect his work as a writer? What influence did close friends like Charles Baxter, Sidney Colvin, Edmund Gosse, and Fleeming Jenkin have on his development as man and writer?

What was it that drove Stevenson to burn the first draft of The Strange Case of Dr Jekyll and Mr Hyde?

Why did RLS lose his closest friend and could it have been prevented?

Might there have been more to his relationship with his faithful stepdaughter and secretary Belle?

A compelling read, The Quest for RLS sheds new light on the complicated life of the man behind the famous stories – Treasure Island, The Strange Case of Dr Jekyll and Mr Hyde and Kidnapped.

The Quest for the Nine Maidens

Stuart McHardy

ISBN 0 946487 66 9 HB £16.99

When Arthur was conveyed to Avalon they were there. When Odin summoned warriors to Valhalla they were there. When the Greek god Apollo was worshipped on mountaintops they were there. When Brendan came to the Island of Women they were there. Cerridwen's cauldron of inspiration was tended by them and Peredur received his arms from them. They are found in Pictland, Wales, Ireland, Iceland, Gaul, Greece, Africa and possibly as far as field as South America and Oceania.

They are the Nine Maidens, pagan priestesses involved in the worship of the Mother Goddess. From Stone Age rituals to the 20th century, the Nine Maidens come in many forms. Muses, Maenads, valkyries and druidesses all associated with a single male. Weather - workers, shape - shifters, diviners and healers, the Nine Maidens are linked to the Old Religion over much of our planet. In this book Stuart McHardy has traced similar groups of Nine Maidens, throughout the ancient Celtic and Germanic world and far beyond, from Christian and pagan sources. In his search he begins to uncover one of the most ancient and widespread institutions of human society.

The Quest for Arthur

Stuart McHardy

ISBN 1 84282 012 5 HB £16.99

King Arthur of Camelot and the Knights of the Round Table are enduring romantic figures. A national hero for the Bretons, the Welsh and the English alike Arthur is a potent figure for many. This quest leads to a radical new interpretation of the ancient myth.

Historian, storyteller and folklorist Stuart McHardy believes he has uncovered the origins of this inspirational figure, the true Arthur. He incorporates knowledge of folklore and placename studies with an archaeological understanding of the 6th century.

Combining knowledge of the earliest records and histories of Arthur with an awareness of the importance of oral traditions, this quest leads to the discovery that the enigmatic origins of Arthur lie not in Brittany or England or Wales. Instead they lie in that magic land the ancient Welsh called Y Gogledd, the North; the North of Britain which we now call Scotland.

The Quest for the Celtic Key

Karen Ralls-MacLeod and
Ian Robertson

ISBN 0 946487 73 1 HB £18.99

Who were the Picts? The Druids? The Celtic saints?

Was the famous 'murdered Apprentice' carving at Rosslyn Chapel deliberately altered in the past? If so, why?

Why has Rossslyn Chapel been a worldwide mecca for churchmen, Freemasons, Knights Templar, and Rosicrucians?

Why are there so many Scottish connections to King Arthur and Merlin?

What was the famous 'Blue Blanket' of the medieval Guilds of Edinburgh?

Did Prince Henry Sinclair get to North America before Columbus?

'The reader who travels with Karen Ralls-MacLeod and Ian Robertson...will find a travelogue which enriches the mythologies and histories so beautifully told, with many newly wrought connections to places, buildings, stones and other remains which may still be viewed in the landscape and historic monuments of modern Scotland....'

Rev. Dr. Michael Northcott, FACULTY OF DIVINITY, UNIVERSITY OF EDINBURGH

'Karen Ralls-MacLeod is endowed with that rare jewel of academia: a sharp and inquisitive mind blessed with a refreshing openness. Her stimulating work has the gift of making the academic accessible, and brings a clear and sound basis to the experiential... from 'Idylls of the King' to 'Indiana Jones', the search for the Holy Grail will never be the same again. This is a 'must read' book for all who sense the mystery and magic of our distant past.'

Robert Bauval, BESTSELLING AUTHOR OF 'THE SECRET CHAMBER', and 'KEEPER OF GENESIS'

ON THE TRAIL OF

On the Trail of Robert Burns

John Cairney

ISBN 0 946487 51 0 PBK £7.99

Is there anything new to say about Robert Burns?

John Cairney says it's time to trash Burns the Brand and come on the trail of the real Robert Burns. He is the best of travelling companions on this convivial, entertaining journey to the heart of the Burns story.

Internationally known as 'the face of Robert Burns', John Cairney believes that the traditional Burns tourist trail urgently needs to find a new direction. In an acting career spanning forty years he has often lived and breathed Robert Burns on stage. *On the Trail of Robert Burns* shows just how well he can get under the skin of a character. This fascinating journey around Scotland is a rediscovery of Scotland's national bard as a flesh and blood genius.

On the Trail of Robert Burns outlines five tours, mainly in Scotland. Key sites include:

Alloway - Burns' birthplace. 'Tam O' Shanter' draws on the witch-stories about Alloway Kirk first heard by Burns in his childhood.

Mossgiel - between 1784 and 1786 in a phenomenal burst of creativity Burns wrote some of his most memorable poems including 'Holy Willie's Prayer' and 'To a Mouse.'

Kilmarnock - the famous Kilmarnock edition of *Poems Chiefly in the Scottish Dialect* published in 1786.

Edinburgh - fame and Clarinda (among others) embraced him.

Dumfries - Burns died at the age of 37. The trail ends at the Burns mausoleum in St Michael's churchyard.

'For me an aim I never fash
I rhyme for fun' ROBERT BURNS

'My love affair on stage with Burns started in London in 1959. It was consummated on stage at the Traverse Theatre in Edinburgh in 1965 and has continued happily ever since' JOHN CAIRNEY

On the Trail of Robert Service

GW Lockhart

ISBN 0 946487 24 3 PBK £7.99

Robert Service is famed world-wide for his eyewitness verse-pictures of the Klondike goldrush. As a war poet, his work outsold Owen and Sassoon, and he went on to become the world's first million selling poet. In search of adventure and new experiences, he emigrated from Scotland to Canada in 1890 where he was caught up in the aftermath of the raging gold fever. His vivid dramatic verse bring to life the wild, larger than life characters of the gold rush Yukon, their bar-room brawls, their lust for gold, their trigger-happy gambles with life and love. 'The Shooting of Dan McGrew' is perhaps his most famous poem:

A bunch of the boys were whooping it up in
the Malamute saloon;
The kid that handles the music box was
hitting a ragtime tune;
Back of the bar in a solo game, sat
Dangerous Dan McGrew,
And watching his luck was his light o'love,
the lady that's known as Lou.

His storytelling powers have brought Robert Service enduring fame, particularly in North America and Scotland where he is something of a cult figure.

Starting in Scotland, *On the Trail of Robert Service* follows Service as he wanders through British Columbia, Oregon, California, Mexico, Cuba, Tahiti, Russia, Turkey and the Balkans, finally 'settling' in France.

This revised edition includes an expanded selection of illustrations of scenes from the Klondike as well as several photographs from the family of Robert Service on his travels around the world.

Wallace Lockhart, an expert on Scottish traditional folk music and dance, is the author of *Highland Balls & Village Halls* and *Fiddles & Folk*. His relish for a well-told tale in popular vernacular led him to fall in love with the verse of Robert Service and write his biography.

'A fitting tribute to a remarkable man – a bank clerk who wanted to become a cowboy. It is hard to imagine a bank clerk writing such lines as:

A bunch of boys were whooping it up...
The income from his writing actually exceeded
his bank salary by a factor of five and he
resigned to pursue a full time writing career.'
Charles Munn, THE SCOTTISH BANKER

'Robert Service claimed he wrote for those who
wouldnit be seen dead reading poetry. His was
an almost unbelievably mobile life... Lockhart
hangs on breathlessly, enthusiastically
unearthing clues to the poet's life.' Ruth
Thomas, SCOTTISH BOOK COLLECTOR

'This enthralling biography will delight Service
lovers in both the Old World and the New.'
Marilyn Wright, SCOTS INDEPENDENT

On the Trail of John Muir

Cherry Good

ISBN 0 946487 62 6 PBK £7.99

 Follow the man who
made the US go green.
Confidant of presidents,
father of American
National Parks, trailblaz-
er of world conservation
and voted a Man of the
Millennium in the US,
John Muir's life and work
is of continuing rele-
vance. A man ahead of his time who saw the
wilderness he loved threatened by industri-
alisation and determined to protect it, a cru-
sade in which he was largely successful. His
love of the wilderness began at an early age
and he was filled with wanderlust all his life.

Only by going in silence, without baggage, can
on truly get into the heart of the wilderness. All
other travel is mere dust and hotels and bag-
gage and chatter. JOHN MUIR

Braving mosquitoes and black bears Cherry
Good set herself on his trail – Dunbar,
Scotland; Fountain Lake and Hickory Hill,
Wisconsin; Yosemite Valley and the Sierra
Nevada, California; the Grand Canyon,
Arizona; Alaska; and Canada – to tell his
story. John Muir was himself a prolific
writer, and Good draws on his books, articles, letters and diaries to produce an
account that is lively, intimate, humorous
and anecdotal, and that provides refreshing
new insights into the hero of world conservation.

John Muir chronology

General map plus 10 detailed maps
covering the US, Canada and Scotland

Original colour photographs

Afterword advises on how to get
involved

Conservation websites and addresses

Muir's importance has long been acknowledged in the US with over 200 sites of scenic
beauty named after him. He was a Founder
of The Sierra Club which now has over ¹/₂
million members. Due to the movement he
started some 360 million acres of wilderness
are now protected. This is a book which
shows Muir not simply as a hero but as likeable humorous and self-effacing man of
extraordinary vision.

'I do hope that those who read this book will
burn with the same enthusiasm for John Muir
which the author shows.'
WEST HIGHLAND FREE PRESS

On the Trail of Robert the Bruce

David R. Ross

ISBN 0 946487 52 9 PBK £7.99

 On the Trail of Robert the
Bruce charts the story of
Scotland's hero-king from
his boyhood, through his
days of indecision as
Scotland suffered under
the English yoke, to his
assumption of the crown
exactly six months after
the death of William Wallace. Here is the
astonishing blow by blow account of how,
against fearful odds, Bruce led the Scots to win
their greatest ever victory. Bannockburn was
not the end of the story. The war against
English oppression lasted another fourteen
years. Bruce lived just long enough to see his
dreams of an independent Scotland come to
fruition in 1328 with the signing of the Treaty
of Edinburgh. The trail takes us to Bruce sites
in Scotland, many of the little known and forgotten battle sites in northern England, and as
far afield as the Bruce monuments in
Andalusia and Jerusalem.

67 places to visit in Scotland and elsewhere.

One general map, 3 location maps and
a map of Bruce-connected sites in
Ireland.

Bannockburn battle plan.

Drawings and reproductions of rarely
seen illustrations.

On the Trail of Robert the Bruce is not all blood
and gore. It brings out the love and laughter,
pain and passion of one of the great eras of

Scottish history. Read it and you will understand why David Ross has never knowingly killed a spider in his life. Once again, he proves himself a master of the popular brand of hands-on history that made *On the Trail of William Wallace* so popular.

'David R. Ross is a proud patriot and unashamed romantic.'

SCOTLAND ON SUNDAY

'Robert the Bruce knew Scotland, knew every class of her people, as no man who ruled her before or since has done. It was he who asked of her a miracle - and she accomplished it.'

AGNES MUIR MACKENZIE

On the Trail of Bonnie Prince Charlie

David R. Ross

ISBN 0 946487 68 5 PBK £7.99

On the Trail of Bonnie Prince Charlie is the story of the Young Pretender. Born in Italy, grandson of James VII, at a time when the German house of Hanover was on the throne, his father was regarded by many as the righful king. Bonnie Prince Charlie's campaign to retake the throne in his father's name changed the fate of Scotland. The Jacobite movement was responsible for the '45 Uprising, one of the most decisive times in Scottish history. The suffering following the battle of Culloden in 1746 still evokes emotion. Charles' own journey immediately after Culloden is well known: hiding in the heather, escaping to Skye with Flora MacDonald. Little known of is his return to London in 1750 incognito, where he converted to Protestantism (he re-converted to Catholicism before he died and is buried in the Vatican). He was often unwelcome in Europe after the failure of the uprising and came to hate any mention of Scotland and his lost chance.

79 places to visit in Scotland and England
One general map and 4 location maps
Prestonpans, Clifton, Falkirk and Culloden battle plans
Simplified family tree
Rarely seen illustrations

Yet again popular historian David R. Ross brings his own style to one of Scotland's most famous figures. Bonnie Prince Charlie is part of the folklore of Scotland. He brings forth feelings of antagonism from some and romanticism from others, but all agree on his legal right to the throne.

Knowing the story behind the place can bring the landscape to life. Take this book with you on your travels and follow the route taken by Charles' forces on their doomed march.

'Ross writes with an immediacy, a dynamism, that makes his subjects come alive on the page.'

DUNDEE COURIER

On the Trail of Mary Queen of Scots

J. Keith Cheetham

ISBN 0 946487 50 2 PBK £7.99

Life dealt Mary Queen of Scots love, intrigue, betrayal and tragedy in generous measure.

On the Trail of Mary Queen of Scots traces the major events in the turbulent life of the beautiful, enigmatic queen whose romantic reign and tragic destiny exerts an undimmed fascination over 400 years after her execution.

Places of interest to visit – 99 in Scotland, 35 in England and 29 in France.
One general map and 6 location maps.
Line drawings and illustrations.
Simplified family tree of the royal houses of Tudor and Stuart.

Key sites include:

Linlithgow Palace – Mary's birthplace, now a magnificent ruin

Stirling Castle – where, only nine months old, Mary was crowned Queen of Scotland

Notre Dame Cathedral – where, aged fifteen, she married the future king of France

The Palace of Holyroodhouse – Rizzio, one of Mary's closest advisers, was murdered here and some say his blood still stains the spot where he was stabbed to death

Sheffield Castle – where for fourteen years she languished as prisoner of her cousin, Queen Elizabeth I

Fotheringhay – here Mary finally met her death on the executioner's block.

On the Trail of Mary Queen of Scots is for

everyone interested in the life of perhaps the most romantic figure in Scotland's history; a thorough guide to places connected with Mary, it is also a guide to the complexities of her personal and public life.

'In my end is my beginning'
MARY QUEEN OF SCOTS

'...the woman behaves like the Whore of Babylon' JOHN KNOX

On the Trail of William Wallace

David R. Ross
ISBN 0 946487 47 2 PBK £7.99

How close to reality was *Braveheart*?

Where was Wallace actually born?

What was the relationship between Wallace and Bruce?

Are there any surviving eye-witness accounts of Wallace?

How does Wallace influence the psyche of today's Scots?

On the Trail of William Wallace offers a refreshing insight into the life and heritage of the great Scots hero whose proud story is at the very heart of what it means to be Scottish. Not concentrating simply on the hard historical facts of Wallace's life, the book also takes into account the real significance of Wallace and his effect on the ordinary Scot through the ages, manifested in the many sites where his memory is marked.

In trying to piece together the jigsaw of the reality of Wallace's life, David Ross weaves a subtle flow of new information with his own observations. His engaging, thoughtful and at times amusing narrative reads with the ease of a historical novel, complete with all the intrigue, treachery and romance required to hold the attention of the casual reader and still entice the more knowledgable historian.

74 places to visit in Scotland and the north of England

One general map and 3 location maps

Stirling and Falkirk battle plans

Wallace's route through London

Chapter on Wallace connections in North America and elsewhere

Reproductions of rarely seen illustrations

On the Trail of William Wallace will be enjoyed by anyone with an interest in Scotland, from the passing tourist to the most fervent nationalist. It is an encyclopaedia-cum-guide book, literally stuffed with fascinating titbits not usually on offer in the conventional history book.

David Ross is organiser of and historical adviser to the Society of William Wallace.

'Historians seem to think all there is to be known about Wallace has already been uncovered. Mr Ross has proved that Wallace studies are in fact in their infancy.' ELSPETH KING, Director the the Stirling Smith Art Museum & Gallery, who annotated and introduced the recent Luath edition of *Blind Harry's Wallace.*

'Better the pen than the sword!'

RANDALL WALLACE, author of *Braveheart,* when asked by David Ross how it felt to be partly responsible for the freedom of a nation following the Devolution Referendum.

On the Trail of the Pilgrim Fathers
J Keith Cheetham
ISBN 0 946487 83 9 PB £7.99

On the Trail of John Wesley
J Keith Cheetham
ISBN 1 84282 023 0 PB £7.99

On the Trail of Scotland's Myths & Legends
Stuart McHardy
ISBN 1 84282 049 4 PB £7.99

FICTION

Six Black Candles
Des Dillon
ISBN 1 84282 053 2 PB £6.99

Me and My Gal
Des Dillon
ISBN 1 84282 054 0 PB £5.99

The Bannockburn Years
William Scott
ISBN 0 946487 34 0 PB £7.95

But n Ben A-Go-Go
Matthew Fitt
ISBN 1 84282 041 1 PB £6.99

The Road Dance
John MacKay
ISBN 1 84282 024 9 PB £9.99

Milk Treading
Nick Smith
ISBN 1 84282 037 0 PB £6.99

Kitty Killer Cult
Nick Smith
ISBN 1 84282 039 7 £9.99

The Strange Case of RL Stevenson
Richard Woodhead
ISBN 0 946487 86 3 HB £16.99

The Great Melnikov
Hugh MacLachlan
ISBN 0 946487 42 1 PB £7.95

Driftnet
Lin Anderson
ISBN 1 84282 034 6 PB £9.99

The Fundamentals of New Caledonia
David Nicol
ISBN 0 946487 93 6 HB £16.99

POETRY

Drink the Green Fairy
Brian Whittingham
ISBN 1 84282 020 6 PB £8.99

The Ruba'iyat of Omar Khayyam, in Scots
Rab Wilson
ISBN 1 84282 046 X PB £8.99

Talking with Tongues
Brian Finch
ISBN 1 84282 006 0 PB £8.99

Kate o Shanter's Tale and other poems [book]
Matthew Fitt
ISBN 1 84282 028 1 PB £6.99

Kate o Shanter's Tale and other poems [audio CD]
Matthew Fitt
ISBN 1 84282 043 5 PB £9.99

Bad Ass Raindrop
Kokumo Rocks
ISBN 1 84282 018 4 PB £6.99

Madame Fifi's Farewell and other poems
Gerry Cambridge
ISBN 1 84282 005 2 PB £8.99

Scots Poems to be Read Aloud
intro Stuart McHardy
ISBN 0 946487 81 2 PB £5.00

Picking Brambles
Des Dillon
ISBN 1 84282 021 4 PB £6.99

Sex, Death & Football
Alistair Findlay
ISBN 1 84282 022 2 PB £6.99

Tartan and Turban
Bashabi Fraser
ISBN 1 84282 044 3 PB £8.99

Poems to be Read Aloud
introduced by Tom Atkinson
ISBN 0 946487 00 6 PB £5.00

Men and Beasts: wild men and tame animals
Valerie Gillies and Rebecca Marr
ISBN 0 946487 92 8 PB £15.00

FOLKLORE

Scotland: Myth, Legend & Folklore
Stuart McHardy
ISBN 0 946487 69 3 PB £7.99

Luath Storyteller: Highland Myths & Legends
George W Macpherson
ISBN 1 84282 003 6 PB £5.00

Tales of the North Coast
Alan Temperley
ISBN 0 946487 18 9 PB £8.99

Tall Tales from an Island
Peter Macnab
ISBN 0 946487 07 3 PB £8.99

The Supernatural Highlands
Francis Thompson
ISBN 0 946487 31 6 PB £8.99

CARTOONS

Broomie Law
Cinders McLeod
ISBN 0 946487 99 5 PB £4.00

LUATH GUIDES TO SCOTLAND

The North West Highlands: Roads to the Isles
Tom Atkinson
ISBN 0 946487 54 5 PB £4.95

Mull and Iona: Highways and Byways
Peter Macnab
ISBN 0 946487 58 8 PB £4.95

The Northern Highlands: The Empty Lands
Tom Atkinson
ISBN 0 946487 55 3 PB £4.95

The West Highlands: The Lonely Lands
Tom Atkinson
ISBN 0 946487 56 1 PB £4.95

HISTORY

Scots in Canada
Jenni Calder
ISBN 1 84282 038 9 PB £7.99

Civil Warrior
Robin Bell
ISBN 1 84282 013 3 HB £10.99

A Passion for Scotland
David R Ross
ISBN 1 84282 019 2 PB £5.99

Reportage Scotland
Louise Yeoman
ISBN 0 946487 61 8 PB £9.99

Blind Harry's Wallace
Hamilton of Gilbertfield
[introduced by Elspeth King]
ISBN 0 946487 33 2 PB £8.99

Plaids & Bandanas: Highland Drover to Wild West Cowboy
Rob Gibson
ISBN 0 946487 88 X PB £7.99

Napiers History of Herbal Healing, Ancient and Modern
Tom Atkinson
ISBN 1 84282 025 7 HB £16.99

POLITICS & CURRENT ISSUES

Scotlands of the Mind
Angus Calder
ISBN 1 84282 008 7 PB £9.99

Trident on Trial: the case for people's disarmament
Angie Zelter
ISBN 1 84282 004 4 PB £9.99

Uncomfortably Numb: A Prison Requiem
Maureen Maguire
ISBN 1 84282 001 X PB £8.99

Scotland: Land & Power – the Agenda for Land Reform
Andy Wightman
ISBN 0 946487 70 7 PB £5.00

Old Scotland New Scotland
Jeff Fallow
ISBN 0 946487 40 5 PB £6.99

Some Assembly Required: Behind the scenes at the Re-birth of the Scottish Parliament
David Shepherd
ISBN 0 946487 84 7 PB £7.99

Notes from the North Incorporating a brief history of the Scots and the English
Emma Wood
ISBN 1 84282 048 6 PB £7.99

Scotlands of the Future: sustainability in a small nation
ed Eurig Scandrett
ISBN 1 84282 035 4 PB £7.99

Eurovision or American Dream? Britain, the Euro and the Future of Europe
David Purdy
ISBN 1 84282 036 2 PB £3.99

NATURAL WORLD

The Hydro Boys: pioneers of renewable energy
Emma Wood
ISBN 1 84282 047 8 PB £8.99

Wild Scotland
James McCarthy
ISBN 0 946487 37 5 PB £8.99

Wild Lives: Otters – On the Swirl of the Tide
Bridget MacCaskill
ISBN 0 946487 67 7 PB £9.99

Wild Lives: Foxes – The Blood is Wild
Bridget MacCaskill
ISBN 0 946487 71 5 PB £9.99

Scotland – Land & People: An Inhabited Solitude
James McCarthy
ISBN 0 946487 57 X PB £7.99

The Highland Geology Trail
John L Roberts
ISBN 0 946487 36 7 PB £4.99

Red Sky at Night
John Barrington
ISBN 0 946487 60 X PB £8.99

Listen to the Trees
Don MacCaskill
ISBN 0 946487 65 0 PB £9.99

WALK WITH LUATH

Skye 360: walking the coastline of Skye
Andrew Dempster
ISBN 0 946487 85 5 PB £8.99

Walks in the Cairngorms
Ernest Cross
ISBN 0 946487 09 X PB £4.95

Short Walks in the Cairngorms
Ernest Cross
ISBN 0 946487 23 5 PB £4.95

The Joy of Hillwalking
Ralph Storer
ISBN 1 84282 069 9 PB £7.50

Scotland's Mountains before the Mountaineers
Ian R Mitchell
ISBN 0 946487 39 1 PB £9.99

Mountain Days and Bothy Nights
Dave Brown and Ian R Mitchell
ISBN 0 946487 15 4 PB £7.50

Mountain Outlaw
Ian R. Mitchell
ISBN 1 84282 027 3 PB £6.50

SPORT

Ski & Snowboard Scotland
Hilary Parke
ISBN 0 946487 35 9 PB £6.99

Over the Top with the Tartan Army
Andy McArthur
ISBN 0 946487 45 6 PB £7.99

SOCIAL HISTORY

Pumpherston: the story of a shale oil village
Sybil Cavanagh
ISBN 1 84282 011 7 HB £17.99
ISBN 1 84282 015 X PB £10.99

Shale Voices
Alistair Findlay
ISBN 0 946487 78 2 HB £17.99
ISBN 0 946487 63 4 PB £10.99

A Word for Scotland
Jack Campbell
ISBN 0 946487 48 0 PB £12.99

TRAVEL & LEISURE

**Die Kleine Schottlandfibel
[Scotland Guide in German]**
Hans-Walter Arends
ISBN 0 946487 89 8 PB £8.99

Let's Explore Edinburgh Old Town
Anne Bruce English
ISBN 0 946487 98 7 PB £4.99

Let's Explore Berwick Upon Tweed
Anne Bruce English
ISBN 1 84282 029 X PB £4.99

Edinburgh's Historic Mile
Duncan Priddle
ISBN 0 946487 97 9 PB £2.99

Pilgrims in the Rough: St Andrews beyond the 19th hole
Michael Tobert
ISBN 0 946487 74 X PB £7.99

LANGUAGE

**Luath Scots Language Learner
[Book]**
L Colin Wilson
ISBN 0 946487 91 X PB £9.99

**Luath Scots Language Learner
[Double Audio CD Set]**
L Colin Wilson
ISBN 1 84282 026 5 CD £16.99

FOOD & DRINK

The Whisky Muse: Scotch whisky in poem & song
various, edited by Robin Laing
ISBN 1 84282 041 9 PB £7.99

First Foods Fast: how to prepare good simple meals for your baby
Lara Boyd
ISBN 1 84282 002 8 PB £4.99

Edinburgh and Leith Pub Guide
Stuart McHardy
ISBN 0 946487 80 4 PB £4.95

BIOGRAPHY

The Last Lighthouse
Sharma Krauskopf
ISBN 0 946487 96 0 PB £7.99

Tobermory Teuchter
Peter Macnab
ISBN 0 946487 41 3 PB £7.99

Bare Feet and Tackety Boots
Archie Cameron
ISBN 0 946487 17 0 PB £7.95

Come Dungeons Dark
John Taylor Caldwell
ISBN 0 946487 19 7 PB £6.95

GENEALOGY

Scottish Roots: step-by-step guide for ancestor hunters
Alwyn James
ISBN 1 84282 007 9 PB £9.99

WEDDINGS, MUSIC AND DANCE

The Scottish Wedding Book
G Wallace Lockhart
ISBN 1 94282 010 9 PB £12.99

Fiddles and Folk
G Wallace Lockhart
ISBN 0 946487 38 3 PB £7.95

Highland Balls and Village Halls
G Wallace Lockhart
ISBN 0 946487 12 X PB £6.95

Luath Press Limited
committed to publishing well written books worth reading

LUATH PRESS takes its name from Robert Burns, whose little collie Luath (*Gael.*, swift or nimble) tripped up Jean Armour at a wedding and gave him the chance to speak to the woman who was to be his wife and the abiding love of his life. Burns called one of *The Twa Dogs* Luath after Cuchullin's hunting dog in *Ossian's Fingal*. Luath Press was established in 1981 in the heart of Burns country, and is now based a few steps up the road from Burns' first lodgings on Edinburgh's Royal Mile.

Luath offers you distinctive writing with a hint of unexpected pleasures.

Most bookshops in the UK, the US, Canada, Australia, New Zealand and parts of Europe either carry our books in stock or can order them for you. To order direct from us, please send a £sterling cheque, postal order, international money order or your credit card details (number, address of cardholder and expiry date) to us at the address below. Please add post and packing as follows: UK – £1.00 per delivery address; overseas surface mail – £2.50 per delivery address; overseas airmail – £3.50 for the first book to each delivery address, plus £1.00 for each additional book by airmail to the same address. If your order is a gift, we will happily enclose your card or message at no extra charge.

Luath Press Limited
543/2 Castlehill
The Royal Mile
Edinburgh EH1 2ND
Scotland
Telephone: 0131 225 4326 (24 hours)
Fax: 0131 225 4324
email: gavin.macdougall@luath.co.uk
Website: www.luath.co.uk